CAPONE'S VAULT

CAPONE'S VAULT

The Real Story of the Biggest Disaster in Television History

WILLIAM ELLIOTT HAZELGROVE

BLOOMSBURY ACADEMIC
NEW YORK • LONDON • OXFORD • NEW DELHI • SYDNEY

BLOOMSBURY ACADEMIC

Bloomsbury Publishing Inc, 1359 Broadway, New York, NY 10018, USA
Bloomsbury Publishing Plc, 50 Bedford Square, London, WC1B 3DP, UK
Bloomsbury Publishing Ireland, 29 Earlsfort Terrace, Dublin 2, D02 AY28, Ireland

BLOOMSBURY, BLOOMSBURY ACADEMIC and the Diana logo are
trademarks of Bloomsbury Publishing Plc

First published in the United States of America 2026

Copyright © William Elliott Hazelgrove, 2026

Cover images: background ©iStock.com/kitsana pankhuanoi,
hotel ©GettyimagesBettmann / Contributor,
inset ©Gettyimages/Steve Kagan / Contributor
Cover design by Jen Huppert

All rights reserved. No part of this publication may be: i) reproduced or transmitted in any form, electronic or mechanical, including photocopying, recording or by means of any information storage or retrieval system without prior permission in writing from the publishers; or ii) used or reproduced in any way for the training, development or operation of artificial intelligence (AI) technologies, including generative AI technologies. The rights holders expressly reserve this publication from the text and data mining exception as per Article 4(3) of the Digital Single Market Directive (EU) 2019/790.

Bloomsbury Publishing Inc does not have any control over, or responsibility for, any third-party websites referred to or in this book. All internet addresses given in this book were correct at the time of going to press. The author and publisher regret any inconvenience caused if addresses have changed or sites have ceased to exist, but can accept no responsibility for any such changes.

A catalog record for this book is available from the Library of Congress.

ISBN: HB: 979-8-2163-7007-9
ePDF: 979-8-2163-7010-9
eBook: 979-8-2163-7009-3

Typeset by Integra Software Services Pvt. Ltd.
Printed and bound in the United States of America

For product safety related questions contact productsafety@bloomsbury.com.

To find out more about our authors and books visit www.bloomsbury.com
and sign up for our newsletters.

For
Kitty, Clay, Callie, and Careen

We had no idea if anything was in Capone's vault . . . nobody knew . . . and that was the whole point of the show . . . Geraldo didn't know . . . I didn't know . . . the audience didn't know . . . it was great television.

Allan Grafman, Executive Producer, "The Mystery of Al Capone's Vaults"

CONTENTS

Acknowledgments xi
Preface xii

Prologue: April 21, 1986, 7 P.M. Central, Chicago 1

PART ONE The Buildup 7

1. The King of Chicago: Valentine's Day, Chicago, February 14, 1929 9
2. The Discovery: 1981 17
3. *The Farm Report*: 1985 23
4. Willowbrook: 1971 31
5. Scarface: 1930 45
6. Signing Geraldo: January 1986 51
7. The Opening of the Safe from the *Andrea Doria*: August 16, 1984 55
8. The Tunnels of Chicago 61
9. Hooverball: 1930 67
10. Hiding at the NAPTE: 1986 73
11. Television: 1909 77
12. The Vault Within a Vault: January 1986 83
13. Public Enemy Number One: 1930 89
14. The Rebel: 1972 95
15. Hayseeds: 1930 101

16 Sailing: 1985 107

17 Capone on Ice: 1932 113

18 Happy Days 117

PART TWO The Broadcast 131

19 Showtime!: April 21, 1986 133

20 A Live Two-Hour Infotainment: April 21, 1986 137

21 Suspension of Disbelief 143

22 Getting Ready to Pull Down the Slab: April 21, 1986, 8:20 P.M. Eastern 147

23 A Safecracking Party 155

24 The Slab: April 21, 1986, 8:25 P.M. Eastern 159

25 The Thompson: April 21, 1986, 8:30 P.M. Eastern 165

26 Digging for Capone: April 21, 1986, 8:50 P.M. Eastern 171

27 Blowing Up the Wall: April 21, 1986, 8:55 P.M. Eastern 177

28 Milk Crate Blues: April 21, 1986, 9:39 P.M. Eastern 183

PART THREE The Aftermath 193

29 War of the Worlds: 1938 195

30 Revenge of the Suits: April 22, 1986 201

31 Redemption: April 22, 1986, 6 A.M. 215

32 Capone's Vault 227

Epilogue 231
Notes 236
Selected Bibliography 253
Index 255
About the Author 261

ACKNOWLEDGMENTS

Many thanks to Geraldo Rivera, Allan Grafman, Clark Morehouse, and Mitch Nednick for taking time to recall an event from forty years before that changed television forever. Special thanks to Allan Grafman for his assistance in procuring interviews and pictures from a moment long ago.

PREFACE

It was the misfit toy of television. A fired television journalist. A start-up media company with two programs, one of them the *The Farm Report*. A syndicated program when syndication was where programs went to die. A premise based on opening a vault in a dirty basement of a dilapidated hotel that may or may not have belonged to Al Capone. A live, two-hour show during the dead zone of television programming on a Monday night. "Capone's vault." Say it to anyone over forty and they will know what it means. The meaning is simple. On a cold night on April 21, 1986, more than thirty million people tuned-in on live television to watch a vault in a crumbling hotel in Chicago get opened. One in three households planted themselves in front of the television to see if Al Capone had left something behind in the basement of the Lexington Hotel. It is now part of our cultural zircon, and the opening of Capone's vault sits on the pop culture reference chart along with Will Smith hitting Chris Rock at the Oscars. It was something everyone seemed to have watched, and if they didn't, they heard about it.

I saw it along with everyone else, but I really found out about the mystique of the colorful Prohibition gangster after I wrote a book on Al Capone a few years ago. I was doing a presentation on my book *Al Capone and the 1933 World's Fair* in New Buffalo, Michigan, when a tall, angular man walked up to me and introduced himself. It was Allan Grafman. He was one of the original producers of "The Mystery of Capone's Vaults," with Geraldo Rivera. We talked for a while and soon after I rewatched the two-hour special on YouTube. There was Geraldo standing outside the Lexington Hotel in a dark jacket with his smoky breath, two microphones pinned to his lapel, and announcing to the world, as only Geraldo can, that *on this night, on live television, the secrets of Capone's vault would be revealed!*

Forty years ago, America was in the middle of an economic boom that mirrored the 1920s. We had a cowboy movie star for president who believed that America was that shining city on a hill and that there were no real problems. There was MTV, Madonna, Michael Jackson, the Go-Go's, U2, Mr. T., *The Cosby Show*, *Hill Street Blues*. Three networks. Four channels, if you count PBS. People still went to theaters to watch movies. VCRs were new tech. The Apple IIc was a personal computer most people had never heard of much less owned. There were brick phones. Few car phones. No one had heard of the internet. *The Cosby Show* and sitcoms dominated the television landscape with a few edgy shows like *Hill Street Blues*. Television stayed in narrow guidelines where *The People's Court* was about as close to reality television as anyone could get. The eighties were yuppies, prosperity, cocaine, the Brat Pack, *Footloose*, *The Breakfast Club*, *Pretty in Pink*, and *Top Gun*. Cyndi Lauper sang that girls just wanted to have fun. In the middle of this *decade of decadence* a cultural phenomenon occurred on April 21, 1986.

Years ago, I was approached by producers who wanted to create a show around Al Capone's missing money. Capone had been shipped off to Alcatraz in 1932 for tax evasion and while there dementia-induced syphilis erased his memory. One of the things he forgot was where he hid his millions. His niece Deirdre Capone would later claim he had hidden the money in safety deposit boxes all around the country but could not remember where any of them were. The legend of Capone's lost millions grew with each passing year. Eventually, Al Capone's missing money would push more people to watch a two-hour live syndicated program broadcast from the basement of the Lexington Hotel than the Superbowl or David Frost's interview with Richard Nixon.

The longest live show in 1986 was *Saturday Night Live*. Everyone thought that the show would fail when it debuted in 1975. There was no reality television in 1986. Not yet. The networks offered tame fare to the American public. The top ten shows were *The Cosby Show*, *Family Ties*, *Cheers*, *Murder She Wrote*, *Cagney and Lacey*, *The Golden Girls*, *60 Minutes*, *Night Court*, *Growing Pains*, and *Moonlighting*. HBO was still three strange letters and cable sat on top of televisions like a foreign black box that most people did not have. Into this buttery, network-driven landscape came a two-hour syndicated show with an unemployed news journalist sponsored by a start-up entertainment company whose biggest program was . . . wait for it, *The Farm Report*.

Geraldo Rivera had been fired from ABC after fifteen years and the live broadcast from Chicago was to be his comeback. "The Mystery of Al Capone's Vaults" was a bet that Geraldo would open a vault in the basement of the nineteenth-century Lexington Hotel and show the world Capone's missing millions, or at least something important from Al Capone. On April 21, 1986, Geraldo broadcast to the world from the catacombs of the Lexington Hotel in Chicago—a live primetime event that for Geraldo was his make-or-break moment. Geraldo was on his sailboat when producers John Joslyn and Doug Llewelyn caught up with him and offered him the job of hosting the two-hour live television event. The intrigue of the broadcast would involve a sleight of hand where only later audiences would realize they had been taken for a ride. There would be outrage, indignance, and then a desire to do it all again.

People all over America and the world tuned-in to watch Geraldo shout over men in hard hats on an earth excavator, blow up walls with dynamite, shoot a Thompson machine gun, and pull down a cement slab to reveal what was put in a vault over fifty years before. It is still the most-watched syndicated event in television history. The buildup had been tremendous, with the media nationwide speculating what was in the vault. The chamber was 125 feet long, 8 feet wide, and 8 feet high. In the bricked basement, a 5,000-pound slab of concrete would be torn down and then a second wall would be blasted apart with dynamite. All on live television.

Every newspaper had built up the opening and every newspaper in America covered the story the day after the vault was opened. Incredibly, many papers featured the story of Capone's vault on the front page. *The Salt Lake Tribune* was typical, with the blaring headline CAPONE'S VAULT TO SHARE SECRETS ON

LIVE TELEVISION.[1] *The Detroit Free Press* led with ASSAULT ON BIG AL'S VAULT.[2] *The Philadelphia Inquirer* announced EXPERTS SPECULATE OVER CONTENTS OF MYSTERY VAULT IN CAPONE HOTEL.[3] A Knight Ridder wire service story picked up by hundreds of papers declared AL CAPONE'S VAULT TO BE PRIED OPEN ON TV SHOW.[4]

Nothing like this had ever been attempted, and the one-million-dollar television production would be available to 94 percent of the nation's viewers and beamed live to the Netherlands, Germany, France, the United Kingdom, Argentina, Italy, Japan, Australia, the Bahamas, the Dominican Republic, Costa Rica, and Paraguay. At 7:00 p.m. Central on April 21, 1986, "The Mystery of Al Capone's Vaults" went live. How this show came about, the saga of a shaman of television named Geraldo Rivera, the lasting impact this broadcast would have on television, and what this moment in time tells us about ourselves, where millions of households tuned-in on a cold night to find out if a gangster left behind a calling card in a vault in a basement of a South Side hotel in Chicago ... is a story in itself.

Prologue
April 21, 1986

7 P.M. Central, Chicago

It was cold for April. Even for Chicago. The temperature had plunged to the twenties. Michigan Avenue still had the feel of Christmas with the twinkling lights of horse-drawn carriages for tourists who wanted to tour the Magnificent Mile. Further down on the South Side, crane-high movie lights blazed on an old hotel at 2135 South Michigan Avenue. Men in yellow hardhats spoke outside with their breath illuminated in the light. Diesel-puffing satellite trucks parked up and down the street. The *whop whop whop* of a helicopter began to get louder. Michigan Avenue was blocked off with crowds of people behind barricades. Mr. T was in the front of the crowd in his trademark gold chains and mohawk. Vendors sold T-shirts that proclaimed I WAS THERE WHEN CAPONE'S VAULT OPENED. They sold out in minutes.

Reporters from all over the world stood around as the helicopter became deafening and everyone looked up. The flashing strobes suddenly appeared in front of the hotel. Then the helicopter with the camera poking out landed on Michigan Avenue. Geraldo Rivera appeared in the front door of the Lexington Hotel as a crane camera moved in. It was Monday, 8 p.m. Eastern in New York and 7 Central in Chicago and people around the world were locked in place in front of their televisions. Geraldo looked like he was breathing smoke in a half-zipped blue coat with a white shirt and tie. He looked at the camera with his trademark Groucho mustache and pointed with his finger.

"I'm Geraldo Rivera and you are about to witness a live television event, a massive concrete vault has been discovered, and some think it belongs to none other than the notorious Al Capone. Well, tonight for the first time that vault is going to be opened. . . . LIVE!"[1]

One hour later in the basement of the Lexington Hotel, it was five degrees colder. A shiny chain had pulled down the five-thousand-pound slab blocking the vault in the first half of the two-hour broadcast and revealed nothing but a bottle of gin. There were ninety minutes to fill and find something, *anything*, that belonged to the notorious gangster Al Capone. The first hour passed to the second hour and for Geraldo, it was all coming down to the 1930s plunger in front of him. Two sticks of 60 percent dynamite had been inserted into a second wall with flashbangs added for dramatic effect. Everything was riding on the dark wood explosives plunger that looked like something out of a bad movie. The city had not given the permit to use dynamite in the city limits of Chicago until four that afternoon. The broadcast had been one of several anticlimactic moments filled with montages of Capone, old gangsters, and women whose husbands had been killed by the Chicago mobster. A highlight was Geraldo shooting off a Thompson machine gun with live rounds.

That was all over. They could only fill so much while the Bobcat excavator and the men dug into the earth behind the slab pulled down by the earth mover. Nothing. Dust. Debris. More dirt. But they knew there was another wall and behind that wall was the chamber; the vault that reached out to the front sidewalk. Millions could be behind the wall. *Capone's millions*. Bodies. Weapons. Cars. No one knew. Geraldo had been using every trick in the book to hype up the tension and barking out orders to the men and cutting away to commercials at key moments. Two hours. They had to fill two hours of live television, and it turned out they needed every minute. Geraldo stared at the plunger that would ignite the sticks of dynamite inserted into the second wall at strategic points. The whole building might come down on top of them. Who knew? But what that plunger really might blow up was Geraldo's career. He had just been fired from ABC when the network refused to run a story by his colleague Sylvia Chase, linking Marilyn Monroe with JFK and his brother Bobby Kennedy. Geraldo had pushed the plunger down by complaining to *People* magazine that his boss, Roone Arledge, had killed the story because of his friendship with Ethel Kennedy. He told *People* he thought the network was cowardly for not running the story. *Boom.* Just like that, he had blown up his fifteen-year job at ABC.

This was now his comeback. It would show the producers at ABC they were wrong to fire him. Geraldo didn't think about the ramifications of not finding anything in the vault under the old hotel. Everyone had assured him something was there. Money. Bodies. Cars. Diaries. Torture machines. *Something* was there. The sonar said *something was there.* The historians said *something was there.* The people having Capone parties all over the country said *something was there.* The newspapers had said *something was there* for months. Psychics said *something was there.* Of course, *something was there.* Capone had used the Lexington for five years as his headquarters and they had found secret stairwells and secret tunnels going to other buildings. *There was something there.* There was no reason for this five-thousand-pound slab of concrete to be in the basement of the Lexington Hotel if not to hide something precious to Capone. Everyone assured each other . . . *something was there.*

Geraldo breathed in the frigid air and looked at the plunger again. When he pressed this down the dynamite would blow the wall apart and there would be no turning back. It was the last ace up the collective sleeve of Geraldo and the producers. They had hoped for something behind the slab, but everyone assured Geraldo the real treasure was behind the second wall they had drilled and put the dynamite in. They were into the second hour and now . . . now it was time to push that plunger and see if he should have just stayed on his sailboat down by the Panama Canal and listened to his agent who initially said Hell NO! when they offered Geraldo the job of hosting the event.

But it was a career restart. That was the way he saw it. He had been flying into Chicago for the B-roll and the interviews and all the fill that would give the guys in yellow hard hats and snazzy blue uniforms time to dig and find the treasure. Even the workers looked like movie stars with trimmed mustaches and glossy swept-back hair. The IRS was there for potential money. The police were there for Chicago's share of the money. A medical examiner was there for potential bodies. Everyone was ready to spring into action the moment they found something. But they had found nothing so far, and people had begun to whisper on the set. Geraldo had seen the increasing expressions of concern on the producers' faces. The doubt was like a creeping disease, a black plague of doubt overwhelming Geraldo; he might have really done it this time. This could destroy what was left of his career after being fired from ABC. He was always a joke to the news establishment, and this would confirm the suspicion Geraldo was nothing more than a charismatic showman.

So this was the climax of the two-hour "Mystery of Al Capone's Vaults." The blasting of the wall was set to be the big dramatic moment, and the supervisor of the blasting crew was calling everyone to clear the area. Geraldo's whole damn career had been this way. One blowup after another, and yet he had landed on his feet and become a television journalist who had walked the line between journalist and celebrity reporter and done very well. He was *Geraldo*. That's how people knew him. Like *Oprah*. One name. The carnival barker. The great drama presenter. *Geraldo*. And now *Geraldo* was about to blow it all up again and see where the pieces landed.

The supervisor gave him the signal and Geraldo pulled up the handle of the plunger. Ever the dramatist, he shouted out, "Fire in the hole!" Geraldo paused, then slowly counted down and dramatically pushed down the plunger. What the world didn't know was the plunger wires led to nowhere. The foreman overseeing the explosives set off the dynamite by pressing a button in his hand.

They were taking no chances. The dynamite exploded with flashes of light from the flashbangs and a deafening concussion sending out a roiling cloud of dust. The men in bright yellow hard hats and immaculate, trim blue suits then went in to see if any of the sticks of dynamite had not exploded and Geraldo waited for the all-clear. The supervisor nodded.

"Okay, Geraldo."

This was it. Geraldo strode into the hanging dust cloud and began climbing across the wall that had disintegrated into a pile of rubble. The cameras followed. Cash. Skeletons. Booze. Torture chambers. Capone's car. The big man himself. Who knew? Geraldo stared into the television lights cutting through the dust. He squinted, smelling the gunpowder and brick dust, then stumbled over the rubble like a blind man looking for salvation.

PART ONE

THE BUILDUP

1

The King of Chicago

Valentine's Day, Chicago, February 14, 1929

He wore a white fedora and had a fifty-thousand-dollar ring on his pinky finger. He had a steel-backed chair in case of an assassination attempt and the only armored Cadillac in the United States. He set up soup kitchens on the South Side of Chicago and had a habit of giving out money to people in need. His suits were impeccable with flashy, colorful ties. He ran an operation that flew in booze from Canada with rum runners bumping off the shores of Lake Michigan. He bottled beer, whiskey, milk, and soda. Whenever he went to court or ball games he was mobbed. He was a celebrity before celebrities. He had only one wife, one son, and many mistresses. His nickname was Scarface, but no one called him that. He had a murderous temper and ran his entire operation from the fourth and fifth floors at the top of the Lexington Hotel from 1927 to 1932. He was the undisputed king of Chicago.

Al Capone's White House was 2135 South Michigan Avenue, Chicago. Like the address 1600 Pennsylvania Avenue, that address meant power. His Oval Office was room 230 in the Lexington Hotel until he moved into room 430, which became his new Oval Office. His Resolute Desk was a large mahogany desk circled by three curved windows that looked down on Michigan Avenue so he could keep an eye on his beer trucks. A picture of George Washington hung behind him along with Mayor Big Bill Thompson. All he was missing was an American flag. The 1892 hotel designed by Clinton Warren was the main headquarters for Al Capone Inc. and the entire fourth floor was occupied by his gang. Room 530 became his private suite where he would entertain and live. In the middle of the room was a crest with the initials AC carved into the oak parquet. The walls were ornately plastered in gold and pink, and an oriental rug ran the length of the room. A fake fireplace and built-in radio set over the mantle allowed Big Al to relax in style. His family would stay on the same floor in another suite when they visited him. He had a private dining room that seated fifty-two people and a private movie theater for first-run films. Men with Tommy guns patrolled the lobby and bodyguards slept on cots outside his suite. Secret stairwells leading to his mistress and to the basement allowed him a quick escape if the Lexington was raided by police or rival gangsters.

Two former employees in 1962 gave an interview to the *Chicago Tribune* but withheld their names. "It was Capone's hotel, although he didn't own it. They paid fabulous rentals for their rooms and suites. All you had to remember was mind your own business and everything was fine. Neither employees or other residents were afraid."[1] Sheet metal lined the elevators to bulletproof the cage when Capone came down. "Some people work with their hands. Some people work with their brains. These people worked with their guns, but not in the hotel."[2] Another employee remembered Capone coming down a back elevator. "He gave me $10 and said go out and put it on a horse. They wouldn't harm anybody, unless they were enemies."[3]

The eviction process of Al Capone from the Lexington Hotel really begins on Valentine's Day, 1929. On this day, snow fluttered down outside a nondescript garage at 2122 North Clark Street. Years later the garage would be torn down and there would be no trace it had ever existed. Still, people would slow down in cars or pause and imagine the men dressed like cops walking into the side door. There were two of them along with two men in long coats. They were the last ones to go into George Moran's (Bugs) headquarters. It was a big day. They were intercepting a shipment of booze from Al Capone and the seven men stood around smoking in the cool, oily darkness of the garage. They wore spats with stickpins and flashy ties. Their hair was smoothed back with pomade, and they wore fedoras tilted to one side.

Prohibition. What a bonanza of money the Nineteenth Amendment had brought to Chicago. One hundred million a year. That's what Al Capone made. Chicago had more speakeasies than any other city in the country, and ever since 1919 the river of booze had been supplied by gangsters, the biggest supplier being Al Capone. Prohibition changed America's drinking habits. Before Prohibition, men drank in saloons with men; after Prohibition, men and women drank in speakeasies with jazz, interracial mixing, sex. America ended up drinking more than ever before and Capone's bottling operation included beer, whiskey, soda pop, and milk. He began stamping his bottles with dates for the milk and started an industry standard. He was not a stupid man. He was a WOP. That's what the other kids called him in Brooklyn. "Without papers." His parents spoke no English, and the WOP bloodied the mouths of not a few kids in Brooklyn, and then he was bloodied himself many times. Stout and built like a bulldog, he could pack a punch early. He was born Alphonse Capone in Brooklyn just down from the Navy Yards in a cold water flat with an outhouse. For fun, he would go down and watch the soldiers march and yell through the fence when one fell out of step. The WOP from Southern Italy had a mouth on him.

"Hey, you! You, long-legged number three! Get in step. You're holding 'em up!" he shouted in a bullhorn voice. The short ten-year-old with the black WOP haircut kept up the abuse until the soldier charged the fence. He would flatten the loudmouth Italian kid if he could, but a corporal stopped him. Most kids would run but Al just stood by the fence and shouted. "C'mon! Let him outside the gate and I'll teach the big sonofabitch a lesson!"[4] The corporal looked behind him in amazement at the pudgy, dark-haired kid who had his fists up. The soldier shook his head and went back. Al Capone didn't back down. He didn't back down when a nun slapped him, and he punched the nun right back. The WOPs had to be controlled. Henry Cabot Lodge said immigrants were pouring into the country like a firehose spouting dirty water. Al was dragged down to the principal, who gave him a beating; then he left and never went back.

School was not for him. He would make his name in the streets. Besides, he was fourteen; time to go to work. His parents moved to Garfield Street into a nicer apartment and in his new neighborhood, Al met Johnny Torrio. Torrio ran some brothels and gave Capone five bucks to run errands. One of the errands had Al going to Torrio's apartment where a stack of money was on the kitchen table. If Capone stole the money, he was finished but if he didn't, then he could join Torrio's Five Points Gang. Capone didn't take the money and eventually followed Torrio to Chicago where he took over "the outfit" after Torrio was shot in an assassination attempt. Within two years he was controlling a vast bootlegging operation from the Lexington Hotel.

The party was on. F. Scott Fitzgerald published a novel about a bootlegger who made vast amounts of money but came from nothing. *The Great Gatsby* encapsulated a new American Dream where it didn't matter how you became rich just as long as you did. Capone saw Prohibition very simply. People wanted to drink, and he was supplying the booze. A favorite phrase of his was that if someone wanted to drink in the Southside of Chicago then it was bootlegging, but if they wanted to drink up on the well-heeled enclaves of the North Shore then it was hospitality. To Capone, it was all the same. He supplied the booze for a price and that price also included murder. Bugs Moran wanted in on the Chicago operation. His Northside gang killed Capone's men and Capone's killed his. After "Machine Gun" Jack McGurn had survived an assassination attempt in a phone booth, Capone and McGurn laid the trap that brought in

Moran's men who were waiting behind the storefront window, emblazoned with S. M. C. Cartage Company.

Moran should have been there by now, but he had stopped to get a haircut. The seven men continued smoking, talking, but they were getting cold. The door opened and they turned when two cops walked in accompanied by the well-dressed men in long coats. Highball began to bark. She didn't like the men and neither did the seven Moran men. They paid for protection and the two cops, and the detectives didn't make any sense.

"Everyone against the wall," the cops shouted, holding sawed-off shotguns.

The Moran men turned slowly to the greasy wall. What did it matter? They had mob lawyers if it came to that. They would be out in an hour anyway. Highball continued to bark tied up to the pipe on the right side of the garage. The single bare bulb cast its shadows against the stained brick, their breath visible in the damp cold. Highball was growling and showing her teeth. The cops nodded to the two men in long coats as they swung up two Thompson machine guns and ripped back the firing bolts. Every one of Moran's men knew the double click of a Thompson machine gun. It meant that the piranha of hell was about to start firing .45 ACP slugs so fast the barrels would turn red from the heat. Invented in World War I by General John T. Thompson to kill Germans, the stout machine guns were adopted by gangsters as the gun of choice. Thompson named his gun "The Annihilator." To the men in the garage on Clark Street, it was simply a Thompson, which meant death.

The clattering exploding concussive blasts echoed back off the brick walls while the shells rained down to the cement in musical succession as the shooter on the right raked the men at skull level and the shooter on the left went across the middle of their backs. Men with firehoses used much the same motion with seventy .45 ACP slugs blowing apart skulls, severing arteries, and perforating lungs as the men fell in a hail of blue smoke and fire, grabbing chairs, falling against each other, kissing the wall in geysers of blood. The crime scene photos that would end up eventually in the Chicago History Museum would be splayed across the papers of the country later in a gruesome concerto of brains, blood, broken skulls, and contorted bodies. Still, the men fired at the bodies lying on the cold cement with the rivers of blood spreading across the garage floor like encroaching ink. The Thompsons ran through their clips and then there was the silence, the blue smoke, the acrid scent of gunpowder, and the ringing in the ears.

The two policemen walked among the bodies and heard one of the men groan. The sawed-off shotgun flashed among the bodies; the faces of men suddenly obliterated. Chipped red-brick fragments from the back wall lay among the men who didn't move, and didn't breathe. The cops took the Thompsons and led the two men in long coats out the door with their hands raised. People outside the garage saw the police and assumed they had already taken control. The four men got into a stolen police car and vanished.

Walter Trohan was working for the City News Bureau when he got the call. Valentine's Day had been slow, but then the phone rang. "I was in the press room when the call came through that six men had been killed at 2122 North Clark Street,"[5] he later recalled. He didn't take a taxi because he wanted to save money and took a streetcar instead. He wasn't sure it was really anything as there were a lot of call-ins that didn't amount to much. He reached the garage ahead of any other press. He heard a dog barking inside the garage and a lone cop at the door looked up as he approached. Trohan flashed his City News badge and walked through an office with no furniture except a desk and a phone. The air had the petroleum scent of motor oil, but then something else. Trohan pulled the door open to the garage and the iron scent of blood filled his nostrils with the dog now barking crazily.

"There were just pools of blood everywhere and the dead guys spread out as in the movies," he wrote later. "I'd seen dead guys before—it was part of my job—but I'd never seen that many before. They were sprawled all over and there was blood all over and this crazy German shepherd was barking and lunging on a heavy chain . . . I was impressed but I was also interested in running to a phone. I did know that that the victims were the Moran gang, and I knew Moran wasn't among them . . . I knew Capone was behind it because they were rival gangsters fighting for chunks of the rope."[6]

The newspapers carried photos of the massacre all over the country. It was bad publicity for Chicago, which was planning a World's Fair in four years. Gangsters dressed up like cops who mowed down gangsters with Thompson machine guns. When questioned in his home in Florida, Capone said, "The only man that I know who kills like that is Bugs Moran." Moran returned the favor by saying, "The only man I know that kills like that is Al Capone."[7] Something had to be done, and Mayor William Thompson was not the man to do it. He was on Capone's payroll. In 1931, Big Bill Thompson lost to Anton Cermak. As mayor, Cermak promised to clean Chicago up and said Al Capone had to go. The King of Chicago in the Lexington Hotel had been given an eviction notice that would come due in a year.

2

The Discovery

1981

At the northeast corner of Cermak and Michigan Avenue was a relic of the Gilded Age. The 1893 Exposition in Chicago required a hotel that spared no expense for the prominent guests of the fair who spared no expense either. Built in 1891, the Lexington Hotel was the epitome of turn-of-the-century elegance, with crystal chandeliers, soaring arches, glittering ballrooms, wrought-iron staircases, and a broad lobby lined with varicolored marble from Italy, France, and Vermont. The 1890s was the high-water mark for the elegant hotel, which hosted presidents and dignitaries from all over the world. Now, like a fast-action movie, the hotel was a dilapidated hulk awaiting demolition or renovation with water leaking inside and a large, gaping hole in the center of the lobby that went straight down to the basement where a former porn store owner, Harold Rubin, was carefully walking in the dank, dark space that had once been the habitat of none other than Al Capone.

"Weird Harold," who had been known as the "Porn King of Chicago," was now the collector of mob paraphernalia. His adult bookstore, Weird Harold's—located in the South Loop—had finally closed after raids by the police and Harold had moved to the suburbs after being arrested many times on obscenity charges. He started collecting anything he could sell that was not nailed down. The Lexington Hotel at Cermak and Michigan Avenue had proved to be a gold mine. Squeezing in between the chained front door, he and his son collected Italian marble tiles from the lobby and stacked them on the side of his house. He was selling the tiles as desk sets under the name Cement Shoes Co. Harold Rubin called himself an entrepreneur, and it didn't matter how many times he was arrested; he always shrugged and said he was just making money.

Now he was just making money in the hotel at 2135 South Michigan Avenue, built in 1892 for the 1893 Chicago World's Fair. He didn't know and didn't care that the Lexington had once been the height of elegance in Chicago with crystal chandeliers, soaring arches, glittering ballroom, wrought-iron staircases, and a broad lobby lined with marble from Italy, France, and Vermont. He didn't know that President Grover Cleveland stayed there during the 1893 World's Fair. But he knew another guest who had occupied the fourth and fifth floors with his own barber chair, private kitchen, chef and food tester, lavender bathtub, washbowl, toilet with gold fixtures, and a gymnasium built on the second floor so his bodyguards could stay healthy.

"The front doors of the hotel were boarded and chained," his son Jules later recalled. "You had to push them open and squeeze through. The downstairs was very grandiose . . . so when you walked in there you had a twenty-foot hole across the ceiling. In Chicago there are rats, and you hear things." Jules and his father had gone to many buildings, and to Jules the Lexington was just another building until he found out that it wasn't. "Once my father realized that a famous crime boss had stayed there that just lit the fire."[1]

Rubin learned all about the hotel and about Al Capone's tenure there, and that was why he had gone into the abandoned hotel that was a crumbling monument at the corner of Michigan Avenue and Cermak Road. The hotel had been renamed "the Michigan" before World War II, but it slipped into squalor, and for a time it became a four-hundred-room brothel, then a third-class residential hotel. When it closed, 150 transients stayed on without electricity or gas. Finally, the hotel became the abandoned hulk that Rubin was making his way through. Broken windows had let in rain and snow for years after scavengers tore out radiators for scrap and cleared out anything deemed to be of value. Men like Rubin were looking for a nugget of gold in a mine ravaged long ago.

Rubin had found some prizes: "Old bullets, hotel keys, shot glasses, and a ledger listing 'Christmas Donations to certain policemen by name and badge number.'"[2] He had heard about the hinged mirror that hid a secret door that led to Capone's mistress and another door that led to the basement and coal tunnels that connected the hotel to other buildings where Capone could escape unnoticed. He had also heard about tunnels that connected the Lexington to Colosimo's Restaurant and Capone's Four Duces Saloon at 2222 South Wabash. Rubin believed there were undiscovered Capone artifacts in the Lexington. He believed the artifacts were in the basement that no longer had a stairwell. His son Jules, who was helping him, refused to go down into the basement. Harold lowered himself with a rope into the dank darkness of the old hotel. He had a cop flashlight he flashed around the bricked walls. More rats scurried in the corners. Harold walked slowly into the catacombs as more animals peered into the light and disappeared. Creepy was not the word. The basement had flooded multiple times and smelled like a crypt to Rubin.

Harold walked further with creatures scurrying away and then stopped. In front of him was a strange white slab of cement. It glowed in the darkness. He shined his light on the giant cement slab that crudely patched a brick wall. Harold shined his light against the slab of concrete, then followed the 6-foot-high wall extending 125 feet along the front of the hotel. Rubin walked the length of the wall, then turned back and looked at the slab of concrete. It made no sense. A masonry expert who later inspected the wall determined there was "no purpose for the strange structure and estimated it took 250 cubic yards of cement and that it was constructed in the thirties." "It's a sloppy job," he would tell the *Chicago Tribune*. "It was done by amateurs."[3] Harold Rubin knew none of this, but he could smell an opportunity. He walked the wall back to the slab. He turned and nodded slowly. Yes. This slab—this rough, pimply, crude conglomeration of cement—was hiding something behind that brick wall and he knew then, like a prospector looking for gold, that *the something* behind the wall belonged to Al Capone. Harold Rubin was certain of it. There was no doubt in his mind. There was a space behind the wall. *There was a vault!* So, it was here, at that moment, in that dark, cold, rat-infested basement in 1981, the mystery of Capone's vaults was born.

Harold Rubin had hit the motherlode. Millions could be behind that cement slab. The millions of Capone's lost money. Harold later returned to pillage the Lexington many times, inspecting, studying, but like an old lady holding onto her purse, the slab of cement was maddeningly impenetrable. Harold had hoped there might be some way to breach the slab, but he needed help. So he told some reporters and fueled speculation on what was behind the five-thousand-pound slab of concrete. An article appeared in the *Chicago Tribune* on June 18, 1981, and announced the discovery of the vault: CAPONE'S OLD HOTEL NOW JUST A TOMB? "Whose bones might be moldering in the 125-foot-long solid concrete vault beneath South Michigan Avenue along the foundation of the old Lexington Hotel?" The article went on to catalog Rubin's finds in the hotel, "old bullets, hotel keys, shot glasses, and a ledger listing 5-dollar Christmas Donations to certain policemen by name and badge number . . . and a library card of Willis Barker, a known swindler." After describing the desecration of the hotel where steam radiators were dropped down elevator shafts for scrap, the *Tribune* announced to the world what Rubin had found:

> It is the concrete vault under the hotels vaulted Michigan Avenue sidewalk that has attracted the chilling curiosity of the souvenir hunters, who believe it could be a gangland burial ground. Six feet high and 6 feet wide, the wall extends nearly 125 feet under the sidewalk to which it offers no support. A masonry expert was cited who estimated it took "250 cubic yards of cement and was poured sometime in the 1930s" called it a sloppy job done by amateurs.

The city was quoted as saying it would cost one million dollars to demolish the Lexington and said it would not be tearing down the hotel any time soon.

The article speculates at the end that federal funds might be required to "help open the secrets of the solid concrete wall hugging the hoary old Lexington's tattered skirts of brick."[4]

Now the world knew, and Rubin began researching, thinking there might be bodies there, but more than that there might be money. *Capone's missing money.* All of Harold's scavenging had led up to this moment. He planned to find out what was in Capone's vault, but fate intervened. One year later, Patricia Porter of the Sunbow Foundation purchased the Lexington for $500,000. The doors this time were locked tight, and Harold Rubin was shut out. The nonprofit construction company that trained minority women in construction skills planned to renovate the old hotel for a planned 1992 World's Fair in Chicago and turn it into eighty-four units of one- and two-bedroom apartments, an international women's museum, and a research center, daycare facilities, and a re-creation of Capone's room 530.

A news story hit the wires again. AL CAPONE SLEPT HERE AND NOW WOMEN GIVE OLD HOTEL A FACELIFT. The article announced:

> at the old Lexington Hotel just south of Chicago's Loop, Al Capone kept a teen aged mistress, played basketball, and got laborers to pour a concrete vault where he may have buried his victims or his money. Now however it's undergoing a pain staking rehabilitation at the hands of a group of low-income single mothers being trained in carpentry by a nonprofit feminist organization that intends to turn the 10-story building into an international women's museum, library and exhibition hall for the 1992 World's Fair.[5]

Pat Porter understood what a gold mine the hotel could be and in 1985 put on a hard hat and led a group of reporters into the basement. Porter had secured a federal grant to start Sunbow, and the hotel was their first large-scale renovation. Never better than raising money, Porter gave finger food to guests, then led them all down for a tour of the basement of the old hotel. The discovery of hidden stairwells and tunnels in the basement had whetted Patricia Porter's appetite for finding the treasures behind the slab of concrete. "My instinct was telling me there was money behind the wall," she told reporters. The planned World's Fair was canceled in 1985 but Patricia Porter didn't give up on her renovation of the hotel. She was no stranger to scrambling for money and hosted a fundraiser for $100.00 a plate in June 1985 in the rickety hotel. Guests "donned bright yellow hard hats and climbed rickety stairs while eating seafood salad in tomato baskets on folding chairs."[6]

But the real attraction for the guests was going down to the basement to see the slab of poured cement and hearing Patricia and others speculate on the money and bodies or even cars that might be behind the slab. Antoinette Giancana was one of the guests. Her father, Sam Giancana, was a mob boss who drove beer trucks for Capone. Porter announced to the crowd and the press, "I have to thank Al Capone because, without his famous name, we wouldn't have gotten any attention."[7] There were plans to open the vault in late summer, but Sunbow was forbidden to use federal funds to excavate the concrete. Several fundraisers fell flat, and the best Porter could do was to keep the press interested in hopes funding would come through. On May 28, 1985, a wire service story described Sunbow's renovation but also speculated on the vault in the basement. "In recent weeks the old hotel's mysterious basement vault has people wandering if it contains human remains, bootleg hootch or a ferreted away fortune. The IRS has been attracted too. Porter recently received papers indicating that Capone owed the government more than 800,000 in back taxes and if there's any loot in the vault the IRS intends to claim it."[8] The legend of Capone's lost money already had people holding their hands out.

Another article in the *Chicago Tribune*, "Capone's Vault Still Dark," quoted Porter: "We're a not-for-profit training program . . . we would love to have donations for the vault search, but no fund has been established to receive the money."[9] It would seem Capone's vault was to remain a mystery, but an article in the *Los Angeles Times* would change everything and give thirty million people the ride of their lives.

3

The Farm Report

1985

All shows begin with a pitch. John Masterson in 1975 had an idea for a show where people would agree to have their differences settled in court on television. He pitched it to Monty Hall, the producer and game-show host of a *Let's Make a Deal,* and his partner, producer Stefan Hatos. An associate producer, Stu Billet, pitched the idea to the networks, but no one was interested in a program where people argued their cases in front of a judge. Eventually the show found its footing with a first-run syndication and a host: the blond-haired Doug Llewelyn, who had been a news reporter in Washington and Los Angeles. Llewelyn soon formed a production company, The Westgate Group, with producer John Joslyn.

On January 24, 1985, an article appeared in the *Los Angeles Times.* CAPONE HOTEL TO BE A WOMEN'S MUSEUM. Joslyn was always on the lookout for an idea for a show. He scanned the article about the Sunbow Foundation developing the hotel into an international women's museum and research center for the 1992 Chicago World's Fair. "Al Capone's Depression Era palace—a once opulent hotel that was home to mobsters and madams—is about to become a museum honoring the virtues of women." One paragraph caught his interest. "While the museum will be a repository of women's history, it will not ignore the storied past of the Lexington, which had 10 underground tunnels and a dozen secret staircases, one of them in the bathroom."[1]

This intrigued the producer, but it was the second article from the Associated Press he read while drinking coffee with his feet up on his desk that made him sit straight up. IRS PLACES A TAX LIEN ON HOTEL TO GET SHARE OF CAPONE'S LOOT. He turned the paper and began reading an article about the Lexington Hotel in Chicago.

> A tax lien issued by the IRS to the owners of a hotel that once served as Capone's headquarters demands $800,000 worth of whatever is found in the basement's vault. "I couldn't believe it," said Patricia Porter of the Sunbow Foundation. . . . Porter said she was shocked by the IRS lien, which applies to the contents of a city-block-long concrete vault the Sunbow crew discovered last winter while renovating the old Lexington Hotel . . . the vault is buried behind a wall in the basement of the ten-story Lexington. For months Porter's foundation has had plans to jackhammer through the vault's concrete walls to reveal its contents, but financing has been a problem.[2]

Joslyn felt the hair on the back of his neck stand up as he read about the vault that might have the missing money of Al Capone, bodies, even a car. The vault had been sealed with a slab of concrete. When his partner Doug Llewelyn came in, he brought the newspaper to his office. Doug Llewelyn was at that time known to most Americans as a tall man with a dour expression and well-coiffed blond hair in an impeccable suit who appeared at the end of the show *The People's Court* and said censoriously, "If you have a dispute you can't work out, don't take the law into your own hands; take them to court."

Joslyn opened the paper on Llewelyn's desk.

"Doug, what do you think about this?"

Llewelyn read the article with interviews of Patricia Porter and mafia "historian" Harold Rubin, describing Capone's hidden vault in the basement of the Lexington Hotel. Doug looked up. It was big. Joslyn recalled, "We ran it by a pal of ours in New York who was in ad sales, and he said, 'that's the funniest thing I've ever heard.'³ He also said we had to do it." Llewelyn flew to Chicago and met with Patricia Porter. "She showed me the entrance to a subterranean basement that had been sealed over, and we thought, 'well maybe there's something there too,'" Llewelyn recalled in a 2016 *Chicago Tribune* interview. "What she said made sense. There was no guarantee but at least it was an interesting theory."⁴ He made Porter an offer after flying back to LA. Fifty thousand dollars up front and 1 percent of the profits. He and Joslyn thought the cost of the production would come to about $1 million.

They wrote up a proposal for a live show that would break into the vault to reveal whatever Al Capone had left behind, then pitched it to ABC and NBC. Both networks declined and said they had to know what was inside the vault before they would sponsor the show. "We gotta know what's inside," NBC told the producers. It seemed they had hit a wall, but then they heard of a small company called Tribune Entertainment. They sent over the proposal that landed on the desk of Sheldon Cooper, president of Tribune Entertainment. The only problem was the pitch was on the bottom of a stack of scripts and proposals no one had touched in the new company with only twenty-four employees.

Allan Grafman, head of finance and business affairs, had just become one of them. He recalled:

> I called Jim Dowdle twenty-three times before he hired me. It wasn't much of a company then. We had only WGN radio and television with three other stations in Chicago, New York, and Denver. We were looking for content and I was brought in to make deals to bring in programming. Our big hit was . . . wait for it, syndicated through the Midwest, *The US Farm Report.*⁵

Grafman in our interviews is very personable, persistent, and affable. Sheldon Cooper, his boss, was the president of Tribune Entertainment.

He probably had ADD and was always saying "gotta keep shoveling, gotta keep shoveling" . . . which meant we had to keep working and find content for our stations to syndicate out. I bought eight shows that had been stage plays that nobody wanted. So, we had the *Farm Report* and *At the Movies*. We bought *Baywatch* and *Fame* through national syndication and I sat down with Oprah Winfrey and her attorney and tried for national syndication rights but they went with King World . . . so basically we had nothing and that's when I went to the stack of scripts and pitches on Shelly's desk and pulled this one out on Al Capone's vault.[6]

Grafman, an angular man with a Christopher Walken East Coast accent, laughed. "I told Shelly I wanted to meet with these guys and he said go . . . gotta keep shoveling." But Cooper liked the idea. "We were generating content for our stations to sell across the country. It was really for stations that couldn't afford original content on their own."[7] Still, Sheldon Cooper was troubled. No one knew if anything was in the vault. Allan Grafman went out to meet with Westgate and hear Joslyn and Llewelyn's pitch.

"We were only a few years old at the time and had syndicated shows but doing something live was unheard of . . . I met with Westgate and thought this could really be something. I knew it was way too out there for the big networks,"[8] Grafman later confirmed. Llewelyn and Joslyn worked on their pitch and returned to Tribune Entertainment and pitched Peter Marino, Vice President of Program Development. This was it. If the Tribune didn't take it on, then they would have no sponsor. Joslyn did more research and upped his pitch again, telling Marino about the secret tunnels that had been found running from the hotel to other buildings and hidden stairwells that had been found by the workers of the Sunbow Foundation leading to the basement and the electrical conduit that went into the slab of cement sealing up the vault. Why would there be electricity in this hidden room? He told him about the legend of Capone's lost money. The pitch worked this time. The Tribune would pay $900,000 to Westgate for the two-hour live show. "It was a big commitment, to do a live show and not know what's in the vault,"[9] Joslyn later admitted.

The Associated Press got wind of the deal and fueled speculation: "*Capone Vault May Be Opened by California Film Company.*"[10] Patricia Porter told the paper she was waiting for a contract and expected filming to begin immediately. It was then confirmed that Sunbow would get $50,000 to let the company film the vault's opening and would receive 1 percent of the royalties from any broadcast. They had already received $5,000 to let Westgate X-ray the vault. The IRS had served Sunbow again with papers seeking $806,000 in back taxes, interest, and penalties owed by Al Capone. The IRS said the tax bill would be paid from the contents of the vault and not by Sunbow.

Allan Grafman went to work and knew he had the ultimate hook to sell the program: Al Capone and Chicago. Capone was known internationally and Chicago for good or bad was known as the headquarters of the gangsters. Grafman would eventually sell it worldwide to twenty different countries. "Al Samuelson was the corporate risk officer, and I had to take him over to the Lexington and take him down in the basement. It was a war zone," Grafman recalled. "A dangerous wreck where stairs or walls could fall over any minute. I mean here was the risk officer looking at this disaster of a building where we want to a do a two-hour live show and blast open a vault in the basement." Grafman paused. "It's amazing he signed off."[11]

The *Tribune*, while taking a chance, did have some assurance. Clark Morehouse, who was then executive vice president, pointed to another live show that had aired the year before. "TPE did a live special and tried to raise a vault out of the shipwreck *Andrea Doria* from World War II. They didn't find a whole lot, but they did a 22 rating, which was very nice, so we were coming on the heels of that."[12] Morehouse oversaw ad sales. "We had 28 commercial units to sell, and they sold incredibly fast."[13] Peter Marino and Grafman pushed the idea of a live show where the excavation of the vault would happen in real-time. Grafman felt if it was taped it would be just another show on Capone.

Donald Hacker, then vice president of Tribune Entertainment, thought it was crazy but intriguing. A live two-hour show where the vault would be revealed in real-time. "They had found secret passages. So, I thought yeah, this could be intriguing. This was long before the History Channel or the Discovery Channel, but it was in that vein."[14]

A format was established for the show that would include the back story of Al Capone in a documentary style while the live excavation of the vault proceeded. Now they needed someone who could pull off a live television show and usher an audience through the unknown vastitudes of a show that depended on intrigue, drama, and building tension, all while the physical digging went on in a nineteenth-century basement under a crumbling hotel. And add to that the biggest curve ball of the whole show: no one knew what was in the vault. They needed a host. The obvious choice was Robert Stack. He had played Eliot Ness from 1959 to 1963 on the television show *The Untouchables*. Sheldon Cooper pushed back on Joslyn's suggestion. "I said that's not a bad idea, but I really think we need someone who can walk and talk at the same time."[15]

Peter Marino agreed, and the consensus became they needed someone from news. "I had seen Robert Stack attempt a morning TV talk show, I felt we needed someone who could do it without cue cards, a real reporter." Sheldon pushed for Mike Wallace of *60 Minutes*, but there were doubts CBS would allow Wallace to star in a two-hour live show digging up Capone's vault under the Lexington Hotel. No, they needed someone good on their feet, part journalist, part showman, part carnival barker. Sheldon pointed out that he knew of someone who might work. "There's this guy who just got fired from ABC, but he won them a bunch of awards."[16]

At first, Geraldo Rivera seemed like an out-of-the-box idea, but Cooper was adamant. "Geraldo was a celebrity. The Tribune company took a real risk. They were these conservative Irish Catholic wingtip shoes guys, and they want this hard charging Jewish Puerto Rican guy," Clark Morehouse, head of Sales at Tribune Entertainment, recalled.[17] "I was living in Brooklyn for a while, and we threw a Christmas party and Geraldo showed up in a limousine . . . the whole neighborhood lit up." Geraldo had made a big splash on *Goodnight America* when he was the first to broadcast the uncut version of the Zapruder film. Sheldon Cooper felt Geraldo had been hit hard by being fired and might want to get back out there. Donald Hacker placed a call to Geraldo's agent, who listened to the pitch patiently.

"Hell no," he responded and then hung up.[18]

Sheldon Cooper told the producers to approach Geraldo directly. But the question was, where was Geraldo? He had retreated from the world after his devastating fall from grace and was somewhere on his sailboat in the Panama Canal. Nobody was quite sure where he was, but Sheldon Cooper told Hacker to contact Geraldo in the Caribbean. The next day Donald Hacker attempted to find Geraldo Rivera to pitch a live two-hour show based on blasting open a vault with dynamite in an abandoned hotel basement in Chicago that might or might not belong to the notorious Al Capone. It was right up Geraldo Rivera's alley.

4

Willowbrook

1971

He was Jewish. He was Puerto Rican. He had a law degree. He was from New York. His name was Jerry Rivera to throw people off from his Jewish heritage, but he changed it to Geraldo to accent his Puerto Rican roots. He fronted a handlebar mustache and long hair. He would smoke pot on television. Cover AIDS before anyone else. He would air the unedited Zapruder film. He was a muckraker of television and fearless. Drug busts. War zones. This would all become the domain of the five-foot-seven Geraldo Rivera. He was the Hemingway of news journalism who covered news and made news. He would meet John Lennon and Yoko Ono and interview them while they were lying in their bed nude, then take them for a ride in a convertible Volkswagen. He would have four wives, make millions of dollars, and spend it all, and he would unknowingly be a pioneer in the way news and entertainment intersected. He would be reviled by people in his own industry, looked down upon by the news establishment; the Cronkites and Brinkleys and Rathers would see him as nothing more than a carnival barker bringing down the standards of television journalism. Through it all Geraldo Rivera would be almost undefinable. Love him. Hate him. He was a celebrity in his own right and would do what no one else would dare to do.

Geraldo was doing it now. Busting into a mental institution called Willowbrook with a camera crew. He was the long-haired young activist reporter looking for a cause and he had found one with reports of abused children in unspeakable conditions. But he had to get inside.

> I always drove when we were out on a heavy story and Mike sat up front giving directions. The crew sat in back and prepared on the fly. Bob Alis, the cameraman, tinkered with his newer, lighter version of the Auricon sound on film camera. Dave Weingold, the sound man, connected his audio lines to the camera. Ronnie Paul, the lighting man, got his portable sun gun ready. We drove past the guard at the gate at high speed.[1]

That's from Geraldo's 1991 tell-all memoir, *Exposing Myself.*

They clear the gate and Geraldo and his crew jump out and race inside with the cameras rolling. He has come far from when in 1970 news director Fred Friendly picked the young lawyer out of the crowd for a new program at Columbia University's Graduate School of Journalism. The legendary producer of Ed Murrow fame, Friendly was running a program "to train young black and brown professionals as reporters."[2] Friendly took Geraldo under his wing; at twenty-seven, he had his first job with WABC TV. And now Geraldo was on his first big story:

> We bounded up the steps and into a washroom area, the smell hit us before we reached the empty room, but it was bearable. I thought to myself, this is nothing. There's no story here. But we kept on. Mike knew where we were going. Next, he turned and opened a heavy metal door with a small glass window. We barreled in after him. There we saw about sixty profoundly retarded children living on a drab, cold ward that looked like an unfinished basement . . . exposed pipes ran the length of the room. Chunks of plaster were peeling from dirty cement green walls. . . .

But what Geraldo saw next knocked him to his knees. "The residents bore only a passing resemblance to children. Some as Mike had warned, were naked, others wore fragments of clothing; others wore straightjackets. Their heads were swollen; their bodies, bent and twisted, and their eyes were blank or rolled back."[3]

In Geraldo's book he describes the horror from twenty years before as he told his cameraman to capture a child drinking from a toilet and "a boy of about eight or ten, lying on the cold floor, curled in a fetal position, his pants pulled down around his ankles, waiting for an attendant to clean the shit from his ass . . . the rank odors of shit, piss, and vomit." Geraldo is staggered when he goes to a row of toilets without seats and caked with filth and "there a small child curled around the rotting porcelain bases."[4] Geraldo and his crew finish up and get back in their cars, passing two squad cars on the way into the institution. When the story started that night it was a sensation, and the station was deluged with calls from viewers. Geraldo's story went national, and he did a follow-up the next night, closing dramatically with the words that would become his signature: hyped, heartfelt, stinging, memorable.

> We showed you that film again, because it comes with the promise that we're not going to let this story die. We're going back to Willowbrook again. We're going to talk to the parents. Again. And look at those horrible wards. Again. And show them to you. Again and again and again. Until somebody changes them. Even with your help we probably won't be able to change the world, but we might be able to make life a little more bearable for some kids living at the outer edges of society.[5]

Willowbrook would close, and Geraldo's life changed forever. "Willowbrook humbled me. It made a made me a different journalist and a different person. It also made me a celebrity." He was already on his way after marrying Kurt Vonnegut's daughter, Edie, but now he was in a different place. John Johnson, a reporter for *Eyewitness News*, summarized Geraldo's sudden fame. "It all started with Willowbrook. It was the right time and the right place. We were going through a very revolutionary era, where the antihero, in a way, was in, where someone who had Geraldo's charisma, he was very attractive to the jet setters. Here he was, almost an outlaw type, who also had the soulfulness to care about the children who were being mistreated at Willowbrook, but who could also get down and boogie. It all fit together."[6]

The man who was to open Capone's vault had just become famous fifteen years before. After Willowbrook, Geraldo had done a series of hard-hitting new stories centered on crime and junkies in the ghetto. The young activist lawyer journalist with the long hair had become famous quickly. It happened that way in New York, where local fame was exported nationally. Geraldo had stumbled into a new style of gonzo journalism just getting started by Hunter S. Thompson and immortalized in *Fear and Loathing in Las Vegas*, and so it was no surprise when he found himself at a party attended by Kurt Vonnegut, Tom Wolfe, and Norman Mailer. "I was strictly a middleweight in a crowd like this, but people seemed to know who I was. I was an odd kind of ghetto pet to New York's jet set . . . I knew the streets and real people and how the other half lived."[7] It was here Geraldo met twenty-two-year-old Edie Vonnegut. Kurt's daughter Edie, wearing a big sheepskin coat, a small waif of a woman with curly hair, she and Geraldo left the party in his convertible Volkswagen.

In twenty-four hours, they were living together. Geraldo was now living with the daughter of one of the most famous men in the literary world. *Slaughterhouse Five, Cat's Cradle*, his novels were never hotter. "I was urban, gritty, dark, and skeptical and she was rural, soft light, and trusting,"[8] Geraldo later wrote, and began to think about marriage. He was also invited to cover the Concert for Bangladesh organized by George Harrison. After meeting Ringo Starr and George Harrison backstage an invitation was extended to meet John Lennon and Yoko Ono. The Jewish Puerto Rican lawyer was moving up in the world. Geraldo went to their apartment on Bank Street.

> I rang their doorbell at the agreed upon time and was met by a big burly guy who led me into another room where I was met by a woman. . . . I had to go through three or four layers of people and through three or four rooms

> before I was led into the master bedroom. And there he was, John Lennon ... he wore fairly thick rimless glasses.... His hair was cut short, and he was clean shaven ... there was a guitar by the side of the bed. Their big television set was on.... [9]

They talked about "world peace and poverty and Nixon and everything else we could think of." Geraldo then offered to take them to dinner, and they dressed (they were nude) and piled into his Volkswagen. This began a friendship between Geraldo and John Lennon and Yoko Ono where he would take them around in his VW with top down into some of the rougher parts of New York.

On November 21, 1971, *The New York Times* did a story on Geraldo Riviera by John O'Connor.

> He knows New York City ... unlike many newsmen who had difficulty telling the difference between a drunk and a heroin mainliner ... television news is part of television show business and Rivera is not the least bit shy about becoming a star.... Rivera himself refuses to be typecast. If he is outraged at certain social conditions, he is generally outraged when a policeman is shot in the back and gets threatening letters when he says so on television. If he is a first-rate activist reporter, he also throws himself into celebrity interviews that bring some entertainment and a change of pace ... directly and emotionally involved, he has tapped into an area that has been given if anything superficial and establishment-oriented coverage on television.[10]

Geraldo had arrived. Still at Channel 7 *Eyewitness News*, he was already pioneering a new type of newsman. Young, involved, passionate, the activist reporter who was banging up against the network white male-dominated culture of news anchors. Geraldo was everything they were not and vice versa. He would never be one of the members of the old boys' club. He had to go his own way and that would be his asset and curse throughout his career. People just did not know what to make of him, but he had arrived and married Kurt

Vonnegut's daughter at the Vonnegut house in Barnstable, Massachusetts, on Cape Cod in December of 1971.

Once Geraldo moved into the celebrity rung of society he and Edie began to drift apart. He became intoxicated with fame and money. "There was no room for Edie in this new world of mine. At least I didn't make room for her," he wrote later. "This was the one great moral failing during this period. I started to leave Edie behind to separate. I justified this behavior by telling myself that most of the society invitations didn't include her."[11] Geraldo had come from a hardscrabble background and now he was going to parties that included Marian Javits, the wife of Senator Javits. When he arrived at the party, "Marian hurried out to the hallway and embrace me, tight and warm. I was flattered . . . this forty-eight year old former actress and model had the dark hair, bright eyes and full lips of a gypsy. I responded to her embrace with great enthusiasm. Sure, I was married but so was she."[12]

Dinners with Henry Kissinger in attendance punctuated the torrid love affair as Geraldo charged ahead and sampled the rarified air of the 1 percent. Still, he was the activist journalist and formed the One-to-One Foundation,

> which became a kind of lobby group and charity fundraiser designed to fundamentally restructure the way intellectually disabled people were cared for in the metropolitan area and throughout the state. Over the next ten years One to One would raise more than five million dollars, open more than one hundred group homes for more than one thousand residents with intellectual disabilities.[13]

Geraldo was never better than when he was driven by a cause. He set up shop in the basement of 77 West 66th Street and recruited college students to raise money and organize events. "We lobbied community boards," he wrote later. "We found reasons to shoot follow up stories for Eyewitness News and other area stations. We fought endless zoning battles in our efforts to secure and convert housing to our needs. We tapped into existing government programs."[14]

In the spring of 1972 Geraldo organized a benefit concert for children with intellectual disabilities. There had been George Harrison's concert for Bangladesh, but no one had attempted a large concert on the scale Geraldo was envisioning. He needed a headliner and had an interview with John Lennon and Yoko Ono the year before. He had lost contact with them but flew out to San Francisco to pitch the idea. Acting as producer, director, and organizer, Geraldo was essentially doing what the Westgate Group and Tribune Entertainment would do thirteen years later: create something out of nothing. He found Lennon in San Franciso recovering from a detox for heroin addiction.

> These were tough times for John. He was already under attack from Attorney John Mitchell who was seeking to deport him. . . . The breakup of the Beatles had now been cemented by several years . . . but hard times or not I went after him, I was relentless in my pursuit. . . . With John Lennon to headline our benefit concert I thought surely we'd get the attention and the money we needed to help the children back home.[15]

Lennon was reluctant but Geraldo wore him down. John played songs on an acoustic guitar while Geraldo pointed out the benefits of the concert in John's apartment. John and Yoko finally agreed to do it, and fifty thousand people crowded into Madison Square Garden to hear John Lennon play. Years later Geraldo was only eight blocks away from the Dakota when he heard the shots that killed John Lennon.

*

Jerry Weintraub became Geraldo's agent and immediately saw him as someone who could blur the lines between news and entertainment.

> I felt Geraldo had a lot to offer . . . he was up in Harlem, he was in the streets, he was banging down doors in drug centers before it was popular. He was

doing a lot of things that were very different, number one. And number two, he had long hair and a moustache, and he was good looking, and he was young and he was three hundred and sixty degrees from everybody that was in the news business. There was nobody like him.

When several news positions at the networks didn't pan out, Jerry told Geraldo, "Look Geraldo, if you can't make it in the news division, fuck the news division. Keep your job at Eyewitness News, take their money, and I'll get something going with the entertainment division."[16]

The line between news and entertainment had been blurred. Jerry Weintraub would sell Geraldo as a "network personality." Geraldo meanwhile interviewed Muhammad Ali, John Lennon, Bette Midler, John Denver, Judy Collins, Stephen Stills, Stacy Keach, Cheech Marin. Many of the celebrities became personal friends as Geraldo landed his first show, *Good Night America*. "A pre-*Saturday Night Live*, late night hipster sensibility... included interviews with all the Beatles and Rolling Stones, the Grateful Dead...." Geraldo broke the rules again when he smoked a joint on the air.

> In an effort to bring to light the growing movement to legalize marijuana I smoked a joint on the air.... I told viewers that the marijuana I was about to smoke was supplied by the federal government for the NYU experiment.... I laid out all the urgent don't try this at home warnings.... It was the only time I would ever appear before a television camera under the influence of drugs or alcohol and the effect was startling....[17]

Promotion pieces of the taped segment smoking pot went out before the broadcast. They teased the audience with the shots of Geraldo smoking a joint and ABC News president Bill Sheehan saw the promo. "He made a panicked call to our office and ordered us to edit the marijuana segment from the ninety minutes we were readying for the broadcast. I refused to edit the piece and Sheehan wound up killing the promotional teases that had been scheduled but not yet run." Eventually Geraldo gave in and cut the piece, but he put CENSORED in its place. He then took out an ad in *The New York Times* with the same CENSORED across the top and explained to readers what happened: "As a direct result of Sheehan's suppression our ratings increased substantially for the second broadcast." It was a lesson learned. Controversy sells even if nothing is delivered to the viewer. "Critics who had in large part been willing to let the show air unnoticed were drawn to our show. . . . I had, it seemed, a hip, new following and the beginnings of a new career."[18]

Geraldo then aired the Abraham Zapruder home movie of the 1963 Kennedy assassination. It was the first network airing of the controversial film, and it stirred the conspiracy pot of assassination theories to a boiling point. Geraldo mixed news with sensational reporting and interviewed Jane Fonda, Grace Slick, B. J. Thomas, Bill Withers, Sha Na Na, Kris Kristofferson, Don McLean, John Denver, Carole King, and others. He was the counterculture darling of news but not the darling of straight news. "As an interviewer of other celebrities," the *New York Times* critic wrote, "Mr. Rivera keeps tripping over anxiety about his own celebrity. The result is too often embarrassing. . . . Mr. Rivera has come a long way from his perceptive and sympathetic essays about the poor and hopeless on the streets."[19]

In 1974 he and his first wife, Edie Vonnegut, divorced and after a series of romances that included Bette Midler, he became engaged to the daughter of a billionaire, Francine LeFrak. A whirlwind romance and a sixteen-thousand-dollar engagement ring pushed the activist reporter yet again into the rarefied air of the ultra-rich.

The very success of Geraldo Rivera damned him for all time to the news establishment. Interviewing Paul and Linda McCartney and fraternizing with the same celebrities after the interview kept him from ever landing the august patriarchal anchor jobs of the big three networks. Instead, he joined NBC's *Good Morning America* in 1976. A former intern for *Good Night America*, Michael Horowitz, recalled that a man was in Geraldo's office, and he demanded someone get him a cup of coffee. "'He's the governor of Georgia, he's gonna be the next President of the United States. Here's a dollar. Go down and get this guy coffee.' . . . [N]o one believed him. And it was him, Jimmy Carter . . . it was an incredible thing."[20]

In 1977 his show *Good Night America* was canceled and after threatening to resign from *Good Morning America*, Geraldo ended up as a reporter on *The Evening News*. He then joined the ABC news magazine *20/20* on Tuesday June 6, 1978. In his own memoir *The Geraldo Show*, he wrestled with his identity as a journalist versus a celebrity. Running through romances like rain even though he was engaged and hanging with Mick Jagger, Kurt Vonnegut, Norman Mailer, Gore Vidal, Tom Wolfe, and Andy Warhol, Geraldo ran the gamut of the high life. One of these romances was with Sheri Braverman. Geraldo wrote later, "Part Sicilian, part Jewish ball of fire who happened to be married at the time to a friend of mine, Chuck Braverman, Sheri was everything Francine was not, a thin brunette with no formal education and a wild heart . . . she was also dynamic and passionate in a way that Francine could never be, at least not for me."[21] Geraldo married Sheri in 1976. The marriage lasted until 1984. He then began dating his associate producer, Cynthia Cruickshank, whom he called "CC."

For the next eight years with a million-dollar salary, Geraldo covered wars, famines, celebrities, all with the fearless Geraldo trademark, and it seemed he could do no wrong. He could do no wrong, right up to the story by his colleague Sylvia Chase on the sex goddess Marilyn Monroe and her relationship with the Kennedys. When ABC killed the story, Geraldo became incensed. Hugh Downs and Barbara Walters told him they stood with him.

> I was incensed . . . even though the Monroe piece was not my story. I looked on the *20/20* show as my show and I did not like anyone, even Roone, tampering with it. . . . I committed professional suicide later that evening in a telephone interview with syndicated columnist Liz Smith. She called

me around midnight, tipped that I would talk about the handling of the Monroe story . . . stoked with moral fury, I charged Roone with cronyism and censorship and questioned his journalistic integrity.[22]

He then responded to a *People* magazine reporter and further criticized his boss. Then Geraldo's girlfriend was caught transporting marijuana using an ABC messenger. The drug allegations added fuel to the fire. "I was fighting for my life. I worked the phones tirelessly," Geraldo recalled. He offered to take drug tests and threatened to sue ABC, but it was over. A press release came out from ABC. "After fifteen years of hard honorable work with ABC, Geraldo Rivera had told us that he wishes to leave to pursue other opportunities. Although we sincerely regret his decision, ABC does not wish to stand in the way of his future plans. We wish him well in those endeavors, including the possibility of freelance work for ABC."[23]

There would be no freelance work. In fact, there were no job offers at all. On November 21, 1985, Geraldo Rivera signed off on his last broadcast. His final words are a summation of his career. He summed up his career from storefront lawyer to becoming an investigative reporter and his path to ABC and *20/20*:

> I'm going to be leaving *20/20*. As one of the founding members of this wonderful program, this is one of the toughest decisions I've ever made. But it's time to go. I've always been sort of a square peg trying to squeeze into the round hole of network news. . . . I have no set plan for the future. Maybe I'll do what my buddy Hugh Downs did when he was my age and go sailing off into the sunset. . . .[24]

Geraldo did just that. He took his sailboat *New Wave* and on January 25, 1986, he began an around-the-world trip with no return date. And now the shape-shifting celebrity journalist lawyer known as Geraldo Rivera was pulling in the jib and correcting the main sail of his fifty-four-foot boat while steering through the Panama Canal. His trademark mustache and locks of brown hair ruffled in the wind that had just come up and heeled the boat over while Geraldo kept his feet planted wide and his hands on the wheel of the ship. His shirt was off in the Caribbean sun, and he felt a million miles away from the man who had been publicly fired by ABC. The Puerto Rican, Jewish, New York-born lawyer turned journalist had left New York to sail around the world. Like Teddy Roosevelt, whose wife and mother had died on the same day, pushing him to go to the badlands of South Dakota with no return date, Geraldo had simply left.

Geraldo steered the sailboat into the wind, then broke off at a forty-five-degree angle as the sails filled. Geraldo turned the wheel and followed the wind. He had been turned down for a spot on *60 Minutes* and a possible role in a Jane Fonda movie. He was turned down for NASA's journalist in space. He shook his head. At forty-two he wondered if his career was over on television. His style had proved "too flamboyant" for another major news network. He had walked the line between sensationalism and news but had yet to successfully combine the two in a way that would show his brand to the world.

Geraldo stared into the glaring sunshine. Maybe this was it. At forty-two he was washed up. It happened. He had begun as a "skinny, asthmatic, pimply-faced mutt" and had ridden the fame train to its obvious destination. He had met "Ronald Reagan, Donald Trump, Muhammad Ali, Elvis, Michael Jackson, and Yasser Arafat," and yet he always felt the tabloid aspect of his career denied him the respect of his colleagues. Now he was on his sailboat with his professional and personal life in shambles. His third marriage had ended in divorce. The word *comeback* had been used by his agent more than once. He did need a comeback. But staring over the leaning sailboat bow he didn't see anyone knocking on his door. To have a comeback one needed a platform, and he didn't see one out there. His brand of reporting chafed against the old journalism. He believed stories should be energized and yes, there was an entertainment factor. It was as if he was waiting for television to catch up to him.

Geraldo came about and the sailboat's main sail went slack and then caught the wind as the jib swung to the other side. He would just keep sailing. That was all he could do right now. The world could move on without him. If his career had taught him anything, it was when he least expected it that things happened for him. The warm air was balmy. He thought about making himself a drink when the satellite phone's shrill voice reached him from the cabin. Geraldo gave the wheel to one of his crew and swung down into the tawny teak-lined cabin. He picked up the phone and heard the voice of his agent.

5

Scarface

1930

Chicago was in a panic. Newspapers had an unofficial rule not to put gory photographs on the front pages. The photos that would eventually make it into the Chicago History Museum were black and white photographs of men with their skulls blown open draped over chairs and on the hard cement of a garage in pools of blood. The newspapers ran with the photos, and worse, they ran with headlines proclaiming Chicago was out of their control and that cops and gangsters were killing people. The panic the officials of Chicago felt was well founded. They were due to have a World's Fair in 1933, there was no turning back, and no one had thought to ask if Al Capone might be bad for business. Worse, people would stay away from the World's Fair, which would be held in the worst year of the Great Depression. Something had to be done, but what? Al Capone ran the city from the Lexington Hotel and had the mayor and just about everyone else on his payroll.

Rufus C. Dawes read Walter Trohan's prose and wondered who had come up with the idea to hold a World's Fair. He stared at the headlines in his office in downtown Chicago. The slaughter shocked even Chicago's hardened cops. "I tell you, I've never seen anything like it," one detective lamented after staring at the twisted bodies. Patrick Roche, a federal investigator, went even further. "Never in all the history of feuds or ganglands has Chicago or the nation seen anything like today's wholesale slaughter." *The New York Times* led the way: "7 Chicago Gangsters Slain by Firing Squad of Rivals, Some in Police Uniforms." The president of the 1933 World's Fair read the lead in the *Chicago Tribune* next: "Chicago ganglands leaders observed Valentines Day with machine guns and a stream of bullets and as a result seven members of the George (Bugs) Moran, Dion O'Banion North Side gang are dead in the most cold-blooded gang massacre in the history of the city's underworld. . . ."[1]

Dawes dropped the paper and groaned. The fair would depend on private-sector money and that meant getting big business to finance the building of the fair, but he couldn't very well ask for money when Al Capone and his gangsters were mowing down people in the streets. He knew if the city's business leaders didn't act fast Chicago would cease to be a viable economic center. But what could he do? Not only did Capone have the power, but the man who lived on two floors in the Lexington Hotel and had a workout gym, a barber, a food taster, and men in the lobby twenty-four seven reading newspapers with Thompson machine guns in their laps was a celebrity. He was a celebrity the way actors or sports figures are today. During his time, he was as big as Babe Ruth and as addicted to media as Donald Trump. He was as popular as a president and crowds had to be held off behind barricades whenever he appeared in court in his trademark white fedora with a fifty-thousand-dollar ring on his finger. He always wore a bulletproof vest and had bars on the window of his Cicero home. He had personally beat two men to death with a baseball bat and shot another man three times in the head for assaulting a man who worked for him.

He was constantly in the press, appearing in newsreels and the papers and would change dress, media, movies, speech, politics, drinking, and eventually, income tax law. He would offer to help law enforcement solve the Lindbergh kidnapping and the famous Chicago murder of the boy Bobby Franks. When the Great Depression hit, he set up soup kitchens all over the South Side of Chicago and fed hungry men and women. He was an employer of thousands of people who would swear Capone saved them when they had nothing to eat. Incredibly, he was chosen as *Time* Man of the of Year in 1930. He was bigger than life and deadlier than a graveyard.

Chicago had a homicide rate higher by 25 percent than anywhere else in the city. Cars mysteriously appeared in quiet neighborhoods, police opened the trunks and found corpses that had been shot fifteen or twenty times with skulls bashed in, eyes burned out, features melted away with acid. The movies were exporting gangland violence at the same time with cars racing around blasting Thompsons out the windows. To be a gangster was to be glamorous and deadly. At a different time, Al Capone might have been a great industrialist. He used the same organizational skills as any corporation and systematically took over bootlegging, gambling, and prostitution. Capone originated as the CEO far removed from his business operations who filtered his income tax through tax shelters. He pioneered the use of offshore accounts and tax havens in his use of checks made out to phony businesses that made their way back into his account. At the time paying taxes for most Americans was a voluntary act and Al Capone showed no income at all.

And now a thousand miles away from Chicago he was sitting in the Dade County office building in Florida. It was hot and his cheeks and forehead shined from perspiration. As the stenographer settled herself, he stared at Brooklyn prosecutor Louis Goldstein, Dade County prosecutor Robert Taylor, and county sheriff M. P. Lanham. He might have marveled at how far he had come. He had just driven in from his palatial estate on the ocean. Just seven years before he was outside a Chicago speakeasy in the snow, trying to lure people in for girls and drinks. Maybe he thought about stealing fruit in Brooklyn so he could eat. Now he was about to be asked if he had murdered seven men in Chicago. Prosecutor Taylor was sitting on a desk and looked at Capone, his voice echoing in the high-ceilinged office with the slow-turning fan.

"Do you remember when you first met Parker Henderson?"
"About two years ago."
"That was when he was running the Ponce de Leon Hotel?"
"Yes."
"Who was staying with you that winter?"
"I don't remember."
"Under what name did you register?"
"My own names."
"You didn't register under the name A Costa?"
"No."
"You left money with Henderson, 1,000 to 5,000 at a time?"
"I don't remember."
"You didn't receive any money by Western Union from Chicago?"
"I don't remember. I'll try to find out."
"Then you keep a record of your money transactions."
"Absolutely."
"How much did you give Henderson to buy your home?"
"Fifty thousand dollars."
"Was that in cash?"
"Yes."
"Besides gambling, you're a bootlegger, aren't you?"
"No, I was never a bootlegger."
"Do you know Jake Guzik?"
"Yes."
"What does he do?"[2]

Capone shifted his weight and pushed up his hat. The room was growing warmer. This was not going as usual. The cops generally asked him if he had killed so and so and he always said he was a peaceful businessman and that was it. But these guys seemed more interested in his money. Taxes. The government's right to tax American income had only been on the books since

1913 with the passage of the Sixteenth Amendment, and most Americans were still not aware of it. Surely, they couldn't be trying to figure out if he paid his taxes.

"He fights."

"And do you know anybody who sent you money under the name A Costa?"

"No."

"But you did receive money from Chicago?"

"That is correct. All of it come from Chicago, from my gambling business."

Capone stared at the prosecutor. "What has money got to do with it?"[3]

In Chicago, Rufus Dawes heard the press outside his office on LaSalle Street clamoring for a statement. Rufus looked at the headlines again. Capone was in Florida and Bugsy Moran wasn't among the dead. His retaliation would be brutal. Dawes stood up, straightened his tie, and walked into the hallway, where the press blinded him with flashbulbs. He momentarily wavered, then smiled. Reporters fired questions in rapid succession. Rufus held up his hands.

"Gentlemen . . . I assure you Chicago will be safe and sound for the World's Fair of 1933. That I can assure you."

A reporter from the *Chicago Tribune* barked, "How can you assure the world Chicago will be safe when Al Capone is gunning people down in garages?"

"Well . . . young man. We have a plan, and I can assure you the gangsters will be gone by the time the fair opens."

Rufus then turned abruptly and walked back into his office, drenched with perspiration, his hands shaking.

His secretary buzzed.

"I have the president of the Chicago Association of Commerce, Mr. Dawes."

Rufus grabbed the phone. "Robert, we have to do something."

Robert Isham Randolph paused. "I know."

Rufus squeezed the bridge of his nose. A real pounder of a headache was beginning. Randolph had ties to every powerful businessman in Chicago.

Nothing happened unless it passed through him. Randolph cleared his throat and Dawes waited.

"I have a plan."

Dawes breathed again and stared at the commotion outside his office window.

"Thank God."[4]

6

Signing Geraldo

January 1986

Doug Llewelyn says he spoke for hours on the phone with Geraldo about the two-hour special. Geraldo came back from the Panama Canal and ended up in the office of his ex-jockey chain-smoking agent, Jim Griffin, to discuss the offer from Tribune Broadcasting for the live syndicated special called "The Mystery of Al Capone's Vaults." In Geraldo's book *Exposing Myself*, he describes the encounter where his agent tries to talk him out of doing the broadcast.

"They want you to host a syndicated special. Two hours live, they've got some deal with a vault that supposedly belonged to Al Capone. It's been sealed for years. They want to open it on live television."

"'What do you think,' I asked. I knew what I thought—even the worst possible deal sounded good to me.

"I think twenty-five thousand dollars is spit. It's syndicated and syndicated shows never do well." He had a whole list of reasons why I should not accept the job, ending with his assessment that my doing this show would not be unlike boxings former heavyweight champion at the end of his career becoming a professional wrestler. "It's beneath you."[1]

Geraldo said he would do it for fifty thousand. He lists off the financial reasons he had to take the money that is equivalent to $122,000 today. "I had three hundred thousand dollars a year in alimony and child support payments. I had lost my house in Malibu, my apartment on Central Park West and a large portion of my other assets in an expensive and bitter divorce a year earlier." Geraldo also had his parents to support, a penthouse on Ninety Sixth and Madison Avenue, and his sailboat *New Wave* that cost a cool fifty thousand a year. He had been making one million dollars a year at ABC, but he had nothing to show for his extravagant salary, and he needed cash. ABC had paid him a $500,000 cash settlement when he left, and he felt the fifty thousand dollars would see him through a month and give him time to consider his next move. He had a tentative job offer from a cable station, but the money was low.

"Ask for fifty," he told his agent. "Then I'll do it."

"Fifty is still spit."

"Jim, I've got nothing else lined up. Nobody is knocking down my door."

"You realize the vault may be empty."[2]

Geraldo had not considered this and hesitated. For the first time he thought about the premise of the whole show. Something had to be in the vault for there to be a payoff. Al Capone had to have left something behind to give viewers what they wanted. Television depended on a reward at the end of a show, a summation, a denouement, a surprise ending, and an unexpected twist. The medium was designed to entertain but more than that to thrill people so they would watch again. In this case it was a one off. The pitch was tune in and see what the great mobster Al Capone might have left in a secret vault in his one-time residence. There had to be something there to reward the audience for sitting through a two-hour excavation. Before television there were World's Fairs and the traveling circus. Then the circus left town, but television remained and to get people to watch, to return again, there had to be the equivalent of the world's strongest man or the man who is shot out of a cannon.

"There's that chance," Geraldo conceded. "But what if it's not?"

He gestured to the horseplayer's credo on the wall. *Scared money never wins.*

"What about that?"

"You'll be standing there on live television, national television with two hours to fill." His agent shook his head. "You better learn a song or a couple jokes, just in case."

Geraldo later rationalized his decision to take the job by telling himself, "it didn't matter if Al Capone's vaults were empty or riddled with cash and corpses. Whatever we would or would not find in the basement of Chicago's Lexington Hotel, I was sure I could produce a great documentary on an intriguing period in American history—prohibition, and the era of the Chicago mob. It was a chance to tell a story that people seemed to want to hear."

"Fifty," Jim Griffin asked, making sure.

"Fifty."[3]

The *Tribune* matched the fee, and Geraldo Rivera was once again employed. The question of whether or not something was in the vault he had conveniently tucked away for now. But there were others who were questioning the same thing. The possibility of nothing being in the vault became the subject not mentioned. Jim Griffin had brought up the one question that the Westgate Group, Tribune Entertainment, Sheldon Cooper, Doug Llewelyn, Allan Grafman all had made an unsaid pact not to consider. Was there something in the vault? *Of course there was something in the vault. There had to be.* The show pitch was too good, and the producer is nothing but positive. Shows are put together on a pitch and then held together with toothpicks and glue and were like a house of cards where one card pulled out can mean disaster. That one card is never questioned. It shall remain in place. Besides, another vault had been opened two years before on live television and things did not go as planned then either. That vault had been on a ship, the *Andrea Doria*.

7

The Opening of the Safe from the *Andrea Doria*

August 16, 1984

A United Press International article proclaimed DORIA YIELDS A SAFE.[1] The seas had been too rough to dive and then when the weather cleared, they descended two hundred feet to the ocean bottom and started back through the sunken Italian liner the *Andrea Doria*. The safe was cut loose from the moorings in the ship with acetylene torches and brought to the surface. It was August 28, 1981. The safe would not be opened until three years later. On August 17, 1984, George Plimpton filled for two hours while the safe was readied for opening. Millions watched on 161 stations and in forty-four countries as gold jewels worth millions were promised to viewers who had sat through droning documentary footage to finally arrive at the moment everyone had been waiting for.

The Associated Press article that appeared the next day told what happened.

It was billed as the live event of the year but what it was was Amateur Night. The safe from the sunken liner *Andrea Doria* was opened tonight at the New York Aquarium while millions watched on the 161 American stations and in 44 countries with visions of stacks of cash and diamonds by the handful. What they got was a few packets of 20 bills and some Italian lira.[2]

It was a dry run for the opening of Capone's vault two years later with the urbane, lanky George Plimpton as the host talking viewers through the tragedy of the *Andrea Dorea*, which had been speared by the liner *Stockholm* on a foggy night on July 25, 1956. She went down by the bow eleven hours later taking 46 lives with her. Some 1,660 people were rescued, and the ship became a favorite of divers. Among them was department store heir, filmmaker, and adventurer Peter Gimbel, who would make it his life's obsession to dive on the ship over and over, and who would bring up the safe in 1981.

The special, called "The Final Chapter," had centered on the back story of the *Andrea Doria* and the subsequent diving operations of Gimbel and his wife. In a parallel to the lost money of Al Capone, ever since the *Andrea Doria* sank there had been intense speculation that down in the murky darkness of the ship's interior there were millions in treasure waiting to be released by divers who would brave the dangerous waters and the labyrinthine interior of the once-elegant liner. When the liner went down in heavy fog fifty miles south of Nantucket it was a one in a million chance she would collide with another ship, but the 697-foot *Doria* could not avoid the Swedish ship *Stockholm*, and her evasive swerving and reversing of her engines only ensured her doom. The *Stockholm* rammed into the *Doria* at 11:10 p.m., and fifty-two people lost their lives, but forty-six were on the *Doria*. A fourteen-year-old Linda Morgan was later found in the wreckage of the *Stockholm* with both knees and her arm and shoulder broken, but she survived.

A documentary was produced about Gimbel's obsession with the *Doria*, which began two days after the sinking when he dove on the wreck. A CBS special in 1976 centered on his passion and role as a filmmaker while he engineered bringing up the safe. He nearly died from an oxygen overdose, and a hurricane almost destroyed the project to bring up the safe. Gimbel pioneered a new salvaging technique and worked from a pressurized bell that allowed the divers to stay underwater for days. When the safe was finally brought to the surface from its resting place 240 feet below the surface of the Atlantic Ocean, Gimbel and his co-filmmaker, Elga Anderson, who had codirected the documentary and organized the expedition to retrieve the safe, determined the safe wouldn't be opened until a television screening could be arranged to help pay for the $2 million expedition. The film and the expedition were covered by ten silent investors for $1.75 million, the show was sold to 161 American stations and 44 countries. The grand opening would take place at the New York Aquarium in Coney Island.

The safe was sealed by US Customs and placed under a bond of $2 million; then it was put on display in the aquarium shark tank and later in a cold-water tank that would keep bacteria from becoming activated and destroying the safe's contents. The bacteria's presence led Gimbel and others to believe millions of paper dollars might be in the safe. Three days before the broadcast the safe was moved into another Lucite tank that would allow the TV audience to see the safe opened. The major networks showed no interest, so the show was syndicated and distributed through an ad hoc network, Telerep Inc., which covered 95 percent of households with television.

But first they had to open the safe. Sal Schillizzi was one of the celebrated safecrackers of his time and had opened many difficult safes. He began working on the *Andrea Doria* safe on July 24. It was the strangest experience he had ever encountered in cracking a safe. The water level was brought down so the door protruded four inches above the waterline. If the water was brought down any further, it would allow the bacteria to consume whatever was in the safe. Like Capone's vault, there was no record of what might have been stored in the safe. There had been rumors of $4 million in cash. Gimbel and other divers never found the motherlode believed to be stored in the first-class safe of deposit boxes, which had been described as containing $1 million in negotiable bonds along with diamonds and gems.

Over the years divers had brought up a 1956 bottle of red wine and gold appliqué Ginori plates, but there had been no gold mine of money or precious gems. So far. The safe Schillizzi was working on was a money safe that was twenty-eight inches and nearly five feet tall and secured with a combination lock and another lock that required two keys. A broken key in the lock led some to believe someone was in the safe when the *Stockholm* rammed the *Andrea Doria*. The bank of the ship was forty feet from the impact. But now the safe was to be opened on live television.

When the 650-pound safe door opened on camera at 8:30 p.m., during a break in Gimbel's film about the expedition, it broke loose from the derrick that was lifting it and fell shut again.

"Let's get some muscles on this thing," shouted Plimpton.

Moments later, at 8:32, crowbars and hands did the job.

All anyone could see was murky water. There was nothing to do but wait for it to clear. Plimpton cut to documentary footage again. Six or eight times he came back to the live action, but each time there was nothing to see but people watching the dark water-filled safe, lying on its back, while occasionally packets of money floated to the surface.

The anticlimax of the moment was broken only by the gurgling of the safe below the surface of the water. Plimpton and others stared gloomily at the water. He cut to the documentary film again, then came back while everyone stared at the dark water. He did this six times and each time the camera cut back there were just people staring at the "dark water filled safe, lying on its back, while occasionally some more liras floated to the surface."[3] Nothing was happening. No more money had floated up. Finally, a worker put his hand down in the water to find the elusive diamonds or gold. The crowd held its breath.

But there were no diamonds, no gems, no amazing valuables that would justify the two-hour wait. There were only the soggy bills. The hundred reporters were invited to stare into the safe that held nothing. The filmmaker, Peter Gimbel, put a good face on the disaster of the moment. "I'm dazzled. I'm thrilled. It doesn't make any difference if its eight cents, it's got wonderful value."[4]

The crowd outside in the rain standing by the shark tank shouted, "you should have opened it." "The Final Chapter" would score a 22 in ratings.

It wasn't a smash hit, but it was enough for Sheldon Cooper at Tribune Entertainment two years later to greenlight another two-hour special that depended on something from another time contained in a vault that would only be revealed on live television.

8

The Tunnels of Chicago

Beneath the city was another world. This was the premise of Capone's vault. Secret stairwells, vaults, and beyond all that, tunnels were promised to the viewing audience. No one knew yet what was in the vault that Geraldo Rivera would open on April 21, 1986, and most people were not aware of the secret stairwells leading down from Capone's living quarters on the fifth floor and no one knew of the tunnels that crisscrossed Chicago forty feet below the surface. Chicago was a city with a strange relationship with the earth. The city had been settled on a swampland with the same elevation as the shoreline of Lake Michigan. Epidemics of typhoid and dysentery plagued the city with an 1854 cholera epidemic that killed 6 percent of the population. A plan was developed for a sewage system that included raising existing buildings to a new grade. Buildings were jacked up off their foundations or relocated to make room for the underground sewers. A row of buildings on Lake Street were elevated using six thousand jackscrews operated by six hundred men.

Still, most people had no idea the city was raised or that there was something forty below the surface until 1991, when pilings driven into the sand under the Chicago River near the Kinzie Street Bridge nicked a subterranean tunnel beneath the river. George W. Jackson understood the risk of flooding. He was an engineer in 1909 who had designed the tunnel system under Chicago and understood the risk of water entering the tunnels and had bulkheads installed at various points where the tunnels went into the basements of Chicago buildings. But that was a hundred years before, and many of the buildings' bulkheads were no longer in use and had been sealed up with regular doors—or worse still, were open. Still, the leak caused by the pilings was slow and the response to it was even slower. Six months later the leak blew a large hole into the tunnel and the world became aware of an elaborate tunnel system built at the beginning of the twentieth century as buildings all over the South Loop of Chicago flooded. Water gushed from the river into the tunnels and filled up the basements of the Merchandise Mart, the Federal Reserve Bank, and the Chicago Hilton Towers. It became known as the Chicago Flood and people were astounded to learn that indeed there was another world beneath the city of Big Shoulders.

This other world was forty feet beneath the surface of Chicago. The underworld of Capone described this perfectly, but before Capone it was the Tunnels of Chicago. In 1898 Alderman Edward J. Novak of the 8th ward introduced an ordinance to grant a franchise to a company to build tunnels to lay telephone conduit to compete with Chicago Telephone Company. A fifty-year lease was granted and a shaft sunk at the 170 West Madison Street. A massive elevator hauled out excavated dirt and sand and it was deposited into Lake Michigan. On the same elevator, gravel and cement went down the shaft. "Upon arrival at the construction site the concrete was forced by hand into the open areas behind wooden forms which had been built then allowed to dry. Once the concrete had hardened in place the forms were removed, and an additional layer of concrete was applied to give the walls a smooth finished appearance."[1]

The tunnels were built forty feet down in the blue clay stratum under the city. Workers had to use knives to cut out the clay, a laborious process that slowed the work down. "Tunneling operations were generally carried out under ten pounds of air pressure to minimize the possibility of cave ins permitting daily progress of 12 to 16 feet at each construction heading. Work forces were organized on a three-shift basis, working around the clock. The two-night shifts cut though the clay with handheld knives while the day shift poured concrete. . . . The excavated clay and dirt were removed in 14" gauge cars which were moved over temporary tracks to the construction shaft for removal. Excavated materials transported to Grant Park reclaimed one hundred acres from the lake."[2] In 1904 train operations began and the Illinois Tunnel Company invited members of the press and distinguished guests down into the Jackson Street Tunnel. The dinner party went down an elevator and were met at the bottom by a special train that took them on a tour and then dropped them off at the intersection of Jackson and Fifth. Here in the tunnels was a banquet hall with temporary overhead lighting and bunting lining the tunnels. Telephones were on the tables for the press to relay the good news that a new railroad running forty feet under Chicago was now operational.

By 1914, fifty miles of cavernous tunnels crisscrossed under Chicago and began hauling coal, ash, mail, and freight. The tunnels were typically seven feet and six inches high and six feet wide with 2 feet 610 mm gauge track. There were nineteen elevators to get customers to the tunnels. One hundred and thirty-two electric locomotives with a pulling strength of 50 horsepower hauled 2,042 merchandise cars. The small electric locomotives pulled the cars along twelve-gauge tracks, and the term *underground railroad* became a literal description of the invisible system. The tunnels were always cool at 55 degrees and buildings brought the cooled air to be pumped in as early air conditioning. The tunnels went under the Chicago River and ended up in the basements of buildings where freight, coal, and cinders were loaded and moved across the city, relieving congestion above. Chicago was a coal-fired city, and the buildings needed massive amounts for boilers. The small electric gauge railroad fed the buildings from the basements and took away the ash. Telephone lines running in the tunnels allowed the phone networks to expand but the Chicago Tunnel Company posted losses as early as 1906 and the building of a subway system later would close many of the tunnels. In 1909 the company was forced into receivership and forced to reorganize.

One of the buildings the tunnels connected to was the Lexington Hotel. Mail, coal, and ashes were carried to and from the hotel. The tunnels invariably became used for bringing booze into various locations during the 1930s. The tunnels had a brief encounter with fame during one scene from the movie *The Blues Brothers*, but other than that they remained a secret swirling around the mythology of Capone until Patricia Porter connected it to the vault in the bottom of the Lexington Hotel. A perusal of articles that began appearing before the opening of the vault has the tunnels making it into the press. "It was also believed that numerous secret staircases and tunnels provided Capone and his associates with easy access and to buildings throughout the area. The tunnels were also thought to connect to Chicago's massive tunnel system that was built at the turn of the century to haul coal and freight."[3] *The Albuquerque Journal* also featured a one-page ad emblazoned with AL CAPONE'S VAULTS. "A cement bunker discovered in the bowels of a rundown Chicago hotel—a former headquarters for the famous gangster—will be opened LIVE."[4]

Other papers followed suit connecting the tunnels with the vault. "The building which is being rehabilitated by a foundation that wants to turn it back into a hotel also contains secret passageways and stairways and exit tunnels which Capone used to elude police and federal agents."[5] Many people felt that the tunnels were more proof that Al Capone had something to hide down in the vault of the Lexington Hotel. The real purpose of the tunnels was forgotten as it was assumed Capone had the tunnels built to escape the law or other gangsters. Another article goes even further in connecting the tunnels and the vault. The *San Francisco Examiner* claimed, "During the 20s the Lexington was connected by an extensive underground tunnel system complete with electric lighting that ran to Colosimo's, a classy club, and the Metropole Hotel, both across the street, as well as to Capone's home. Legend has it that the tunnels reached as far as Chicago City Hall and police headquarters. It was said that Capone could get 1,000 people out of here in 15 minutes without anyone hitting the streets. Porter says the tunnel system will be opened and explored during the television special."[6]

The tunnels used to haul coal and mail and still operating during Capone's time were now part of the great mystery that would be solved when the vault was opened on April 21, 1986. No one knew what was in vault. "And we didn't want to know," Allan Grafman of Tribune Entertainment said years later. "We thought there was something there. Everyone did but in another way, we didn't really want to know for sure one way or another."[7] Still, the producers brought in X-ray equipment, sonar and scanned the vault, but there was no conclusive evidence that anything was there other than dirt and empty space. The papers immediately began carrying pictures of the cemented archway in the basement of the hotel, tantalizing readers that the vault had not been opened since Capone left on May 5, 1932.

The tunnels were loaded into Capone mythology, with many thinking Capone imported workers from Italy to complete them. The same Sicilian laborers were suspected of building the brick wall in the basement of the Lexington and sealing it with a slab of concrete. It was all coming to a head quickly. Doug Llewelyn and John Joslyn had four months to do the necessary construction, get the permits, and get Geraldo to Chicago to begin filming the back story that would anchor the two-hour special while excavation was going on. The networks had all turned down the producers because of the very real possibility that something might not be in the 125-foot, sealed-up vault. "Nobody... I mean nobody wanted to think about that," Allan Grafman said, shaking his head. "That was simply unthinkable."[8]

9

Hooverball

1930

President Hoover liked to play medicine ball with members of his cabinet. Every morning on the White House lawn he and the cabinet would throw the six-pound medicine ball back and forth and discuss the issues of the day. The court was sixty-six feet long and thirty feet wide with an eight-foot net. Teams consisted of two to four players who hefted the ball back and forth and points were scored when the other team failed to get it over the net. Americans really didn't work out at this time in our history. They did fun things like ride a bicycle but rarely was it for exercise. Hoover stood on the court and caught the heavy ball and hefted it back. He just had an amazing meeting. Frank J. Loesch and other prominent officials of Chicago had come to plead with him to get personally involved in restoring order in Chicago. "They gave me chapter and verse for their statement that Chicago was in the hands of gangsters and that the police and magistrates were completely under their control that the governor of the state was futile that the federal government was the only force by which the city's ability to govern itself could be restored."[1]

The president stared across the sunny court and shook his head. It was amazing. City officials had lost control of their city and now one man ruled the city by murder and intimidation with citizens cooperating because he gave them what they craved most: booze. Mayor Thompson was in Capone's pocket after his thugs used murder and pineapple bombs thrown at the opposition's polling stations. The real mayor of Chicago was relaxing on the fifth floor of the Lexington Hotel getting a massage, a haircut, or having fifty people over for dinner in his dining room. He was watching the beer trucks down below while tallying up his profits before going down to see his barber or disappearing into a secret stairwell behind a mirror that led to his syphilis-infected teenage prostitute one floor up, or he was going down to his gymnasium where his bodyguards could get a little exercise and play a little medicine ball. He was walking through the lobby full of men with newspapers with Thompson machine guns in their laps; or waking up the bodyguard on the cot outside his door; or going down in his bulletproof elevator to his bulletproof Cadillac and waving to the press, who obliged with cameras; or dropping $100 bills to homeless people, saying "go play the horses, Bub" while heading downtown once again to court or to see the DA, who always had nothing because everyone either worked for him or were paid off, in the Chicago River, or down along some deserted beach in the trunk of a car.

President Hoover just couldn't believe one man could take over a whole American city, and he began asking around during Hooverball, "Did they get Capone yet?" They had not. In fact, Capone had just come down to see Attorney General George Johnson and started a small riot outside his office. Flashbulb smoke curled outside his office. *Pop pop pop!* The flashbulbs bleach the celebrity. The streets are already crowded with people trying to get a glimpse of the man in the white fedora with the fifty-thousand-dollar ring and flashy ties and immaculate suits. So Chicago was having a fair in a few years. So what? The fair was right here with Al Capone. People could not get enough of him. They still can't to this day. Some kind of blend of Robinhood gangster celebrity antihero and Capone looks great. He is tan and lost some weight and looks like a successful, confident businessman. His hair is still black and his eyes rove over the reporters easily, but there is that glint of something darker.

Something brooding, smoldering behind the easy smile that would have him beat two men to death with a baseball bat. The police had to be called to control the crowd outside the courtroom that had already swelled to 1,500. There is no television. No internet. No influencers, or whatever that means. Chicagoans just know he is town, and Al may not be a movie star but lately he has been thinking about selling his story to the "pictyahs." Autographs are given all around and for the rest they have a moment they will talk about for the next forty years. "Yeah, I saw him. I saw Al Capone." What did he look like, Grandpa? "Big. Big man. Nice guy though." I had met a man in Barnes & Noble during a signing. "You know my mom used to date Capone." I would ask what he was like. "Nice guy. Big. Nice guy." Capone would later muse, "I ought to go into vaudeville. Look at the crowd I get." A president almost a hundred years later would fashion himself a modern-day Al Capone. Mass communication is just getting started, and right now celebrity is the new drugs. For a poor WOP from Brooklyn it is nothing short of amazing. Fame. Money and dames and bullets are nothing compared to this drug.

"Just my good side, boys."

Pop pop pop!

George Johnson bursts into the room and clears out the area. "Get out of here! Get out of here! This isn't a photograph gallery for hoodlums!"

Capone laughs. "So long, boys."[2]

Johnson keeps Capone waiting all day. He goes to his lawyer's office in the Marquette building for a corned beef sandwich and a glass of milk. He goes back later and sits in front of a grand jury for an hour and a half. He has received immunity for his testimony but says, "I don't know," or "I don't remember." Johnson tells him to come back in six days. He is nowhere close to finding out about the Saint Valentine's Day murders. Capone heads back to Florida. Meanwhile in Hammond, Indiana, a couple of cops are driving along Sheffield when two black sedans blow past them. They see a black Cadillac up ahead on the side of the road and get out. Two open the trunk and see two men beaten with bats and shot and then shot again. Their skulls are mush; their ears are bloody stubs. Another car nearby has another body in the same condition. They are John Scalise, Joseph Guinta, and Albert Anselmi. A scene from the 1987 movie *The Untouchables* speculates on their execution at the hands of Capone and a baseball bat after showing up for a meeting. Everyone remembers the scene.

But now Capone is headed down to Atlantic City for a meeting with a gangsters from all over the country. The theme is violence like the Saint Valentine's Day Massacre is doing no one any favors. After the meeting Big Al and Frankie Rio start driving for New York where they are going to catch a train back to Chicago. It's raining. Capone is wearing his dark long overcoat with a .38 caliber snub nose revolver in his pocket. The car breaks down in Camden, New Jersey, and they decide to hop a commuter train to Philadelphia scheduled to leave around 9:05 p.m. They kill time and catch a movie, *Voice of the City*. It's a detective story starring Willard Mack. The Stanley theater is on Nineteenth Street and two detectives drive by in an undercover car. John Creeden and James Malone see the oversized fedoras and long overcoats. They look like mobsters; more than that, they look like Al Capone and his men from Chicago. The Philadelphia cops pull over and hoof it over to the theater, but Capone and his men are already inside settling in with some popcorn.

The detectives wait outside for the movie to end. They don't want a shootout and watch an hour and a half later as people stream out. They are nervous, but at 8:30 Capone and his men emerge into the drizzling night and they flash their badges. Creeden grabs Rio and pins him against the wall. Al puts his hand in his right pocket, Malone grabs it, and they lock eyes. "Easy there, Al,"[3] he says. They slowly pull out the .38 together. The other two bodyguards melt away. Capone is booked on weapons possession. He still wears his white fedora in the mugshot. He lights up a cigarette and stands before a magistrate who orders him held on $35,000 bond. Lemuel

B. Schofield, director of public safety, interviews Capone and gets some publicity for himself. Capone tells him:

> I went into the rackets four and a half years ago. During the last two years I've been trying to get out. But once in the rackets you're always in it. I have a wife and an eleven-year-old boy I idolize and a beautiful home in Florida. If I could go there and forget it all I would be the happiest man in the world.[4]

Capone sleeps on a bench with Rio. Ten big Philadelphia cops guard their prison cell. The next morning as they await trial a man asks how much the ring on his finger is worth. "About fifty thousand," Capone says with a shrug, about what the average American would see in his lifetime. Capone pleads guilty and is sentenced to one year in prison. He gives the diamond ring to his lawyer. "It's the breaks, kids,"[5] he says to Rio as he is led away. The biggest gangster in America is now in prison for carrying a gun into a movie theater. The Philadelphia police fire Capone's gun into a barrel to see if the bullets match the ones at the Saint Valentine's Day Massacre. They don't. Some said Capone wanted to go to jail for his own protection. Capone's sister Mafalda said that was crazy. He would never have himself incarcerated intentionally. Chicago was embarrassed. The cops in Philadelphia had put Capone in jail for a year while Chicago couldn't put him in jail for a day.

10

Hiding at the NAPTE

1986

Geraldo Rivera stood in the booth at the National Association of Television Producers and Executives, or the NAPTE convention. After working for ABC for fifteen years, Geraldo had been oblivious to the grind of selling a syndicated show to local stations. "I hadn't counted on this,"[1] he would say later in his autobiography *Exposing Myself*. "I had a down and out sinking feeling when you brought this show up,"[2] Geraldo said to me during our interview almost forty years later. Geraldo had interviewed John and Yoko, Muhammad Ali, presidents, movie stars, and been paid a million dollars year. Now he was in a musty convention hall in New Orleans selling the two-hour infotainment program "The Mystery of Al Capone's Vaults." It was like being dropped from the majors down to the minors—or worse, being cut altogether. "It seems to have a lot to do with pomp and flash and sirens and bathing beauties and clowns and fresh popcorn,"[3] he wrote later. Geraldo was now right in the middle of the carnival. After signing the deal to host the two-hour event, he had returned to his sailboat with the promise to return for the NAPTE convention and the interviews that would be the B-roll between the excavation in the basement. He had agreed, but now he was in a convention hall with everyone else who had plastic name tags on their jacket, blouses, and shirts. Geraldo had one too. "Hi, my name is Geraldo Rivera."

Clark Morehouse, the senior vice president of ad sales, recalled, "We had an antique Ford with two gun models holding fake guns and sold most of the advertising to these small independent stations." It was Geraldo's job to help sell the show, but standing in the Tribune booth Geraldo felt like hiding. It was akin to going back to high school after leaving college. "There I was, battling malignant embarrassment, flanked in the Tribune booth by two gorgeous models, immodestly dressed in Roaring Twenties style."[4] Tribune Entertainment had set the booth up with pictures of Al Capone and a 1926 Pack touring car. Behind all of this were pictures of Geraldo blown up. This was the nuts and bolts of the television industry. Programming was produced and then, much like a colorful cereal box sold to prospective supermarkets, the show was packaged and presented to the conventioneers who had come looking for programming for their stations. "The Mystery of Al Capone's Vaults" was the cereal and the Tribune company had to recoup their investment and sell it to independent stations. Clark Morehouse was then executive vice president of Tribune Entertainment. He was the ad sales guy, and he was in charge of selling the twenty-eight commercial units to advertisers who wanted national exposure. "Each unit cost one hundred thousand dollars and they sold incredibly fast,"[5] he recalled in an interview years later. But the stations had to be sold, and Geraldo and Capone's vault were the bait. Geraldo went to work. "To me the whole thing made me feel small and humiliated, but I held up my end of the deal. I always do. I glad handed the endless swarm of conventioneers—mostly network affiliated independent station managers considering our program for their air."[6]

Geraldo the showman kicked in and he talked with the station managers' wives and answered their questions. He felt their wondering stares and ignored the questions on everyone's lips: how could he be involved in a program like this? Some were not above asking Geraldo how his career had come to this. "But my career had come to this," he wrote later. "After everything I had done, Al Capone was all I had going and as distasteful as the whole NAPTE circus was, I was determined to make a success of it."[7] Geraldo was nothing if not a realist, and his hardscrabble roots kicked in as he pushed the show onto the independent stations. He was just beginning to adjust to his new reality when he was blindsided. Judd Rose, a former correspondent at ABC News, came walking across the convention floor with a camera crew. Rose had come to highlight the very embarrassing aspect of the convention: "On what had become the perennial pick of network assignment editors; the annual trip to NAPTE to mock the blatant hucksterism of syndicated television."[8] The networks viewed syndication as where programs went to die. These syndicated programs were the orphans no one wanted, the misfit toys of television that would make their way to the NAPTE, where not unlike someone selling trinkets from the trunk of their cars, the hawkers called out and made their pitches to the rubes from the rural stations. And now Geraldo had become one of the hucksters that Judd would show his colleagues and they would all laugh and wonder how Geraldo had fallen so far and so fast.

"My heart and pride raced each other to new depths," he wrote later. "I was horrified at the thought of being found out. Of course there was little hiding my involvement with the program—it had been announced in all the television trade magazines and the show would after all be syndicated nationwide... but I did not want to come face to face with a recent peer."[9] In Geraldo's mind he had lost his position at network news and he had fallen down to the junkyard of television where he was pandering to station managers in loud ties and cheap suits. But Judd Rose was coming straight toward him, and he had to act fast, or he would be on camera explaining why he was hosting a two-hour special opening a vault in a dilapidated hotel in Chicago that once belonged to Al Capone.

So, Geraldo Rivera, who had ridden to the top of the television world and rubbed shoulders with the rich and famous for years, crouched down and hid in the corner of the Tribune booth like a little boy while the ABC News crew passed by. He was sweating by now, crouched down under the booth with his *Hi, my name is Geraldo Rivera* badge. His face was burning up with embarrassment as he kept his head down and imagined what the interview would be like. He would pitch it as a documentary to Rose, but he knew by the time he brought the interview back to the offices of ABC he would be laughed at and ridiculed. The burn was moving down from his cheeks to his chest. Maybe it was all a mistake. Better to fade away than have your failure held up for ridicule.

> I started to wish for my old job, for Judd Rose's job, for anything that would take me off that convention floor. I was willing to start over again. I would have taken anything as long as it held the faint promise of getting back into network television. But I had burned my bridges at ABC News. I had been the object of competitive tension at CBS and NBC for so long there was no way they would hire me; CNN couldn't afford me. What was I going to do? This? Host sensational syndicated specials at $50,000 a pop?[10]

Judd Rose passed by, and Geraldo waited, then stood up slowly. He realized then how much shame he felt at what he was doing, "that I actually had to hide from a former colleague."[11] Every night in his hotel room Geraldo checked for messages. The flashing light on the phone next to his bed never lit. He was desperate for a job offer where he could tell the Tribune folks, he had another job and maybe Roone Arledge changed his mind or someone else in ABC wanted him. But after four days at the convention there was no message, no job offers. For good or for bad, Geraldo Rivera was going to have to swallow his pride and open Capone's vault in a dirty basement in an old hotel in Chicago. He didn't want to think what would happen if it was empty. He couldn't go there. Television depended on the payoff. People needed a reason to turn on the box that had landed in living rooms all over America. It had been that way since the beginning when after World War II antennas all over America began to spider in the sky.

11

Television

1909

What is this device that—aside from sleeping—takes so much of our time? In the United States, people who are fifteen and older watch 3.1 hours of television a day. Adults over sixty-five watch for four hours. Teenagers from fifteen to nineteen watch the least. If you work, you watch less television. If you are unemployed, you watch more. If you live in the Southeast, you watch more television than the average. During the cold months we all watch more. Weekends are prime watching time. Black Americans watch more than Hispanic or Asian Americans. Most people, 96.7 percent, watch at home. We tend to watch television with others, about 54 percent; the rest of us are staring at the flickering images by ourselves. During the pandemic people watched a whopping five hours a day.

The word itself comes from Ancient Greek. *Tele* is far and *vision* is sight. The first confirmed use of the term *television* was in a paper presented in Paris at the first International Congress of Electricity by Russian scientist Constantin Persky. The English term *television* was first documented when it was defined as "a theoretical system to transmit moving images over telegraph or telephone wires." Other names were considered, *telephote* and *televista*, but television became the ubiquitous term for sitting down and watching images on a screen. The invention of television moved along quickly from Georges Rignoux and A. Fournier's demonstration in Paris of letters of the alphabet. In 1911 crude images were sent over wires to a Braun tube (cathode ray tube) in a receiver. Moving images were not possible. Then in 1921 Édouard Belin sent an image over radio waves with his belinography. A big jump came in 1925 when Scottish inventor John Logie Baird showed silhouette images moving at a Selfridge department store in London. Even from the beginning television had a novelty effect on people that retailers recognized could pull people into stores. In 1928 Baird broadcast the first transatlantic signal between London and New York. The first television company was formed in France, Television-Baird-Natan, and in 1931 Baird broadcast the Derby.

In America the first television station was created in 1928, WRGB broadcast from Schenectady, New York, and was soon known as WGY Television. Electronic television moved in with Philo Farnsworth's image dissector. In 1928 Farnsworth held a demonstration for the press. Philo then staged the first public demonstration of all electronic television in Philadelphia on August 25, 1934. The early television sets using electronics were giant boxes with cathode ray tubes protruding out the back that shot electrons toward a curved low-pressure screen. The developments of transistors and the first solid state television was an 8-inch Sony TV8-301 produced in 1959. The smaller televisions ushered in the solitary viewer versus the community viewing of the larger sets. Color, digital, then smart televisions were part of the natural progression as technology and viewing habits evolved.

What was amazing to people was that television was free. People paid for movies. They paid to go to the theater. They paid to hear music. But television, like radio, was free entertainment. For most people how television paid for itself was a mystery. The viewer didn't pay. Not in the obvious way. Television was monetized through the concept of advertising. The early television shows were named for the brand or sponsor who would fund the show. *To Tell the*

Truth was funded by Geritol with large bottles of the vitamin elixir in front of the contestants and celebrities. The host of the show sat in front of a large Geritol placard and would intermittently pick up a bottle and hawk the benefits. In these early shows the one sponsor was the advertiser and the bet was the money they put up to produce *To Tell the Truth* would pay for itself with sales of Geritol. The popularity and reach of television and the fact viewers could now see the products they were to buy made television a powerful medium for retailers. Televisions stations began to sell blocks of broadcast time to their advertisers and as television evolved these blocks or commercials were sold not just to one sponsor, but to many.

Viewers came to hate and love and endure commercials. The common complaint of too many commercials would be echoed across the viewing landscape. On July 1, 1941, the first televised commercial was on New York station WNBT before a Brooklyn Dodgers and Philadelphia Phillies game. Bulova watches paid for the advertisement to be in the form of a WNBT test pattern changed to look like a clock with the phrase "Bulova Watch Time" in the lower-right corner. Single sponsorship dominated the 1940s and 1950s, but after the quiz show scandals in the 1950s networks went to the format of breaking a show up by different advertising spots. A single sponsor no longer identified shows.

At some point the term *idiot box* came into the vernacular to define television as being a cheap form of entertainment for a nation of illiterate people. This was never truer than when the quiz show scandal broke in 1957. The show *Twenty-One* became a hit when noted intellectual Charles Van Doren went on the show and producer Dan Enright told the reigning champion, Herbert Stemple, to take a fall so Van Doren could become the champion. Stemple had been given answers beforehand as well as Van Doren. When it was revealed the show was rigged there was a public outcry, and a grand jury was convened to investigate the game shows. Television itself came under assault as a new medium that was bringing down the cultural level of the nation. The same had happened twenty years before when Orson Welles broadcast on October 30, 1938, that Martians were invading America and exterminating the human race. The resulting backlash had called for censorship against the new medium of radio and that with programs like *The Edgar Bergen and Charlie McCarthy Show*, where a dummy made jokes, radio needed to be reined in as it was playing to the lowest common denominator. When it looked like Welles was about to be blamed for all of radio's ills, popular columnist Dorothy Thompson wrote a letter exonerating Orson and blaming the ignorance and gullibility of the American public.

Television would never shake the idiot box tag, even though its popularity soared. A famous study found that watching television produces the same brain waves as sleeping. Television was a passive medium that required no engagement by the viewer as opposed to reading, which required the reader to create the world. All that came out of the quiz show scandals was an amending of the Communications Act of 1934, where it "declared illegal any contest or game with intent to deceive the audience." Orson Welles would go on to Hollywood to make *Citizen Kane* and the producers of *Twenty-One* went on to produce *Let's Make a Deal* later. The American public would continue to be harangued about the degradation of culture and absolute lack of erudition on the part of the average watcher of television. As programming changed and the lowering of standards were bemoaned by the gatekeepers of culture, the ratings soared.

The advertising rates for shows became tied to Nielsen ratings, which soon became the bible of the industry where decisions to cancel or renew a show depended on Nielsen Media Research. The company Nielsen Media Research measured audiences for radio, theater, and television, but the *Nielsen ratings* pertain only to television. The New York company began sampling television in 1950 and measures which programs are viewed by audiences in different regions of the company. Surveys were sent out to the viewers during the "sweeps" months of February, May, July, and November and asked viewers what they watched during a one-week period. Each year until 2018, Nielsen processed approximately two million paper diaries from households across the United States for November, February, May, and July—also known as the "sweeps" rating periods. The term *sweeps* dates from 1954, when Nielsen collected diaries from households in Eastern United States first; from there they would "sweep" west. Seven-day diaries (or eight-day diaries in homes with DVRs) were mailed to homes to keep a tally of what people watched on each television set and by whom. Homes received new diaries each week over the course of a sweeps period. At the end of the month, the viewing data from the individual weeks were aggregated.

In 1980, a Nielsen Homevideo Index (NHI) was added to track cable and pay cable programming. The sweet spot of viewers quickly became the age eighteen-to-forty-nine range, which was more important than the total number of viewers. Demographics drives pricing for commercials. A commercial during *Friends* was three times more expensive than *Murder She Wrote*. Nielsen ratings could make a star, destroy a career, cancel a show, make a show, get producers and executives fired, or bankrupt a network.

Tribune Entertainment had paid almost a million dollars to the Westgate Company for a two-hour syndicated program on a bet that something was in an old vault from Al Capone in a Southside hotel basement. The bet was that the advertising blocks would pay for the show and that people would watch the syndicated program the networks had turned down. Promises were made to the stations and advertisers that a 20 NTI (Nielsen television index) rating could be expected. Rating points equal the percentage of people who have televisions or watched a particular program. "We thought that was high, but we wanted to get them excited. We would be very happy with a 20 NTI but most of us thought a 15 was more likely; a disaster would be a 10 NTI," Allan Grafman said later.[1] The highwire act of a start-up production company and a television journalist who had been fired from ABC was all dependent on the ratings that would be available the next morning. Ratings were simply everything. They dictated how much could be charged for advertising, among other things. The breakout show, the surprise hit—these were all vouchsafed by the recorded reactions of viewers. The NTI rating of "The Mystery of Al Capone's Vaults" would determine the careers of producers and one Geraldo Rivera on a show where a vault from a gangster would be opened on live television. One could already hear the cultural titans groaning that television was taking another turn for the worse.

12

The Vault Within a Vault

January 1986

The *San Francisco Examiner*, on January 19, 1986, blared in a one-page article, CAPONE'S LEGACY. Al Capone's hiding place has not been opened since May 5, 1932, the day he left his headquarters on Chicago's South Side bound for Alcatraz. The article then dropped down, *The Plan to Open Gangster's Long Forgotten Vault*. "Worldwide the name Al Capone is synonymous with Chicago. You're from Chicago? Ahhhh, yes. Bang, bang. Al Capone." The article then summarized the discovery of the vault and the contents hidden in the "sealed 125 foot long, eight foot high and eight-foot-wide vault that jutted out from the hotel foundation under the sidewalk of the Chicago's busy Michigan Avenue." The article tantalizes readers with a quick history of Capone's residence at the hotel and then explains "the vault has not been opened since its six entrances were crudely but effectively sealed with cement and tar on May 5, 1932, the day Capone last left the hotel for Alcatraz Island where he was being imprisoned after being convicted on federal charges of tax evasion. 'We don't know what's in there. It could be money, documents or bodies,' says Pat Porter founder of the Sunbow Foundation." The article then announces that the world will find out April 14 when the vault is blasted open and notes the IRS is standing by with an $800,000 tax lien for Capone.

Doug Llewelyn quips, "Could be the largest wine cellar in the country's history." The paper paints a time when Chicago had "20,000 speakeasies, 3,000 brothels, 300 large gambling houses and 2,000 bookies." The article references the tunnel system that ran "to Colosimo's, a classy club, and the Metropole hotel both across the street as well as to Capone's home. Legend has it that the tunnels reached as far as Chicago's city hall and police headquarters."[1]

What is amazing is that this article is preselling the two-hour docutainment *four months* before it was scheduled for April. Buzz is everything. A full page devoted to a syndicated show that would not happen for at least four months was unheard of. The story of Al Capone's vaults in the basement of the Lexington Hotel grew more with each article. This was a viral campaign before the internet to create buzz. Radio spots, television spots, articles, interviews began to circulate through the media universe. *Entertainment Tonight* did a segment from the hotel hyping the special and waving around the IRS lien for $800,000. The IRS lien generated immense interest. This claim by a government agency legitimized the vault opening and lent credibility to the possibility that Capone's millions might be in the sealed vault. Geraldo and the producers began to appear on talk shows leading up to the April 21 date. "I'm a pretty normal average person and if I am interested in what is in the vault then I assume other people will be too,"[2] Geraldo stated later.

News outlets ran with their own stories about what could be in the vault. "Chicago's equivalent of King Tut's Tomb," one promo spot blared. But for all the hype there was a massive amount of preparation still to be done for the show. Geraldo had signed and then disappeared on his sailboat, *New Wave*, again. He had agreed to return in early March to begin five weeks of preproduction. "I began receiving urgent messages at sea, from Tribune execs anxious to keep tabs on and drag me back to dry land as soon as possible. I had begun to look on the Capone show as a paycheck and a lifeline," Geraldo later wrote. "It was the only thing I had going, and it was everything. It was my one chance back. When I finally did arrive at the Hyatt Regency in Chicago, my body was calloused and sunbeaten from more than a month at sea, my hair was long, tangled and out of control, a full beard masked my tentative enthusiasm."[3]

Geraldo, besides having to attend the NHE conference, had to get the interviews for the back story of Al Capone. The seven weeks before the show became a whirlwind of getting the Lexington ready and filming the various segments.

> We began our documentary fieldwork the next day reporting various sidebar stories to complement the live excavation of the hotel basement. The show was scheduled for two hours, and half of that time was to be filled with packaged pieces to fill the space between blasting and digging. I traveled the country to interview Capone's surviving friends and enemies. I interviewed mob experts and depression era historians. I talked to Internal Revenue Service agents who had placed a lien on the property in the hopes of collecting the nearly one million dollars in back taxes and penalties owed by Capone. I examined virtually every square foot of the Lexington Hotel until I was knowledgeable about its structure as any landmark's preservationist.[4]

Simultaneously, the hotel had to be ready for the broadcast. The upper floor of the hotel had to be cleaned up to allow Geraldo to walk through and make space for cameras and crews, but the real work entailed getting the basement and the vault ready for the dramatic moment of pulling down the five thousand pounds of cement sealing the vault. For all its ballyhoo live unveiling of the vault, the producers wanted to know what they were dealing with in the basement of the Lexington. The twenty-two-inch-thick slab of cement would not just fall down. The wall around the slab had to be precut with saws to ensure that when the Bobcat bulldozer yanked the wall down with a chain it would fall. The cement adhered to the surrounding brick and without precutting the vault the Bobcat bulldozer would not have the weight or strength to pull down the slab, which would actually be like pulling down an entire wall. The miniature bulldozer they lowered down into the basement would be a star player in the excavation drama.

In January, the producers attempted to get an idea of what if anything might be behind the bricked wall and the vault. They took soil samples, examined them, and brought in Tim Samuelson, an architectural expert with Chicago's Historical Society who examined the vault and confirmed that a soil sample came from the time Capone occupied the building. They drilled holes to try and see into the vaulted area. In February, a heat-sensitive infrared monitor was brought in to see if areas behind the vault were hollow. Unfortunately, many of the areas were found to be solid concrete. The producers then brought a seismic survey—the same kind of devices used in oil exploration—to scan the surface outside the vault and bounce soundwaves into the vault. The results came back that the area behind the vault was solid. The producers had to probe further, desperately looking for some confirmation that there was indeed a vault to be opened.

They began an exploration of selected parts of the vault. More dirt. This was when the bulldozer (the Bobcat) was dismantled and lowered into the basement. The excavation of the basement under the Lexington had begun with tons of dirt being removed. More brick and cement-cutting saws were brought in and holes drilled that revealed another wall behind it and another vault. In the basement of the Lexington Hotel was a vault within a vault. It was a sealed thirty-foot section, and the tests indicated this time it was most likely hollow. At first, they had thought the 125 section was all a hollow vault, but as the tons of dirt were removed and the ceiling propped up, they uncovered secret spaces including stairwells. A lone blue bottle from the Capone era reinforced the belief they were finally on the right track. The second wall had no reason to be there and this along with the tests showing space behind the wall excited the producers. Like King Tut's tomb, the first door, the slab, would be the doorway to the riches in the second vault that now was the repository of

Geraldo and the producers' hopes and dreams that Al Capone had brought in Sicilian masons to create a space to keep his millions hidden from the world. As Geraldo would later tell the world on April 21, "maybe it will be those missing millions of Capone's we will find here or the bones of his criminal rivals or documents or weapons, bootleg booze, or paraphernalia."[5] At this point, only Al Capone knew that answer.

13

Public Enemy Number One

1930

Frank Wilson sat in the old Chicago Post Office building smoking cheap cigars at a steel-topped desk. A wan sallow man, he was blind as a bat and couldn't shoot straight. So, he was a revenue investigator and would sit for hours quietly at his desk smoking and going over confiscated ledgers looking for income where supposedly there was none. Elmer Irey, his supervisor, later testified that Wilson "will sit quietly looking at books eighteen hours a day seven days a week, forever if he wants to find something. Wilson would sit in a small, cramped office no bigger than a closet in a haze of blue smoke, stubbing out one five cent cigar after another."[1] His agents had been hanging around the Lexington Hotel to see what they could find and Wilson had come to admire Capone, who was smarter than he thought. "He did all his business through front men,"[2] he later said. It was not a glamorous job and didn't hold a candle to the story of *The Untouchables*.

Ask someone of a certain age and they will tell you Eliot Ness was responsible for bringing down Al Capone. In the movie *The Untouchables*, Kevin Costner presented an image of the crusader as pure as the driven snow. Author Oscar Fraley would have been pleased with the movie, as well as the series with Robert Stack. He was technically the cowriter but he more than anyone was responsible for creating the mythology of the incorruptible lawman. The truth was that Fraley was a sportswriter for UPI who knew a good story when he heard it. The book, the movie, the television stories all took the untouchables to the bank. But another story is just as interesting. It involves a shadowy group of men known as the Secret Six. They were six Chicago millionaires who banded together to get rid of Al Capone. Chicago was having a World's Fair in 1933, and they couldn't risk their investment in the fair that was being built on the lake front. Capone had to go. Julius Rosenwald, the founder of Sears, bankrolled the Secret Six. Robert Isham Randolph, the president of the Chicago Commerce Commission, was another member. Robert McCormick, the publisher of the *Chicago Tribune*, would become the third member, but not until Jake Lingle was murdered.

Jake Lingle was a mob reporter who invested heavily in the market and bet on horses. The *Chicago Tribune* building fronts Michigan Avenue and down below is Billy Goat Tavern; this is where the Illinois Central Train used to pull in. On June 9, 1930, Lingle left the Sherman House Hotel and ducked down into the cooler air of the Randolf Street Terminal to grab the 1:30 p.m. train to Washington Park Racetrack in Homewood. He walked quickly with a cigar clenched between his teeth and didn't hear the footsteps behind him. A blond-haired man came up behind Lingle, pulled a .38 from his pocket, and fired. Lingle pitched forward with the cigar still clenched in his teeth.

Colonel Robert McCormick, the publisher of the *Chicago Tribune*, saw the murder of his reporter as an assault on the press. He posted a $25,000 reward for Lingle's death and blasted a headline across the front page of the *Tribune* the next day: GUNMAN SLAYS ALFRED LINGLE IN I.C. SUBWAY.[3] McCormick followed this the next day with an article titled "The Challenge," which elaborated on the cold-blooded murder and declared war against the gangsters who had taken over Chicago.

> The meaning of this murder is plain. It was committed in reprisal and was an attempt to intimidate. Mr. Lingle was a police reporter and exceptionally

well informed. His personal friendships included the highest police officers, and the contacts of his work had made him familiar with most of the big and little fellows of gangland. What made him valuable to his newspaper marked him as dangerous to his killers. . . . The *Tribune* accepts this challenge. It is war.[4]

Capone was still sitting in a jail cell in Philadelphia and had no idea the Secret Six and the government were now gunning for him. When he was released, he headed for Chicago and the *Tribune* ran a banner that read "Capone Speeds for Chicago." Capone, who was media savvy, gave an interview to the *Chicago American*, "I'm not telling anybody how to run the country, but . . . if people did not want beer and wouldn't drink it, a fellow would be crazy for going around and trying to sell it."[5] Even as Chicago was seen as out of control his popularity grew. Movie stars wanted to meet him. Mayors posed with him. South Dakota invited him to come stay in Rapid City if he was tired of Chicago. The world knew of Chicago's gang culture of tommy guns and speakeasies. People believed they would be shot down five minutes after their arrival in Chicago.

After all the murders attributed to Al Capone there was not one case brought against him. Taxes. The best the government could do was go after him for not paying his taxes. It seemed absurd to go after the biggest bootlegger in the country for his taxes, but gangsters like Al Capone had become bigger than life. In 1931 Warner Brothers released *Public Enemy Number One* starring James Cagney. The antihero had arrived, and Humphrey Bogart and Edward G. Robinson boasted a new twist on the Robin Hood motif. Bonnie and Clyde would take it home during the Great Depression when people had homes foreclosed on by the banks and turned out of their farms. Cagney dressed like Capone with flashy suits and a beautiful Jean Harlow on his arm. The rags to riches story where Cagney fought against the powerful appealed to the Depression-era audiences.

The outlaw in American culture has one foot in the Robin Hood camp and one in the underworld. The appeal of James Cagney, Edward G. Robinson, Humphrey Bogart, and Al Capone is they confirmed something the public had come to suspect: that the game was rigged against them by the rich and the powerful and it was good to see someone fighting back and winning. Politicians know this and many demagogues have risen to power proclaiming to fight the status quo. Capone's appeal in 1930 is the same as it was in 1986: a smart man who played by his own rules, triumphed against the entrenched powers, had swag and style, and lived the way he wanted in a posh hotel that he basically had taken over. And if this man happened to leave something in the basement of the Lexington Hotel, then everyone wanted to be there to see what it was.

White fedoras, diamond rings, flashy cars, and beautiful women while glad-handing judges, mayors, and senators. Who would not be taken in by the man who could buy anything he wanted and was so dangerous no one would ever testify against him? He was Teflon, and while the world watched the Chicago World's Fair get built on the lakefront, the Secret Six set up their own speakeasies to get information and their own mob informants and studied Capone's operation. At this point, a lot of people had a vested interest in evicting Al Capone from the Lexington Hotel.

Meanwhile, Frank Wilson sat in his office in the old Chicago Post Office and listened to the traffic outside his window. The green shade of the desk lamp creased his eyes. He had been trying to find something on Capone for two years, and now his mouth was dry and tasted like the inside of an ashtray from one cigar after another. Wilson leaned back and stared at the ink-smudged files. He could not tie Capone to any of his money even though he made $100 million a year. Wilson rubbed the back of his neck and slipped his fingers under his glasses. He knew Washington was running out of patience. Every day during the medicine ball games, President Hoover wanted to know what progress was being made against Al Capone. Nothing yet. They had nothing that would put Al Capone in jail. Frank Wilson lit a cigarette and stood up to put the files away. He pulled the file drawer open but accidentally bumped it with his hip and it slammed shut. He didn't have the key and went to put the files in a musty storeroom. He opened the door and pulled the cord on the overhead light. He found an old dusty file cabinet and pulled open the drawer. Large manilla envelopes lay at the bottom. Wilson picked one up and it was unexpectedly heavy. The package had string binding it from four sides like a Christmas present. The treasury agent took it back to his desk and fished some scissors from his drawer and clipped the string. He pulled off the brown paper and pulled out three dirty ledgers. He opened the first ledger and sat down and slowly began reading. He felt heat rising up from his neck. Wilson looked up then down. My God. It was Christmas.

14

The Rebel

1972

Geraldo Rivera was not the talking head America was used to. He was a gonzo journalist who went where his heart took him. But Walter Cronkite, no. His long hair and trademark mustache and swagger were the opposite of the WASPY suited-up newsman who Americans sat down to be soothed by at 5:30 every evening. Polite. Urbane. Staid. The anchors told America what they wanted to hear; that the world was still under control by a patriarchal news organization filtering out the unpleasant facts of a world changing under their feet. Vietnam had gone south and demonstrations on college campuses had broken out. Martin Luther King had been assassinated along with George Wallace and Bobby Kennedy. It was a time of great upheaval, but in the wan evening hours across America across the placid suburban landscape as the world settled down, people could hear the dulcet, stentorian tones of a newsman who looked straight out of 1950.

Then came Geraldo. Still plugging for eyewitness news in New York, he was interviewing junkies and prostitutes and toking up on television. He was a one-man band of upset. He was Jewish and Puerto Rican and didn't look like those men of old who ushered America through the turmoil of the Nixon years. Now George McGovern was running for president. He was the liberal against Nixon's conservative legions and young people were excited again. Maybe there was some light in the darkness of the meat grinder that was Vietnam. Geraldo looked like one of the demonstrators that danced on the television screens every night burning draft cards and bras. His celebrity was such that he was commanding $1,200 speaking fees and enjoying the early perks of celebrity. New York was a bastion of pro-McGovern sentiment and when Geraldo gave a speech at Queens College, he endorsed McGovern and didn't think twice about it until a group of right-wing students called Young Americans for Freedom complained to management at WABC. "The complaint wasn't over something I said, it was over the fact I'd said anything at all. I was a newsman, the students maintained and had no business taking a stand on a political election," he wrote later. "I was not actively campaigning for McGovern at this point; I was merely expressing my admiration for him and his candidacy in a very fiery way."[1]

Geraldo had agreed to speak at a celebrity benefit for McGovern at the Palace Theatre in mid-October and his name was already appearing in ads. A reporter picked up on the complaint at the Queens College speech and connected it with his upcoming appearance. The network gave Geraldo an ultimatum. Pull out of the McGovern benefit or face suspension without pay until after the elections. "The election was nearly a month away and with my recent raise the loss in salary would have approached ten thousand dollars . . . I've always had a 'let's go!' mentality or trigger point and having made a 'let's go!' decision having gone forward, there was no question that I would follow through even if it meant being fired."[2]

Geraldo was suspended and the broadcast community lined up against him. *Daily News* television columnist Kay Gardella interviewed the prominent newsman of the day. Mike Wallace was quoted.

> I think it's dead wrong. We're all Caesar's wives and particularly in this climate, we have to be viewed as impartial. Privileges and responsibilities

go with any job. So, we are not discussing just the fact of impartiality but the appearance of impartiality as well. If Rivera or any other newsman goes on television and voters know him as a McGovern man that taints *Eyewitness News* coverage.

John Chancellor of *NBC Nightly News* agreed. "People involved in news should not endorse. We have public and private roles to play. To be a journalist one must suspend the private part." The god of news, Walter Cronkite of the *CBS Evening News*, lowered the boom. "Basically, I'm on the company's side in that they have a right to ask newsman to refrain from campaigning, since people are not sophisticated enough to accept that a man can wear two hats." Sam Donaldson of ABC News threw in with the pack. "I think it's just awful . . . there are basic tenants of journalism over which you do not cross. You learn them as you grow in the business. If Rivera did not know them, someone should have told him." Marty Berman, the executive producer for Geraldo, summed up what he saw as the real issue in the controversy.

> Professionally I always thought there was a danger that Geraldo had become too big a celebrity, that his celebrity would become so big it would be very difficult to be out Sunday night in a tuxedo at the opening of the Met, or whatever and then on Monday have to cover some drug story in East Harlem . . . I think maybe part of the reason that there was this Geraldo backlash, at some point, was that somehow he didn't wear his celebrity correctly at the beginning . . . all that superstar stuff hurt the other image, the journalist image.[3]

The lines were clearly drawn early on. Geraldo would never break into the old boys' club. He would have to forge his own path, his own identity. The "Capone's Vaults" gig was another event in the serendipitous career of Geraldo Rivera. He had been fired from ABC, but now he was to anchor a syndicated, two-hour, live event for which he was now prepping by traveling the country and filming the video pieces that would be inserted between the blasting and excavation. Another crisis surfaced during the early preproduction days.

Geraldo was beginning to warm up to the project in the preproduction work and was thinking about future projects with the Tribune Company. "I began to talk in broad general terms about follow up specials although there were no offers on the table." Still, Tribune Entertainment was the only company that offered him a job, and he was grateful. On March 19, he went to Las Vegas and ran into Bill Murray in the parking lot and began to chat with the actor comedian. Jim Dowdles, the CEO of Tribune Entertainment, walked up to him and Murray abruptly left. Dowdles stopped in front of him

"Geraldo," he said. "I'm not going to beat around the bush with you because that is not my style." Jim was a big hulking man and seemed embarrassed with what he had to say. He put his hands in his pockets.

"I'm listening," I said.

"I hear you've got a problem with cocaine," he announced.

"What," I stammered.

"Well," he said, "that's what I've been hearing. I've been hearing that's the real story behind your departure from ABC." He skipped a beat and then continued. "Look, Geraldo, I don't know you well, we've only worked together a couple of weeks, but I need to know if there is any truth to these stories. There's no other way to ask than to just ask."

"Jim," I started in as calmly as my seething rage would allow, "that's an absolute fucking lie."

"It is," he said, awash in relief.

"I'll go down and take a drug test right now. I've never used cocaine. It's absolute bullshit."

"I can't tell you how glad I am to hear that," he said extending a meaty palm.

I shook his hand thinking, Jesus, when is this thing going to go away and thanking the Gods of syndicated television that I had partnered with a group of people so willing to believe in me.[4]

This was how Geraldo recalled it in *Exposing Myself*. The smear campaign against him had started the minute he left ABC. The old boy network was alive and well and no matter how high Geraldo Rivera might climb there was always someone there to trip him up. But this time he was in a boat with people who had just as much to lose as he did. For Geraldo Rivera, it was his comeback, and for Tribune Entertainment it was a million-dollar bet that something had to be in a dirt-encrusted tomb that construction crews were cutting toward and drilling with only weeks to go before the world would know if Alphonse Capone had left something behind before he departed for prison. It was winner-take-all bet with disgrace and bankruptcy for the losers.

15

Hayseeds

1930

Frank Wilson leaned back and lit another cigarette in the dusky office and put his wingtips up on the steel desk and read the ledger he had found in the dusty file cabinet. It was amazing. Some $500,000 had been paid out over a twenty-four-month period with $6,537 going to "Town"—probably payoffs to the police. "Then came four payments of $5,720.22 each to Frank, Lou, D, and JaA." Wilson noticed the figures were subtotaled at the bottom. He turned the page and stopped. Across the top in bold ink was written "Frank paid $17,500 for Al."[1] It was the strike of lightning in the coalmine for Frank Wilson. He had the smoking gun now, but he had to find who fired it. That would be Leslie Shumway, who was found hiding in Miami. Wilson went to his home and then brought him to the federal building in Miami.

"I'm investigating the tax liability of one Alphonse Capone," Wilson told Shumway as the men settled in.

"Oh, you're mistaken," he said finally. "I don't know Al Capone."

Wilson put a hand on Shumway's shoulder.

"I know you're in a helluva spot."[2]

Wilson painted a grim picture. The bookkeeper could either testify or Wilson would have him arrested publicly and Capone's men would make sure he never made it to trial. Shumway confessed and said the reason they didn't pay Capone directly was because of his habit of betting on the horses. Shumway testified before a secret grand jury and then was shipped to California to keep him alive. Capone was charged on March 13, 1931, with evading taxes in 1924. But it was the second break that Frank Wilson caught that would allow him to put the mobster behind bars. Capone's lawyer Lawrence Mattingly unwittingly did his client in when he threw an envelope on the table during a meeting to deal with the charges.

"This is the best we can. Mr. Capone is willing to pay tax on these figures."[3]

Wilson read the letter that was a summation of the finances of Al Capone. "I am of the opinion that his taxable income . . . might be fairly fixed at not to exceed 26,000." This was an estimation of what he owned; then Mattingly did his client in by estimating Capone made no more than $100,000 during 1928 and 1929. Frank Wilson filed away the letter with its admission of guilt, but now with the ledger he had a case. One hundred thousand dollars in 1929 was a lot of money, with Babe Ruth only making $70,000 a year. On June 5 a federal grand jury indicted Al Capone on twenty-two counts of tax evasion for 1925–1929. The unpaid taxes now came to $215,030.00. Capone posted a $50,000 bond.

Capone's attorney Michael Ahern offered a plea deal. Capone would plead guilty if they could come up with an acceptable sentence. Eighteen months was offered as a prison sentence. The term was bumped up to two and a half years and they had a deal. An indictment of Al Capone was announced on June 5. "Between 1924 and 1929, the government alleged Capone had earned at least $1,038,654.84. Capone had failed to pay taxes of $215,080.48 for which the maximum penalty was 'thirty-two years in jail and $80,000 in fines.'"[4]

Two and half years was a light sentence for tax evasion on the largest bootlegging operation in history, but it was the best the government could do. On June 16, 1931, Al Capone entered the federal courtroom in a loud yellow suit. Crowds outside the courtroom had been held back as people strained to get a glimpse of the big man. *Little Caesar* with Edward G. Robinson had just come out, and the popularity of gangsters was at its zenith. The man passing through the crowd with a phalanx of police around him was as popular as any movie star.

"Alphonse Capone," proclaimed Assistant District Attorney Dwight Green, "you are charged with attempting to evade and defeat your income taxes for 1924. Do you plead guilty or not guilty?"

Capone rose from his chair.

"Guilty," he said quietly.

"In indictment 23,232 you are charged with attempting to defeat and evade your income taxes for the years 1925, 1926, 1927, 1928 and 1929, and with willful failure to file returns for the years 1928 and 1929. Do you plead guilty or not guilty?"

"Guilty," he murmured.

Then Assistant US Attorney Victor LaRue faced Capone.

"Indictment 23256 charges you with conspiracy to violate the National Prohibition Act. How do you plead, guilty or not guilty?"

"Guilty," Capone answered.[5]

That was it. The biggest gangster in history had just admitted he had not paid his taxes. The *Chicago Herald Examiner* later wrote, "In those quiet few minutes... Chicago was throwing off the shackles of a man and an organization that has represented lawlessness, viciousness, and a flout to its self-respect for ten years."[6]

Judge Wilkerson set the sentencing for June 30 and Capone went down the elevator to the crowds below. No one knew Capone was only going to jail for two and a half years. A man who punched his wife or stole a car got a stiffer sentence. But the big man was free and went back to the Lexington Hotel where he went up to the fifth floor, passed through a secret passage behind a mirrored door, and went up the stairs to his teenage prostitute. It was a hot day and Capone and the prostitute enjoyed sex on top of the grand hotel. Why not?

He was going away for two and half years, so he might as well get some now. Capone's lawyers meanwhile went to work slowing down the sentencing. *The New York Times* interviewed Capone at the Lexington.

"Why don't they go after all those bankers who took the savings of thousands of poor people and lost them in bank failures.... Isn't it lots worse to take the last few dollars some family had saved, perhaps to live on while the head of the family out of a job than to sell a little beer?"[7] Many agreed but on July 30, 1931, a line of dark police cars escorted Al Capone from the Lexington Hotel to the federal building. People lined the streets again hoping to get a glimpse of the big man. Chicago was hot and sticky as Capone went up the back elevator to a courtroom full of reporters, lawyers, and court personnel. Judge Wilkerson entered and after some preliminary business told the astonished courtroom he was not bound by any plea bargain. Capone's lawyers protested but Wilkerson said he would only hand down a sentence after hearing evidence. The bottom line was that the two-and-a-half-year sentence was off the table.

Al Capone was going to trial for tax evasion and as he left the courtroom for the first time he had nothing to say. The word was President Hoover had let Judge Wilkerson know that he had to put Capone away longer than two and a half years. Capone went to a football game at Northwestern on October 3, 1931, and was heckled. On November 2 he made his way to the courthouse again where telegraph wires had been run to tell the world Al Capone might be convicted. In the movie *The Untouchables* the judge swaps one jury for another, but in real life an informant had told Frank Wilson that Capone had gotten to the jurors. "The big fellow is going to outsmart you ... they're passing out $1,000 bills. They're promising political jobs. They're using muscle too," Wilson told the judge, and he cagily switched the juries. For the first time the fix was not in. The new jurors were from downstate Illinois, from the small-farm towns. They did not look at Al Capone as a celebrity. They were churchgoing men and saw Capone as the devil incarnate. One juror from Edisonville wrote after the trail, "I had formed a pretty fair picture of Capone ... I understood that he was a terrible man who did not hesitate to murder those who stood in his way . . . to me he epitomized evil."[8]

A reporter from New York wrote that he detected the "fragrant whiff of green fields and growing rutabagas and parsnip in the courtroom . . . the jurors were a bunch of hayseeds horny handed tillers of the fruitful soil, small town storekeepers, mechanics and clerks."[9] On October 17, 1931, at 10:50 p.m., Al Capone entered the courtroom and stood next to his lawyer. The jury filed in, and the verdict was read by the clerk. "We the jury find the defendant guilty on counts one, five, nine, thirteen, and eighteen in the second indictment. . . ." Capone stood in front of Judge Wilkerson with his hands clasped and listened to the sentencing. At the end, he was sentenced to eleven years and fined $50,000. A newspaper reporter said Capone trembled and turned white. Then he turned to his lawyers and shook their hands. "Well so long," he said. "Goodbye."[10]

A bailiff took Capone from the courtroom and just like that his tenure at the Lexington Hotel ended. The most famous guest of the grand old hotel had left for good and the fourth and fifth floor would never be the same. Legend and mythology immediately moved in to occupy the Southside hotel.

16

Sailing

1985

In sailing the wind is everything. Sailing is instinctual and some people can never quite get it. The best sailors learn to take advantage of the wind and ride it as long as they can. But even the best sailors make mistakes. Sometimes a freak storm will hit the sails and spin the boat around in a 360-degree circle. I have been sailing on a forty-four-foot boat the size Geraldo was on when he was first contacted about Capone's vault, and had it spin in a full circle. The trick is to ride the vortex of the wind without allowing it to overwhelm the sailboat. This is done by feel and instinct and knowing how to sail out of bad situations. Geraldo had been sailing through choppy seas all his life and sailed out of most of them, but on June 9, 1977, the last show of *Good Night America* aired. Geraldo, who had been given the show, had become the man of hip late-night programming. When Geraldo found out the show was canceled, he stormed into Bob Shanks's office. He had been part of an ensemble on *Good Morning America* and *Eyewitness News,* but he was the star of *Good Night America*. The numbers were down, but Geraldo demanded to know the reason they were pulling the plug.

"I can't believe it," I told Bob Shanks. "I can't believe you're pulling the plug."

"I'm sorry," he said. "We have to trying something else."

Geraldo fumed and said he was thinking of leaving the network. The next day Shanks called him back to his office. It was a beautiful spring day and Gerado thought they might have reconsidered or were thinking of him for another news magazine vehicle. He sat down across from Bob behind his desk. Geraldo writes about the encounter in his book *Exposing Myself*.

"We've decided to accept your resignation," he said bluntly.

"What the hell are you talking about," I demanded.

"I've spoken with Fred Silverman and he and I are in complete agreement."

"Complete agreement about what?" I had no idea what he was talking about.

"About our conversation yesterday. And how we don't love you or understand you. About all these other things you wanted to do with your career. About how you were going to resign."

"But Bob," I tried. "I wasn't offering to resign. I was just . . ."

He cut me off. "We accept your resignation," he said more firmly and pushed some papers across the desk.

"I'm not signing anything."

"You said you were resigning, and you have to resign."[1]

Geraldo at this point was making $600,000 a year. ABC wanted out of his contract. Sailing is the easiest thing in the world until it isn't. Geraldo's agent Jerry Weintraub became involved, and Geraldo was called back the next day for a meeting with Roone Arledge, the new president of ABC News.

"I want to put you on the Evening News," Arledge announced, taking my hand as I stepped into his office. "I'm a big fan of your work."

Geraldo later wrote, "My career was made over in one roller coaster day. I woke up as a roving correspondent for a fluffy morning show and I went to bed a network newsman."[2]

Geraldo had arrived as a respected newsman on the ABC network. One of his first stories on the Son of Sam murders was singled out for sensationalism and Geraldo stumbled right out the gate. A story covering the death of Elvis Presley pulled him back up with his youthful looks and rock-and-roll background and high ratings. A gust of wind and he was sailing again. Geraldo let go of his longtime agent for a higher profile agent who promised more money. Jerry Weintraub was out for Jon Peters. Roone Arledge then came up with a news magazine format show that would be called *20/20*. Geraldo jumped into the news show that better fit his gonzo journalism than network news. The show premiered June 6, 1978. It was here he met Sylvia Chase, who was one of his colleagues on the show and who would play a big role in his final act at ABC.

"He was always very friendly, never held himself apart or acted in anyway lordly. I've seen people who have far less ability and who put on all kinds of airs," she said in interview. "But Geraldo. Never. . . . There were some things he did on camera, some of the approaches he took to stories, that I found not to my taste at all."[3] Geraldo took on assignments in the Mideast and in war-torn parts of the world. He was unflinching. An investigative piece into Elvis's death from drugs, "The Elvis Cover-Up" on *20/20*, became the most watched program of the 1979–1980 television season. Another great gust of wind spurring the good ship Geraldo into fine smooth sailing seas. Geraldo's salary skyrocketed to a million dollars during the eighties. Job offers from CNN tried to woo him away. Ten years after he had entered the business as an activist lawyer, he was now making nine figures a year.

Geraldo lived the high life and bought the forty-four-foot *Gulf Star* sloop in Miami he christened *New Wave*. During this time, he had bounced from one marriage to another, each time his next wife was more beautiful than the last one. In 1985 he was the star of *20/20* with fifteen years under his belt at ABC. The trouble at ABC began when Sylvia Chase, his friend and colleague, prepared a story on Marilyn Monroe. "The piece was the buzz of the newsroom and promised hard proof of Monroe's affair with President John Kennedy and later with his brother, Attorney General Robert Kennedy." Geraldo had been sailing along now for years. On the Monday before the segment was to air, his secretary, Jo Ann Torres, told Geraldo that Sylvia was getting a hard time from the network on the Marilyn piece.

"What kind of hard time?"

"Word is they might not run it at all."

"Shit."[4]

Geraldo found out the story had been canceled and flew into a rage. "I was incensed and reacted with every inch of righteous indignation I could muster. Even though the Monroe piece was not my story. I looked on *20/20* as my show." The wind is blowing again as the sailboat picks up speed. "I did not like anyone, even Roone tampering with it. We were a news program and this was news."[5] Geraldo assumed Roone had canceled another Kennedy story out of his friendship with Ethel Kennedy. Geraldo enlisted Barbara Walters and Hugh Downs to support him, then spoke to syndicated columnist Liz Smith. "Stoked with emotional fury I charged Roone with cronyism and censorship and questioned his journalist integrity."

Barbara Walters later commented, "Geraldo had a very emotional relationship with Roone...but somehow that relationship had deteriorated.... It was his way of saying I'm not somebody you can push around.... Geraldo was like a child trying to get attention and he got it. I thought he had great courage to take the stand that he did...."[6]

After Geraldo trashed Roone he realized his new contract had not been signed. He then added insult to injury by attacking Roone in a *People* magazine interview. At the same time Geraldo's girlfriend CC had been caught using an ABC messenger to pick up some marijuana from a friend of hers at CNN. ABC had all the ammunition they needed to get rid of Geraldo Rivera, who had no contract to back him up. Roone called Geraldo the next day. Stormy seas and a wind that could sink a forty-four-foot sailboat had arrived. Geraldo details the conversation that followed.

> "I want you to quit," he announced.
> "Bullshit," I said. "I'm not quitting."
> "You can't continue. Not after this."
> "I have a contact."
> "You have no contract."
> Roone then pivoted to the drugs.
> "That has nothing to do with me, and you know it."
> "It's relevant here. The police are going to investigate."[7]

The media ran with the story of drugs and the feud between Roone and Geraldo. Geraldo fought for his job, but in the end, he left with both sides agreeing to say he was resigning. ABC put out a press release: "After fifteen years of hard work, honorable work with ABC, Geraldo Rivera has told us that he wishes to leave to pursue other opportunities. . . ."[8] Geraldo was now back on his boat without a job. Like any good sailor he began looking for another safe harbor from the storm. But he found nothing, no job offers, no immediate course to sail for. He was now sailing blind like the man who was heading for prison after a conviction of tax evasion and who would never return to the Lexington Hotel where Geraldo Rivera would have a rendezvous with destiny.

17

Capone on Ice

1932

Al Capone sat in Cook County Jail eating plates of corned beef and cabbage, which was a long way from the steaks and lobster at the Lexington. While he was in jail the *Chicago Herald* announced CAPONE RUNS UNDERWORLD FROM CELL. Then Warden David C. Moneypenny was spotted taking Capone's Cadillac to Springfield. When the Lindbergh baby was kidnapped on March 1, 1932, Capone offered his services to help catch the kidnappers, but he had to be released to do it. Not a chance. Frank Wilson killed that proposal and said Capone had no information that would help authorities. Capone's appeals failed and the US Supreme Court declined to hear his case. He was headed for Leavenworth and Eliot Ness escorted him to the train station. The station was mobbed with people trying to get one last look at the Big Man. The Dixie Flyer departed Union Station on May 3, 1932, with Al Capone handcuffed to a car thief named Vito Morici.

Federal agents watched him as he chatted with reporters, smoked cigars, and posed for photographs. At every stop people peered into the Pullman car to catch a glimpse of Al Capone, who waved and smiled much like a baseball player heading off to training camp. When asked about his thoughts on his conviction, Capone replied, "I'm not sore at anybody, but I hope Chicago will be better off . . . they'll find that sending me away won't help Chicago much."[1] Capone said what he always said, people wanted to drink, and he was supplying the booze. Was that such a crime? He was a celebrity, and it would have been fitting if he was headed for Hollywood or baseball camp, but he was headed for Leavenworth.

The federal prison had been built and opened in 1903 and designed to break the spirit of the inmates with walls four feet thick and thirty-seven feet high. Capone gave up his $231.00 in his pockets as well as "religious medals, a rosary, a nail clipper, a fountain pen, a wallet and a single key. He received a pair of blue denim overalls with the number 40866 stitched on a trouser leg. His medical examination showed he weighed 255 pounds with 20/20 vision in his right eye. He was suffering from arthritis and a swollen prostate gland. He had an IQ of 95 and tested positive for nervous system syphilis." In 15 percent of the cases, syphilis caused brain damage leading to dementia. The prison hospital immediately put Capone on bismuth therapy and a series of other chemicals.

Attorney General Homer S. Cummings decided that the government needed a prison that would keep prisoners from communicating with other criminals on the outside. The prison would be escape-proof and inaccessible. Off the coast of San Francisco was a rock. A giant rock that was an island called Alcatraz. It sat in the middle of San Francisco Bay. It was an old military prison that was converted with guard towers and gates. So there Alcatraz sat with fishing boats and ferries churning by in rough icy waters that ensured no one could escape. Al Capone and forty-two other prisoners were loaded onto a train, chained to their seats, and taken to San Francisco. Alcatraz was for the violent offenders, but in Capone's case it was more of a public relations move. Al Capone was famous. Capone got press. What better way to showcase this maximum-security prison than to ship off public enemy number one to Alcatraz?

Capone entered the prison in late August as prisoner eighty-five and moved into cell 181. His cell was "nine feet long and five feet wide with bars overlooking the cell block and little natural light. Prisoners woke at six thirty each morning. They had no radios. They were permitted to shave three times a week with razors passed through the bars then immediately recovered by the guards."[2] Capone began working in the laundry. The prisoners weren't allowed to congregate but they could smoke and talk when not working. As syphilis took hold of Capone the doctors tried an experimental way of treating the disease with no known cure. They would infect Al Capone with malaria and when his temperature rose it would kill the syphilis organism. They would bring down his temperature with quinine before it could kill him. The experiment did not go well, and Capone nearly died. His syphilis was left to develop and slowly Capone began to lose his grip on reality.

Capone had made plans before he went to prison for eleven years. His contingency plan ensured that his enormous fortune would be waiting for him when he was released. He hid his millions to prevent the government or his criminal enemies from taking them. When Capone came out of Alcatraz after six and a half years, he could not find any of his hidden money. The dementia came on fast, and Al Capone began to lose his memory. Over the years the disease progressed and soon he could not remember people from his own family. Soon he could not remember where he had deposited or hid millions of dollars that was the Capone fortune. Al Capone's niece wrote a book, *Uncle Al Capone: The Untold Story from Inside His Family*. Allegedly Capone told his grandniece, "I buried the box but when I went to dig it up after I got out, I couldn't find it. Then I thought I had buried it in another place, but when I looked, it wasn't there either."[3] When he was released from prison in 1947 because of the advanced dementia, he had no idea where his money was. He plopped a fishing line in his pool in Florida and sat for hours. People questioned him about the money and implored him to give them just a clue where it might be. No dice. Al Capone simply could not remember where all the money he had amassed had been hidden. Some thought the money had been deposited in safety deposit boxes all over the country. But nothing ever turned up. Others claimed it was buried in a secret place in the country. Still others thought it might be in a vault in a basement in a hotel on the South Side of Chicago. It was logical. Al Capone had lived and ran Chicago from the hotel. And now there was a vault in the basement that ran out to the sidewalk. Yes. *There.* That was where the lost money of Al Capone was. Down in the Lexington Hotel basement. On April 21, 1986, all they had to do was open the vault and there would be the vast, ill-gotten gains of one Al Capone. Everyone believed it was there. In fact, the whole country was betting on it.

18

Happy Days

The 1980s were like the 1950s. Small things were big things. It was an incubatory decade of fun and prosperity led by a movie star president Ronald Reagan. Vietnam had ended and so had social upheaval. Yuppies were born. Making money was good again. Big hair was good again. Madonna was new. Rock went alternative and Halley's Comet was on the way. The big problems of the sixties and seventies had vanished. *Top Gun* dominated the box office. *The Phantom of the Opera* made its debut in London. Oprah made her debut in Chicago. Cocaine was everywhere and really fun. *The Breakfast Club*, *Pretty in Pink*, and *About Last Night* summed up youth culture as urbane, hip, alternative. We had won the Cold War and there was no more evil empire. Pet rocks were a hit, and the postcollege generation went to the cities with a new novel as their anthem: *Bright Lights, Big City*. Michael J. Fox went *Back to the Future* and people began to put phones in their cars and carry gray brick phones that worked half the time. Pot was still illegal, but everyone got stoned, and AIDS was a problem for Africa and gays. Girls just wanted to have fun, and even though we still only had four channels there was something called cable and if you paid for it, you could watch new movies at home. Going to the video store was a Saturday night ritual for families and couples.

The landscape was placid, even, and fertile ground for a one-off event where the biggest concerns were: was Michael Jordan the greatest basketball player of all time, and did the Chicago Bears really win the Super Bowl? This

1950s landscape might also be compared to the twenties in terms of optimism and prosperity; this was the cultural tabula rasa on which "The Mystery of Al Capone's Vaults" beamed out on the cold night of April 21, 1986. We just wanted to be entertained.

America's obsession with entertainment begins with the World's Fair. We loved World's Fairs. The 1893 Columbian Exposition in Chicago was a big one. Everyone knows about it now after the book *Devil in the White City*. Then came the 1933 Chicago World's Fair. Now that Al Capone was in jail, Chicago could have its 1933 World's Fair. The World's Fair brought people from all over the world. People didn't travel much then. In 1933 only 10 percent of the population had a car and nobody flew. Many people stayed on their city blocks for their entire lives. But the World's Fair of 1933 was a moment to see the exotic, the strange, the world. There were houses from the future and preemie babies in incubators along with Sally Rand and a Pullman car that crossed the lagoon 625 feet up. There were lights and boats and a telephone that called coast to coast along with assembly lines where cars were assembled and peas were canned. The fair was a marvel and there was something else that was there ... *television*. It was a mechanical television that used a rotating disc to throw pinpoints of light on a screen where a faint image flickered. It was amazing and the equivalent of seeing a spaceship. People could not get enough of it, and now fifty-three years later people all over the country, and all over the world, were gathering in front of that same magic box to watch Geraldo Rivera promise to unveil the secrets that Al Capone had left behind in a vault.

The buildup in the press had been extraordinary for weeks. A wire service story from United Press International as early as December 21, 1985, proclaimed "Capone's Vault Still a Mystery," then went on to speculate that:

> Capone's underground vault in the old Lexington Hotel is rumored to contain millions of dollars, perhaps a few dusty corpses, but whatever treasure is there, the IRS wants its cut of the money. Capone sealed the

8-by-8, 125-foot-deep vault with concrete and asphalt before starting a prison sentence at Alcatraz Prison on May 5, 1932 . . . the vault in the old Lexington Hotel on the near South Side will be opened during a live television broadcast April 14. . . . The vault and its contents are the subject of a two-hour live syndicated television special called *The Mystery of Al Capone's Vaults*. . . . Harold Rubin and the Sunbow Foundation own the hotel and hope to share in the treasure of the vault.[1]

A couple of details the article got wrong. The date for the broadcast was April 21, not April 14, and Harold Rubin never owned any part of the Lexington Hotel, but we can see in these early days there was great confusion as to who would share in the spoils. The IRS. Rubin. The city of Chicago. The Sunbow Foundation. The Westgate Group. Tribune Entertainment. In 1985 the speculation was intense and everyone foresaw millions. Another wire service story surfaced on April 20, 1986, in the *Spokane Review*: "Geraldo Rivera Returns to TV with Capone's Vaults."[2] Geraldo had vanished from the public television world when he was fired from *20/20* and now, he was back.

> When you look up the word *hero* in the dictionary Geraldo Rivera's picture isn't there. But he's the sort of fellow who wishes it was. For a decade and half, with his long hair flying in the wind, he's ridden in on his white horse to save damsels in distress and slay corporate dragons with his terrible swift sword disguised as a television camera.

Then the article goes through his getting fired from *20/20*: "I forgot that I was an employee of a network, and you don't bite the hand that feeds you." The article says Geraldo is "tan and fit and ready to get back in front of the camera." When asked what he thinks is in the vault:

> "Oh it could be nothing," he replied with a smile. "In which case I'll be like Hamlet contemplating that skull. That's the exciting part. Nobody knows what's inside. A lot of people don't like risks, which is why most television

is done on tape. But I like risks. I like live television. I love to rock and roll and see what happens...."[3]

Another wire story on the eve of the broadcast in the *Wichita Eagle* is more ominous: "Opening of Capone's Vault May Close Rivera's Career."[4] Geraldo had done an interview in *Esquire* magazine where he took some shots at his old employer.

> I was reading an article about Geraldo Rivera titled, *whatever happened to Geraldo Rivera?* The story was a sad one, detailing the slights and petty humiliations Rivera suffered during lengthy tenure at ABC News ... now in *Esquire* he is ruminating about his career at ABC. He never fit in, see, because he had long hair and was an ethnic minority and a radical and didn't go to the right schools like snotty Peter Jennings and that group. Rivera claims he didn't play office politics and didn't kiss the right behinds. He was a fighting journalist, a throwback to the days when reporters didn't merely report but became personally involved with their stories. Rivera paints himself as a pugnacious pit bull in a kennel full of emasculated poodles ... if you tune in at 7 PM Monday on KSAS Ch 4 you'll find out just what happened to Geraldo Rivera. He is a host of a live syndicated special called "The Mystery of Al Capone's Vaults."[5]

The article then sums up how the show came to be produced and then winds up with a warning for Geraldo.

> Sillier still is Rivera's involvement in this effort. Here's a guy in *Esquire* lamenting that his work was never appreciated agreeing to host *Hidden Vaults of Crooked and Deceased*. Being host of this kind of contrived special isn't going to exactly send his stock as a reporter soaring. For all his phony melodrama, his unctuous patronizing, his name dropping, Rivera did some solid work. You don't win three national Emmy Awards, a Robert F. Kennedy Award, and a Columbia Dupont Award for posing in front of a

camera. Now he's host of the opening of Al Capone's vaults. For Rivera, the opening of that vault could signal the closing of his career as a legitimate investigative reporter.[6]

Geraldo, though, is just following the tide. Americans love spectacle. That is why no matter how cheesy the Superbowl gets we watch it year after year. That is why people in the beginning of the twentieth century went to see a man named Buffalo Bill ride around a tent with cowboys and Indians and dream about being cowboys themselves. That's why P. T. Barnum put together a circus composed of clowns, elephants, tigers, and freaks, went from one small town to another, and took people's money so they could just for a moment see the exotic, the weird, the strange. That is why people began tuning-in on that cold night on April 21, 1986.

Geraldo Rivera was now getting ready inside the lobby of the Lexington Hotel while a helicopter's *chop chop chop* was getting progressively louder with the skyline footage already beginning as the helicopter came down from the sky and STROH'S BEER flashed up as a sponsor and people with only four channels tuned-in on the East Coast at 8 p.m., in Chicago at 7 p.m., and in California at 5 p.m. And all over the world in the middle of the night, in the morning, in the evening, people settled in to watch the show they had been hearing about for the last year.

Never before had so much ink been devoted to a television show. Speculation ran wild. In the *Sun Journal* in Lewistown the front-page wire-based headline said it all. AL CAPONE'S SECRET MAY ONLY BE STALE AIR.[7] Knight Ridder publications sent this story to every subscribing paper in the country. That meant that all over America people were sitting down to a Sunday morning breakfast with Capone's vault staring back at them. The article is a tour of fancy the day before the broadcast.

The bimbos and bottom dealers and alky cookers are dead. The busy brothels and smoky wire rooms have been bulldozed into silence and the sweet-sour scents of perfume and cigar smoke had been recycled into the environment. Sure, it was a toddling town Chicago . . . but it became a toppling town . . . about all that is left of the days when Capone ruled Chicago is the old Lexington Hotel. The Lexington and whatever booze or bones or boodle is found in the hotel's basement Monday night.[8]

People were now writing down the time.

On live television across the nation Monday at 8 PM EST a massive concrete crypt that is being called "Al Capone Vaults" will be opened. What is in there is anybody's guess. And there's a lot of guessing going on.

"A bunch of skeletons if there's anything," said Ven Whaley, 78, who was a newspaper reporter when he came to know Capone in 1928. "I can't believe that Al Capone's stupid enough to bury money in a concrete, sealed-up vault. If he had any extra big bills that he wanted to save, he probably buried them down in Florida."

"I'll tell you what's in there," said author Jay Robert Nash, whose writing on gangsters makes him a Mafiologist. "Nothing."[9]

The wire article goes on to describe what is actually going to be opened. "It's not really a vault." Somebody finally cleared that up. Ever since Weird Harold discovered the cement slab in the basement of the Lexington and named it a vault the world had been envisioning a vault not unlike a bank vault. But in reality, the vault was:

> a long concrete chamber that runs beneath the Michigan Avenue sidewalk alongside the hotel. It's 125 feet long, 13 feet deep, and 8 feet high. In the basement facing Michigan Avenue, the outline of nine archways are visible. But they're sealed with cement. Old electrical wiring was found running along the top of the chamber, suggesting to some that it may have once been booby trapped.[10]

This is new. Boobytrapped. But it adds to the suspense, doesn't it? The article then describes what has been accomplished so far.

The Westgate Group, a California company that is producing the two-hour television special with Tribune Entertainment Company of Chicago, already has cut out one of the archways, conducted high-tech probing, and determined that there was another concrete chamber inside the vault.[11] So what they'll do on television between documentary footage from the era, taped interviews with folks who feared and revered Capone, and commentary from host Geraldo Rivera, is remove the archway they've already cut out, then either jackhammer or dynamite their way into the inner chamber. The president of the Westgate Group, John Joslyn, swears that he himself won't know whether the inner chamber holds any surprises until Monday night.[12]

Allan Grafman put it this way: "We didn't know what was in the vault. Right up to show time we didn't know. We didn't want to know. We had run tests that proved nothing either way. We didn't know if there was something or nothing and we told the audience that. There might be something. There might be nothing."[13] And so that was the approach. Benign neglect. John Joslyn put it this way: "That we were going to leave intact (the vault) and do it live for the sake of our audience, for the honesty and integrity of the show. It's conceivable that it's a big zero. A big zero," Joslyn said. "Stale air. Absolutely. Stale air. That's the risk we take."[14]

The syndicated article that ended up on the front pages of newspapers all over the country framed up the contradictions of Capone's personality. "To some he was a cold-blooded killer who owned virtually everyone who had power and killed those he couldn't." "He is Neapolitan by birth and Neanderthal by instinct," Fred D. Pasley, a newspaperman who knew Capone, wrote in *Al Capone: The Biography of a Self-Made Man* in 1930. Pasley described him as "rather doggish-churlish—disputations inclined to belligerency. He was in a word, crude." But to others he was a kind patron who dumped free coal in poor neighborhoods during winter, provided soup kitchens during the Depression, and started a system of milk dating so children could be assured of fresh milk.[15]

John Joslyn covered his bet by saying, "If nothing else, all the interviews and research into Capone and the era as well the excavation of long forgotten and in some cases previously unknown tunnels running beneath the streets have produced what he calls, 'the definitive piece on Al Capone.'"[16] But that is not what people around the world were tuning-in for on the night of April 21, 1986. They didn't care about the definitive piece on Al Capone; they wanted to see what was in the vault. It was time to find out. An article in *The Washington Post* entitled "TV Stations Eager to Air Vault Opening" showed how the dearth of programming was in favor of the shows:

> "Tribune Entertainment Company, which aired the *Andrea Doria* safe opening special in August 1984, says the two-hour 'The Mystery of Al Capone's Vaults' with host Geraldo Rivera tonight will be the biggest syndicated special ever airing on 181 stations, half of which are network affiliates and covering 95 percent of the national TV audience. Some 40 ABC affiliates have signed for the 'Vaults' special. As a result, ABC moved the movie *Alex: The Life of A Child* from Monday to Wednesday night instead.[17]

Then Geraldo gets in on the act, framing up his return to television in an article with the *Oakland Tribune* that showed how he saw the two-hour show as a reset for his career. *Recess Is Over: TV Viewers Will See a New Geraldo Rivera*—the headline blares with a reflective, thoughtful picture of Geraldo in a polo shirt.

Geraldo Rivera is back. After fifteen years as a brash investigative reporter for ABC after a bitter exit from *20/20* over the cancellation of a story on

Marilyn Monroe's alleged affairs with John and Robert Kennedy, after 77 days at sea, the world will see a new and improved Rivera, he says. A more reflective Rivera. A changed Rivera. A better Rivera.

Someone had been whispering in Geraldo's ear, probably his publicist.

In town recently to film scenes for his latest project, *The Mystery of Al Capone's Vaults*, the New York City poverty lawyer turned journalist spoke optimistically of his future in cable television, bemoaned the wispiness of TV's investigative journalism, and swore like a boy scout that his post-ABC adventure, which consisted of sailing his 45-foot-sailboat the *New Wave* from New York City to the Panama Canal, had made a new man of him . . . "I discovered my reflective side" said the 42-year-old Rivera, sipping a light beer and nibbling on the lunch provided by the San Francisco hotel. "I don't say that it wasn't there before, but to protect myself I ignored it. I felt if I let my guard down someone could hurt me. So, I stayed swashbuckling. I stayed hot."[18]

The article then covers his past work at *Eyewitness News* up to his firing and then his trip on the *New Wave* with his six-year-old son and his girlfriend, CC, after having left New York on December 12.

"There was definitely a machismo, a warrior aspect to my personality . . . but I'm a mature man now," he continued. "I'm evolved. I'm not a revolutionary anymore . . . I don't have to be part of the system. I don't want to be in the corps de ballet anymore. I want my own program. . . ." At the moment Rivera's days are spent working on "The Mystery of Al Capone's Vaults" . . . "I think of myself as a modern-day archeologist exploring King Al's Tomb." The fact that the program is independently syndicated is another example that the public will seek out programming if it's not on network television. . . .[19]

This is the first time Geraldo has revealed his motivation for doing the syndicated show. He needed the money, but he saw it as a fork in the eye to the networks.

His next project will be either to start a nightly cable talk show or a weekly one-hour news magazine. . . . The timing is right for this type of programming, Rivera said, and he is the man to do it. He held up a letter showing he and other newscasters have more credibility than Ronald Reagan. "I'm not arrogant. I have a very sober sense of where I stand."[20]

The strange brick wall discovered by Harold Rubin in a hunt for artifacts had by now taken on mythic proportions. This was Capone's vault. This was where the money, the bodies, the cars, the stills, the Thompson machine guns were all stored. This idea began in a dark, condemned basement of a nineteenth-century hotel. Weird Harold, like any treasure or gold hunter, was convinced that the motherlode was to be found somewhere in the catacombs of the old Lexington Hotel. So, after Harold Rubin lowered himself down into the darkness with his son waiting at the top, he flashed his light around looking . . . looking . . . looking, he flashed his light around and came to the brick wall and that glowing, five-thousand-pound slab.

Here it was. This wall that ran the length of the basement out to the sidewalk had no reason to be here. There was a gold mine on the other side. The Forty-Niners who panned for gold in the Yukon had nothing on Weird Harold. He had a sixth sense, an extra eye for opportunity. Forget that he had been arrested more times than he could count; he had savvy, that knack for smelling a deal, a money-making scheme, a treasure. And so, he named it there and then "Capone's Vault." And it was his. Forgetting the fact there was no vault, just a crudely patched-up brick wall, but no matter. *This was a vault.* It was Capone's vault, and now it was Harold Rubin's, and so what does he do? He goes back and he goes back, but he cannot get past that slab, sealing up the riches that are to be his if he can just penetrate the brick and mortar.

And so he goes to the press, and the Chicago press knows a good story. Capone sells. He always has, and so the article of the secret vault comes out in the *Chicago Tribune* with quotes by Rubin. Just like that, Capone's vault comes into being. If Weird Harold had just said there was some wall down in the basement it would have stayed *da wall*, but he named it and the press named it and now the Lexington Hotel—that hulking, massive, condemned structure—took on a second life as other papers picked up on the story. *Capone's Vault.* It had a ring of mystery and intrigue and promised riches, booty, bodies, whatever.

It didn't matter, because now a wall that had no real significance at all that the Chicago architect Tim Shepardson would nail right off and say, "Yeah, they have these sidewalk vaults where they load in goods on the sidewalk and a lot of times, they fill those in because the sidewalk could cave in."[21] He was ignored. Later in an interview he would recall:

> They called me once and said, "We found a torture chamber!" I go over there and it was a fuse box. They actually brought in Irene Hughes, who was at the time the biggest psychic in America next to Jeane Dixon. She was going to try to pick up the spirit of Capone in the building. We go to the basement, she walks toward the middle of the wall, and says, "Capone is behind it in a garden under glass, laughing, laughing, laughing." Now, I have researched the hell out of that building. I told her there had been nothing there but a yard. Fifteen years later, the city found some old real estate atlases. What was in the middle of the Lexington? A greenhouse. Honest to God.[22]

And then a World's Fair is being planned for 1995 in Chicago and Patricia Porter buys the building for her training ground for young women learning construction and she needs money and publicity and she locks Weird Harold out and takes Capone's vault to the big time and sells the mystery like hotcakes to investors because she needs money for her nonprofit organization and she contacts the media and brings in more reporters and has a dinner complete with a tour of the crappy dark basement where Harold Rubin stumbled onto the wall and the story goes out over the wire and is picked up by newspapers all over the country and now Capone's vault is national news and Doug Llewelyn and John Joslyn in LA are smoking and reading the morning paper and they know that perception is reality and the perception is this is Capone's vault and something is in that vault and so they create the pitch and take it to the next level and it becomes "the mystery of Capone's vault" and they contact Patricia Porter and pitch it to Tribune Entertainment in Chicago, which happens to be looking for programming for their stations, and they take it to the next level by investing almost a million dollars into the idea of Capone's vault because, really, that is all it is—*an idea* that a wall hides a vault that hides something from Al Capone—but never mind, they know that basic maxim of show business, and that is *you will never go broke underestimating the intelligence of the American public,* and so they take it to the bank, and sell the idea to stations all over the country that a two-hour special on the mystery of Al Capone's vault will rake in viewers like fish in a barrel, and then they find an unemployed newsman carnival barker who had just been fired and is sailing in the Panama Canal to host the show for $50,000 and they create a lot of B-roll to fill and lower a bulldozer into the basement and conduct tests that, of course, turn up nothing because there is nothing, but that doesn't matter, because the idea, the germ that was created by Rubin with his cop flashlight in the basement of the decrepit hotel is now about to beam out all over the world, and people all over the world are sitting down to watch "The Mystery of Al Capone's Vaults" be revealed and everyone who has anything to do with the show now believes something is really here because if you drink the Kool-Aid long enough you convince yourself it tastes pretty good and the alternative is unthinkable and Harold

Rubin and his son are at the Hyatt in Chicago watching on a big-screen television at a safecracking party, but they were not invited to be part of the infotainment broadcast even though Harold Rubin discovered the slab and named it "the Vault," as his son Jules says years later in an interview that bothered his father. After all, Weird Harold, the Porn King of Chicago, really was the one who created the show that was just about to beam out all over the world, "The Mystery of Al Capone's Vault."

The Lexington Hotel where Capone took over two floors and ran his operations.
© Brettmann / Royalty-free / Getty Images.

The publicity for The Mystery of Al Capone's Vaults *was unprecedented. Courtesy of Allan Grafman.*

Geraldo Rivera had just been fired from ABC. ABC / Photofest © ABC.

Capone left the Lexington Hotel when he went to jail for income tax evasion in 1931. Photofest © Photofest.

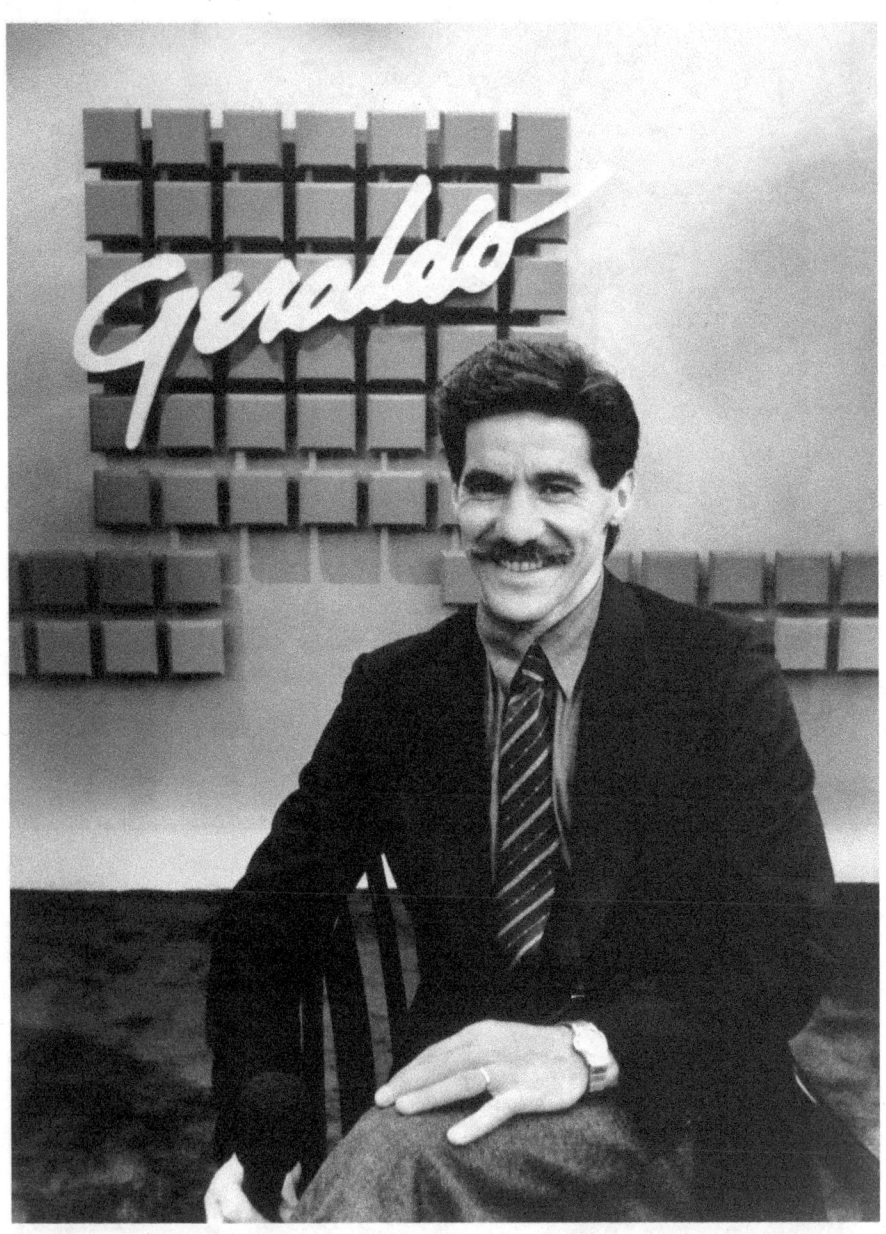

After the biggest disaster in modern television, Geraldo ended up with his own show. Photofest © Photofest.

Al Capone ran Chicago with an iron fist and was famous for his white fedora. Photofest © Photofest.

Geraldo Rivera was a hard-charging journalist who changed the role of the traditional television news anchor. ABC / Photofest © ABC.

Geraldo was a star on 20/20 and was devastated by his firing. ABC / Photofest © ABC.

Producer Allan Grafman (right) of Tribune Entertainment, which took a huge risk on the production. Courtesy of Allan Grafman.

Tribune Entertainment had the highest-rated syndicated show in history. Courtesy of Allan Grafman.

PART TWO

THE BROADCAST

19

Showtime!

April 21, 1986

Geraldo was ready. The networks were moving prime-time movies away from the two-hour live presentation. They were moving shows. Up to 181 stations were waiting to broadcast "The Mystery of Al Capone's Vaults" along with stations around the world. It was going to be the biggest syndicated special ever. Everyone said so. It was now, finally . . . *showtime!* So now we are back to where we started. It is a cold night in April and Geraldo Rivera is getting double mic'd while cameramen position themselves along with the lights while satellite trucks parked outside make sure their feed is right while stations across the country wait for the signal. "The moments leading up to our live broadcast on April 21, 1986, were charged with adrenalin and drama," Geraldo later wrote. He added:

> The stakes were enormous. Everything hinged on my performance and on my ability to sustain viewer interest, which was expected to be high. There is a certain opening night urgency, a palpable nervousness to any live broadcast, even a newscast but especially a prime-time extravaganza. My butterflies . . . typically take the form of cold hands; here, as the world waited and my future hung in the balance, my anxiety moved to other extremities . . . viewer projections promised a huge audience and it was my job to hold

their attention until we determined what, if anything was entombed behind the sealed wall that had been possibly used by a legendary mob figure.[1]

Forty years ago, in 1986, your television had a protrusion-like, extended eye out the back. It was called a cathode ray tube (CRT), which was really a low-pressure vacuum tube containing an electron gun that shot electrons at a fluorescent tube. Your screen was curved to keep the pressure from the atmosphere from imploding your screen. Your television smelled of electricity when you went to change the channel. It had a dusty, foreign smell of old radios. You might have been watching a black and white television even though color sets dominated more than half the homes in 1972. You might have been banished to that old, paneled, half-finished basement where the older television sat like a discarded statue. The newer, bigger television is upstairs where Mom and Dad are watching the network programming. If you bothered to open a *TV Guide* or looked at the listings in the paper, you saw that on ABC at 8 p.m. there was *Hardcastle and McCormick*. But it was a repeat. At 9 p.m. there was *Monday Night Baseball*. You really aren't that into sports. On CBS at 8 p.m. Eastern there was *Scarecrow and Mrs. King*. Another repeat followed by *Kate & Allie* at 9, then *Newhart* at 9:30, then at 10 a cop show, *Cagney & Lacey*. Everything was a repeat and NBC wasn't much better. At 8 p.m. there were *TV's Bloopers and Practical Jokes* and at 9 was the TV Academy "Hall of Fame." Whatever that was.

And you only have four stations in the Chicago area. And your television with the rabbit ears struggles to pick those up while Mom and Dad watch a crystal-clear picture with no problem at all. But then you see it. Right there in the newspaper that lists the cable stations as well, of which you have none. AL CAPONE'S VAULTS. It's on WGN. A 50-thousand-watt Chicago superstation that comes in loud and clear on the basement set and you have heard about this vault for a while now. Some vault in a hotel basement that the guy with the mustache, Geraldo Rivera, was going to open. You looked at the listing sandwiched between *Sacred Ground* on TMC and *Lord Jim* on WOR. The listing says 8 p.m. Eastern, but you are in the suburbs of Chicago and its 7 p.m. Central.

You switch on the television and there is a commercial, but right away the promo is hawking the opening of Al Capone's vaults, and you hit the couch that is musty and old with your bag of potato chips and even though the image on your television is faded from time there is something different about this. Suddenly the screen goes blank, then *bam*, a helicopter is flying above a dark blue Chicago, and you see the city below. Now the helicopter is descending toward the hotel and what you don't know is that all over America and all over the world people are watching the same event. You look up the stairs. Could Mom and Dad stay occupied for two hours because you just hit the motherlode. Some cheesy spooky event about a gangster with that cool guy Geraldo Rivera and what you don't know is satellite trucks are throwing the signal that you just watched up to a satellite that is fanning it out to stations all over the world. The 181 local stations that paid for the programming are getting it off the satellite feed or getting it through a cable feed or ATT long lines. The satellite is busy taking that feed and shooting it down to stations in foreign countries that have bought the show and are now presenting it with their own commercials. The networks are moving shows around to accommodate the one-off syndicated special. Movies have been bumped. Sitcoms have been bumped. Repeats have been bumped. Talk shows have been bumped. The stations are all making a bet that people will be more interested in seeing what's in Capone's vault than some rerun of *Scarecrow and Mrs. King*.

And now the floating helicopter shoots up and down and then starts to float down down down down right onto Michigan Avenue among the crowds of onlookers, reporters, and television cameras. The *thwock thwock thwock* of the helicopter is deafening and the Lexington Hotel is lit up with giant, pale spotlights and looks haunted. Suddenly there's Geraldo Rivera in a white shirt and tie walking out the front door in a trim dark jacket, double microphones clipped to his lapel, and staring at the camera. What you don't know is that just before Geraldo went on he was panicked. He had just realized there was no teleprompter and he would have to ad-lib the entire broadcast. In an interview years later, he told me, "Minutes before I went on, I realized there was no teleprompter. Which I found surprising and disconcerting. Pete Simmons, a cool older producer . . . minutes before we went on . . . grabbed me by the arms, looking at me ferociously, eyes blazing, and said, 'you know this shit! Now nail this motherfucker!' Which had the curious effect of firing me up and calming me down."[2]

So Geraldo walks into the glare of the spotlights without a teleprompter and from here on he has to make it up as he goes. He stabs the air with his right hand, flashing his pearly whites under his trademark mustache. *"I'm Geraldo Rivera and you are about to witness a live television event; a massive concrete vault has been discovered! Some think it belongs to none other than the notorious Al Capone! Well tonight, for the first time, that vault is going to be opened live!"*[3]

And now the music comes up and you are back in a helicopter high above Chicago that is circling over the darkened city. *Live from the Windy City, a Worldwide Two-Hour Television Event from Al Capone's former headquarters in the Lexington Hotel. Tribune Entertainment and the Westgate Group are proud to present the mystery of Al Capone's Vaults!* Then the spooky, fuzzed title comes up on the television. THE MYSTERY OF AL CAPONE'S VAULTS. Then the sponsor flashes up. STROH'S IS SPOKEN HERE AND BY THE HYATT REGENCY OF CHICAGO. "The Mystery of Al Capone's Vaults" is hosted by Gerald Rivera![4]

And now you have settled in with your potato chips to inhale the eye candy and to wonder along with thirty million other people around the world . . . *what in the hell is in Capone's vault?*

20

A Live Two-Hour Infotainment

April 21, 1986

"The Mystery of Al Capone's Vaults" was live, and it was like stepping off a cliff. For most television shows the fix was in, like the quiz shows in the fifties. You gave the contestants the answers first because you cannot trust the unexpected and you have to manipulate audience reaction. So when a show is taped, the producers and the talent know where it is going, but on April 21, 1986, no one knew where the show was going. Not the producers. Not Geraldo. Not the workmen. Not the IRS. Not the medical examiner. Not Tribune Entertainment. Everyone was stepping off a cliff and the skeptics said nothing was there, but there were those uncovered stairwells leading to the basement from Capone's room and there were the electrical wires going back into the vault and there were the historians who painted the era of Capone as gangsters trundling down those tunnels that did exist that did connect the hotel to a famous gang hangout run by big Jim Colosimo. So Geraldo was right. He was stepping off a cliff.

And outside the crowds had gathered with Mr. T at the front and journalists from around the world and the lined-up satellite trucks beaming that helicopter landing right on Michigan Avenue, but we just saw the footage landing and then the zoom-in on Geraldo emerging and telling the world that we were all going on a journey together to unveil the secrets of Al Capone tonight and we have two hours to do it. People paid $10 a head at the Hyatt down the street from the Lexington and dressed up like flappers and gangsters to watch on a wide-screen TV with Doug Llewelyn hosting. So let's get to work. Geraldo walks inside the Lexington Hotel and they lock the doors for security. For the next two hours no one gets in or out . . . but hold on! Rivera is coming out again into the camera glare and explains that Capone lived in the hotel and that directly beneath him:

> in the rubble-strewn hotel a massive concrete vault has been discovered and what this vault contains we don't know. This is an adventure you and I are going to take this journey together, and there is evidence to suggest that that vault once belonged to Al Capone, the richest and most powerful gangster of his time. Now what if anything that vault contains we don't know . . . because one way or another the mystery is going to be solved tonight, and we're going to break open that vault, and we're going to step inside. We're also going to step back into history. . . .[1]

The hook is set. Geraldo has told the audience the purpose of the broadcast and now he has just under two hours to fill with excavation and video clips. He cuts immediately to the first video montage and Geraldo promises us that we will explore the private rooms and the hidden staircases and descend forty feet below the streets of Chicago into a little-known tunnel system, one that may have been used by Scarface Al Capone. Then he promises we will talk with people who knew Al Capone personally. "He was an evil man," one bearded gentleman resembling Rip Van Winkle relates. "He was just like a big roly-poly teddy bear to me," a blowsy blonde says, smiling. "He was loveable, he was sweet," another man remembers while a woman says that Al Capone killed her husband. Geraldo then points to where Capone lived on the fifth floor and identifies the hotel's most famous guest again, Al Capone.[2]

Now after telling the world Capone is a ruthless killer and public enemy number one, Geraldo goes inside and takes viewers with him to imagine the opulence of the hotel in its day. Now we can close the door and lock it. We will not be going outside again. We will be going down to the basement next . . . but not so fast! Was the hook set? That is the aim of the first five minutes of the two-hour broadcast, or really any broadcast. Get people hooked so they don't bail out. People all over the world are considering now what Geraldo Rivera just told them.

Now that he mentions it, there could be something in the vault. Secret tunnels. Al Capone. A massive vault running under the hotel. He lived on the fifth floor of the hotel and had secret passageways to the basement. Millions. Bodies. Booze. I'm not moving. The other side of the mystery is the Tim Samuelson side—the Chicago architect historian who believes the vault is just the same old vault hotels had for loading in coal and supplies. This is not the side that Harold Rubin identified with or that Patricia Porter identified with or that the newspapers identified with. The twenties were crazy with booze, broads, gangsters, and millions and millions of dollars flowing around. It was just like the eighties, and why not stash some of those millions down in the vault of the basement of Capone's headquarters? Besides, *Geraldo thinks it's there.*

Geraldo walks inside and takes us on a tour, describing the hotel with ornate chandeliers and armed men with Thompsons in the lobby and lookouts in the elevator and bookies with .45 automatics. He explains then, still walking, "we have crawled through the whole hotel" and the handheld camera is now going with him, which in 1986 was a new way to film. Now we are moving as Geraldo descends stairs and describes escape passageways through which Capone could escape, and now we are descending into the belly of the beast, into the dust-filled basement as Geraldo shows us secret stairs that are visible after the walls have been torn down "during our process of exploration and excavation." He then goes to another stairwell. "There's another one over here, check it out," he says, picking up a strategically positioned flashlight. "Look, a hidden staircase. . . ."[3]

But Geraldo is done with this and is now heading for what he calls the main event. "This is what you have come to see, and this is why you are here," he says. Geraldo walks into the glare of light and stops in front of a massive, pale slab of concrete with what looks like a shiny lock with chains dangling. Geraldo grabs up a piece of conduit leading back into the vault. "Look at this electric wiring," he observes, and says he has talked to the son of the electrician who put it in, who says his father was working for Al Capone.

Geraldo then points out an obvious question: "why do you need electricity if nothing is behind the slab?"[4]

Geraldo then tells us the slab weighs five thousand pounds, is twenty-two inches thick, and is coming down tonight. This is the show we have come to see! Here is the vault. Here is the entrance to Capone's gold, the King Tut of gangsters. But wait! There's more. Due to the thickness of the wall or the vault the slab has been presawed to make sure it will come down. Full disclosure. No gimmicks here. Geraldo faces the camera. "But now we are ready to tear this wall down and we are going to do it with a miniature bulldozer." The bulldozer, or "this baby is called . . . a Bobcat, yes a Bobcat."[5] As Geraldo explains, the Bobcat will actually do the pulling that will take down the wall. Cue the Bobcat. The Bobcat comes bouncing over with a roar of smoke and noise with well-coiffed young men in brilliant blue suits and bright yellow hard hats. The Bobcat begins to position itself in front of the slab.

Geraldo has done his work well. He tells the audience that as they are hooking up the chains to the Bobcat, we are going to take our first commercial break. Geraldo puts one foot up on the wheel of the Bobcat and tells us when we return, "that wall is coming down." He then claps his hands like a football coach. "*Okay guys let's do it . . . get it set . . . get it set.*"[6] Now we go to commercial, and the hook has been set. Will anyone click those new remotes or stand up and change the channel? Not a chance. There is something behind that eerie concrete slab with the bright steel chain in the middle. You can feel it. Besides, the fix is in. *There has to be something.* They know what's back there. No one would promise what they could not deliver. *It's television, for Godsakes!* Just don't move. Stay in your La-Z-Boy, your couch, your floor, your basement, your living room, or keep drinking at the Hyatt in your spats with your girlfriend dressed like a flapper or in the pub in Ireland where you are watching or in London or France. No one. I mean *no one* was going to move now. Was the hook set? You bet. And we are just seven minutes into the show.

One hundred and thirteen minutes to go.

21

Suspension of Disbelief

And while Geraldo goes to commercial, we go to ours on the local stations.

It may be the equivalent of King Tut's Tomb for Chicago. It belonged to the king of a criminal empire. [bullets fired] *Its massive, 125 feet long, 20 feet high.* [camera panning over wall and concrete slab] *It's a mystery.* [more bullets fired, Geraldo standing in front of the wall, hands hooked in his pockets] *What secrets lie hidden in Al Capone's vault? Find out when we open it on live television. A world premiere television event. "The Mystery of Al Capone's Vault." Tonight at 7 only on TV 9!*[1]

These local spots have been going off all over the country like firecrackers. Guess what we are going to show you? CAPONE'S VAULT. *Top that!* We bought it from Tribune Entertainment and had to bump some old movie from our 8 Eastern spot but so what . . . *it's Al Capone's vault in a two-hour live special from Chicago, the shoot 'em up city itself.* The advertising spots the station could sell make it a no brainer. Al Capone. Old hotel on the South Side. Money. Bodies. Booze. Bullets. Americans love Al Capone. Besides . . . there is nothing else on a Monday night across the nation! *All reruns.* Nothing good to watch. This thing is set to make a killing.

Suspension of disbelief. The calling card of every realm of entertainment. The local station spot invites us into a mysterious landscape. Bullets.

Gangsters. Vice. Evil. All of it is in the vault in Chicago and now that the local station has the broadcast, they want people to watch it. So, they make their own commercials to push the show. In an interview with Bill O'Reilly on the thirty-sixth anniversary of the original 1986 broadcast, Geraldo has to defend himself against O'Reilly, who does the same thing every show. *He entertains.* Geraldo points out he needed the money. Bill O'Reilly ignores him and keeps it up. Who is he kidding? Television is a setup in itself. A flickering image we are programmed to watch by our genetics. Something moves in the forest, and we notice it. Television is always moving and tricking our eyes with all those pixilated dots. We are cats. Movement attracts us. Professional wrestling attracts us because it is a setup. Big men in tights beating each other up and smashing chairs over their heads and they gave Geraldo hell for getting his nose broke by a Nazi at one time and the irony is That Was Real.

But in wrestling nothing is real. *And we know that!* These guys screaming and taking dives off the ropes and the crowd going nuts. Our president loves this stuff, but we know it is not real; yet we watch it knowing the falls, the kicks, the flips are all staged, but our mind does not accept this. To us the wrestling *is real* even though intellectually we know that is all fake. We read a novel knowing none of it happened, yet we believe in that world so much we reread a good novel over and over or watch a good movie over and over. And yet, what tantalizes us even more is the unknown. It's rare. The fix is usually in, and it was in game shows at one time, but people got upset so the fix was taken out. That's why sports are amazing: because we cannot predict the outcome. No one could until they fixed the World Series in 1910. That really upset people because we were supposed to not be able to control the outcome. People in sports have to watch to the end for the payoff. We watch a show that has the possibility of things going wrong, and this keeps us glued to the set. *Saturday Night Live* was great because it *was live,* and things did go wrong as people lost it on television until Sinéad O'Connor tore up a picture of the pope. That went really wrong, and she never recovered from it; in fact, it almost did in

Saturday Night Live. But that is what we watch for. We watch a stunt to see if it will go wrong. We watch Geraldo Rivera in a Southside hotel basement blasting open a vault because many things could go wrong. The hotel could collapse. Dynamite could blow up the whole building. Suspension of disbelief here is not necessary because we really don't know if something is in that vault. *Nobody does.* And the medical examiner is there for the bodies. And the IRS is there for the money. And Geraldo is there for the hype. And we are there to lose ourselves. It is not the Academy Awards, where the winners are kept in a vault. This vault contains the dark secrets of the past. Or so we are told.

Local stations are the reason people watched "The Mystery of Al Capone's Vaults." I interviewed Mitch Nednick, who ran KTLA, the Los Angeles-based Tribune station at the time. Our conversation is wide ranging, but it is the view of the local station on a national event. Mitch gives us the view of television as I asked him why the show succeeded and if it could ever happen again:

As big a deal as it was just as big as a letdown . . . in a world where there was no streaming. It could never happen today. Do you know what's big today sports, the Academy Awards . . . things like *American Idol* are making a comeback. Linear television is on the decline. Live television is on the decline. 9,000,000 for a two-hour show. Chump change. I watched the special. There was no there there. There was all this buildup, and you feel like you get sucked in for what? I don't think it was fake news. They didn't know what was in there. Al Capone is a villainous hero. There might have been millions of dollars in there. Everyone knew who Al Capone was. Look at *The Godfather*, these guys in the mafia became antiheroes. You couldn't do this today. *Nobody cares.* Sports. Big award shows. The driver to local stations to get the most rights to live sports, you can't scroll through those. Live linear television, that business is hurting. It was a great play to syndicate "Capone's Vaults." They sold big rating guarantees to the local stations. Magazines were big. Newspapers were big. Premedia. No online instant media. Things moved slowly. Four channels. HBO was in its infancy. Local station. Split the units for commercials. Time was set. Nostalgic to look back. . . . CNN might cover this. . . . I wish I could remember more but that's forty years ago. Think about it today, a big interview like when Oprah interviewed Harry and Meghan . . . one-off specials can work . . . but many shows are broadcast the next day on Netflix. NBC has Peacock. CNN has Hulu. Television viewing has changed. . . . Linear television works best for political advertising . . . all politics are local . . . during an election, big demand. The sitcom is done except for syndication . . . economic success . . . huge curiosity factor with Capone's vault because everyone wanted to know . . . everyone was keenly interested in what was in the vault . . . never happen again."[2]

And now back to our regularly scheduled program.

22

Getting Ready to Pull Down the Slab

April 21, 1986

8:20 P.M. Eastern

And we are back. The program is humming along now. Everyone from the construction workers to the cameramen to Geraldo feel like they are closing-in on something. We had been promised that the wall was coming down when we came back . . . but not so fast. Geraldo wants to talk to Tim Samuelson, our architect historian of Chicago. He is a smiling, slight, balding thirty-something with that Chicago veneer. Smiling with a hard hat while he pulls at drywall and Geraldo confirms that a soil sample taken from the vault could have come from the period of Al Capone. The voice-over continues while Tim rips out more drywall. "Still, there were many unanswered questions." Geraldo is now facing Tim and holds up his arms. "So . . . what do you think?"[1]

Tim Samuelson smiles. He is wearing a windbreaker and a tie. Tim knows exactly what he thinks; in fact, he has told the producers what he thinks, that the vault was in fact a sidewalk vault where goods and coal were loaded into the hotel basement. But the lights are bright. He is talking to none other than *Geraldo Rivera* in front of an audience of millions. He will not be on television again. This is a one-off. In the basement the producers and cameramen and lighting technicians and assorted assistants and construction workers all watch Tim. Is he really going to throw a hand grenade into this beautiful wedding cake Weird Harold created back in 1981? He does what any person in his position does. He plays for the team.

"Well, in these old buildings I see similar things [sidewalk vault unsaid]. I just got to dig through and interpret the different layers, it's just all kind of stacked up and just have to sort it out."[2]

So, there you go. A nonanswer. So, what Tim is saying is that maybe and maybe not and I'm on camera and I'm not going to take the wind out of the sail. As an architect historian for the Chicago History Society, he has never had so much attention or notoriety than in the last few months. He too has been brought out of the basement into the glare of the spotlight and damned if he is going to shoot his own foot off. "You just have to dig through and interpret the different layers." Perfect. The company line. *Do you know we paid a million bucks to dig around in this old basement and you are going to tell us we are wasting our time? I don't think so.* So, Geraldo runs with it through a montage where he is drilling into a wall, a sonar is dragged over snow, and a heat-sensitive infrared monitor is pointed at the wall with men staring at what looks like an old oscilloscope "trying to learn if some of the entrances to the sealed vault entrances were solid or hollow; unfortunately many of the areas were solid concrete."[3]

Geraldo tells the viewing audience who have come back from commercial break that much of the vault was proving to be solid. Like a balloon losing air people all over the world are watching Geraldo carefully modulate their anticipation. One young viewer later wrote,

"I was 7 . . . and I remember my mom glued to the TV and then dad cracking up at her and saying, 'what did you expect?'"[4]

But wait, Geraldo *did* find something. An artifact. A bottle from the time of Capone. Onward. The Bobcat bulldozer waits while cutting saws begin slicing through the concrete. And now the payoff: Geraldo tells us after hours and hours of digging they have found *a vault within a vault . . . a sealed, self-contained thirty-foot section and our tests indicated it was probably hollow and so our excitement mounted.*[5]

Now the video montage of excavation has ended, and Geraldo is explaining what all this meant. At first, they thought the whole length of the 125-foot wall was hollow. One hell of a big vault. Geraldo is walking to the wall now. "This is the section that turned out to be packed solid," Geraldo says, walking among concrete pillars. So, what is going on? Tribune Entertainment has paid a million dollars for "Al Capone's Vaults," Harold Rubin's invention. But the wall turned out to be just that, a wall. So, like any producer, they panicked; or like a mad treasure hunter who believes there is treasure somewhere, they began digging holes everywhere. Doug Llewelyn and John Joslyn and everyone involved became frantic and began almost excavating *the whole basement*. As Geraldo explained to the audience, "We've literally moved tons of fill out of here; this is where we have found the artifacts [a bottle, a stop sign] and other things we've also propped up the ceiling of this old hotel so it wouldn't fall down on us . . ."[6] he says, pointing to a steel girder running across the ceiling.

Translation. In an attempt to find anything to open they have been digging out the foundation of the Lexington Hotel itself, and it might fall in on them. But the show must go on and Geraldo promises us secret spaces they discovered. But now he is walking again, and he crosses over and explains, "This is what I was talking about, a chamber within a chamber of the vault that our tests have indicated is probably hollow." We are breathing fresh oxygen now. *So, there is a vault!* Geraldo is now standing in what looks like a dark corner with his flashlight and explains how "this brick, for instance, has no structural reason for existing." He now restokes the boiler. "It is here it seems for one reason and one reason only, and that's to seal this space." Geraldo swirls his flashlight over the wall. "This space, this is our vault within a vault; this is where we are going to go in when we pull that slab down."[7]

So basically, Geraldo and crew have dug out all the dirt right up to the slab and come to another brick wall behind the slab that is protecting a hollow space. Hallelujah. The folks at Westgate breathe a collective sigh. As Allan Grafman later said in an interview, "We didn't know what was in that vault and we didn't want to know."[8] That may be, but you need a vault to open a vault and until all that dirt was dug out and until they determined a space was back there . . . they had no vault! Now, after excavating half the basement there is indeed a vault. Television could continue. It was a little like promising a football game and not having the teams show up. You at least need the teams even if they are going to lose. All you have then are irate fans, and the fans are all over the world, and everyone is saying the same thing: *when is that frigging slab going to come down?*

Geraldo walks out of the darkness and misses a camera cue and then puts down his flashlight. The screen briefly goes dark, and Geraldo comes back and gives us some more background on Capone. He was in the hotel from 1927 to 1932 and when they dug out the basement, they found artifacts like this one that date back to that Capone era. Geraldo picks up a shiny blue bottle put there by someone on a brick shelf and for a moment looks like someone hawking a tonic to cure all ills. But he is hawking something much bigger. He is hawking an idea born in the darkness of a cold basement and then packaged up on a medium that turns the mundane world into something magical. The distortion of humans and terrestrial existence is heightened by the compression of television that glorifies the everyday world. That pumped and colored world is otherworldly to the viewer. It is magical and comes from a distant place called Chicago, and now that world is in our living room.

The Bobcat is rumbling in the background as Geraldo explains that Capone made $100 million a year and remember, he didn't pay taxes. *Taxes?* Yes, taxes, and then Geraldo explains that the intelligence unit of the Internal Revenue Service that was investigating Capone at that time believes Capone may have not paid taxes on $20 million . . . but where has he hidden it? So, the hidden money of Capone is now with us. A number has been given. *Twenty million.* There could be twenty million sitting behind that slab where the Bobcat is huffing and puffing out exhaust. And as people eat pizza, fill Cokes, drink beer, smoke cigarettes, smoke pot, eat hotdogs, popcorn, Ho Hos, Twinkies, chips— that five-thousand-pound slab is waiting. Children and adults are waiting. But now Geraldo is walking toward the wall, and he rolls the grenade into our lap. "Maybe those missing millions are what we will find in here."[9]

Finally, someone says it: this is where Al Capone hid his famous lost money! Then Geraldo points us another way. "Or maybe we will find the bones of his criminal rivals." The thought that on live television a skeleton might be dragged out of the dark recesses of the Lexington Hotel has parents looking at their children. A gangster skeleton dressed like Edward G. Robinson with shoulder holsters still on. It's too much to imagine. *When is Geraldo going to tear down that fricking wall?* But Geraldo is on a tear now. "Or maybe weapons or bootleg booze or paraphernalia . . . who knows? I don't; not even the IRS knows."[10]

Geraldo is walking now and explains that "Capone didn't go to prison for the six hundred homicides he is allegedly responsible for: he went down like so many of these hoods do on an income tax evasions rap."[11] Geraldo just went into *vintage Geraldo rap* that he would come to perfect one day on his show. "And right now here in Chicago on the off chance there is something great, there is something of value. . . ." A balding man with a combover in a blue drab seventies suit walks up to Geraldo. "The local tax man has shown up; Dennis Sansoni, special agent in charge in the IRS here."[12]

The collective groan is there. People in knotty pine dens, living rooms, basements, bedrooms in front of flickering black and white and color televisions look at their watches. *The tax man? Really.* Everyone is growing impatient. But really, only twenty minutes have passed, and we have already excavated half a basement and found a bottle of gin. We are making progress and now Dennis Sansoni has announced the IRS has put an $800,000 lien against anything found in the basement of the Lexington Hotel. This works in Geraldo and the producers' favor. If the IRS *believes* Capone's money is in the vault . . . *then money is in the vault*. The IRS does not mess around. You got to file your taxes, or you go to jail. That is what people in the middle class believe. There is no messing around with the IRS and Al Capone found out the hard way and went to prison and special agent Dennis Sansoni is saying unequivocally if anything is found there then the IRS gets their cut first. The lien had come in early to Patrica Porter and the Sunbow Foundation and fairly freaked her out. She believed she was on the hook for $800,000 until the IRS explained no, only if Capone's money is found.

So, Geraldo and the man who could have a clip-on tie are chatting it up. The Bobcat's motor is even louder now as Geraldo asks Dennis if he has any personal guess as to what is behind the slab of concrete. You can almost see people around the world saying through gritted teeth, "*Come on Geraldo, come on*." Dennis takes his fifteen seconds of fame and mulls over the questions. "Well, I think it might be Prohibition paraphernalia, stuff that is from the old booze days, possibly trucks, maybe some old cars."[13] Wow. Dennis is really out there. Geraldo is holding up one little bottle and Mr. IRS thinks there are whole cars and trucks back there in the darkness. You never know who these IRS guys are really.

"Okay, but the first $800,000 goes to the government, Uncle Sam," Geraldo confirms.[14]

Dennis Sansoni nods and then walks off. Now. Finally, Geraldo starts walking to that rumbling Bobcat. Yes. It is time. "Okay, over here this slab that seals this mysterious vaulted area is ready to come down. . . ." Geraldo pauses and turns to the camera. "Just one word of caution. . . ."[15]

Let's hold there before the word of caution as people sit down from eating crackers, Twinkies, pizza, cookies, cereal, popcorn, and anything else because if television does nothing else it makes people eat. Something about the total immersion and relaxation television provides. And remember, this is *Monday*.

The week has just started over with that five-day march to the weekend beginning again. But now there is this detour. This is making Monday a holiday. A two-hour fantasy trip and we are just twenty minutes into the broadcast and Geraldo has just stopped by the Bobcat manned by a handsome mustached Geraldo lookalike in a white shirt under a spanking new blue suit. And he is giving us a word of caution before he reveals to the world what is behind the slab. And if television is good at anything it is stretching out the moment. Ever watch the end of a basketball game when seconds are stretched into minutes? How do they do that? Magic.

So . . . we wait with 105 minutes to go.

23

A Safecracking Party

You can't make these up. The stories that follow Al Capone like gum on his shoe. I have heard many stories since I wrote my first book, *Al Capone and the 1933 World's Fair.* They walk into Barnes & Noble and announce themselves. One gentleman told me his mother used to date Al Capone. He said she and Capone would get in fights. After one fight some gangsters showed up and kidnapped him from his home. He was ten. They blindfolded him and took him to a bar and took off the blindfold. He said a big Italian sat in front of him and slapped him a few times and then he was taken back home. He said that it was Al Capone. "What was he like?" I asked him. "Nice guy," he responded. Or the wife of a dentist who told me how Capone used to get dental work. She said he and goons would come into her husband's office and go right in and pull out whoever was in the chair. Al would then sit down. A pistol was placed on the counter and the dentist began to work. When it came to a painful procedure the dentist told the gangster standing by Capone, "*this is going to hurt.*" The gangster then told Capone, "*this is going to hurt.*" And so, it went. When the procedure was finished an envelope with a wad of money was left with the dentist. Or the girl who used to shovel his walk in Cicero and he would give her candy, or the many people who made bathtub gin for Capone and said he saved their families during the Great Depression. People who went to his soup kitchens would later say in newsreels, "Al Capone was a great man and he saved my family."

Across town while Geraldo is mucking around in the basement of the Lexington old associates of Capone are drinking in the Chicago Hyatt at a "safecracking party" waiting for the vault to be opened on the big-screen television. Harold Rubin and his son Jules are there but they don't appear on television. There are camera crews working the crowd and Doug Llewelyn giving it a dash of celebrity with his long microphone. Ninety-one-year-old Carmelita Esposito is there with her daughter, Jeanette Braun, and recalls how Diamond Joe Esposito was gunned down in front of his daughter in 1928. Braun would tell the *Philadelphia Inquirer* that her father, who was a prominent Cook County commissioner and lawyer, handled favors for Capone for years. "He used to always have to get up at 12 midnight or two o'clock in the morning and bail out Capone, and this went on for years." Carmelita, who came to the party wearing "an antique lace dress and a black flapper hat," claimed she learned thirty years after her husband's death that Capone had ordered his execution.

"He had him killed," she said. "He rose to such fame, and he couldn't do Capone any more favors." Her husband tried to quit working for Capone "because they were getting into too much trouble, killing people and all," she said. By the time a dying mobster told her of Capone's fingering Esposito for death, she said Capone was also dead.[1]

Carmelita had accepted a mausoleum as a gift from Capone, and he paid her $1,000 a month until he went to jail. Here is where the connection occurs with the Bobcat that is about to pull down the slab on the South Side of Chicago. Carmelita gave Capone, the man who killed her husband, "one of her dearest possessions, an eight-carat diamond ring that had belonged to her husband, who gained his nickname because he loved diamonds." Carmelita had come to the party to revel in a moment of notoriety, but also "her deepest hope was that the vault would reveal if nothing else the diamond ring."[2] There were other Caponites at the safecracking party waiting for the wall to come down. Rio

Burke, aged eighty-two, was the former wife of Dominick Roberto, who was a mob henchman, and Rio remembered Al Capone hiding out at their house when he was on the lam. "He would stay with us for days," she said. "There has never been a finer gentleman." The booze is flowing freely now while men in fedoras and spats mingle with flappers. Carmelita loved the party, but she said with Capone and her husband "when it came to parties, the mistresses went, and the wives stayed home." Burke remembered asking her husband about a gunny sack full of machine guns in their closet. Her husband responded, "Some of the boys are going hunting."[3]

Okay. Back to the show.

24

The Slab

April 21, 1986

8:25 P.M. Eastern

When King Tut's tomb was discovered in 1922 it set off a frenzy of interest, exploration, and speculation. It was a hot and dusty day on November 26, 1922, when archaeologist Howard Carter held up a candle to peer inside a small hole through a plaster door not unlike the holes drilled into the vault in the basement of the Lexington. No one had seen inside this tomb for three thousand years and light glinted on golden objects. We are fascinated by those who went before us and what they leave behind. It is our only chance to sample that other world where bygone travelers have vanished. Breadcrumbs from our existence and Howard Carter believed that King Tut's tomb was somewhere in the Valley of Kings in Egypt. He enlisted the support of a wealthy British man, Lord Carnarvon, which would be our Tribune Entertainment and Howard Carter would be the Westgate Group. And they began digging all the way down to the bedrock in each section searching for Tut much the way the earth was excavated out of the basement of the Lexington. Years went by. And Carnarvon's financial support had its limits. Howard asked for just a few more months and then three days later he stumbled onto stairs buried in the sand. He uncovered the stairs that descended to a plaster door that is our five-thousand-pound slab.

One could make the case that Capone was called the King Tut of Chicago, and the slab guards the entrance to the untold riches of Capone. When Howard peered into the room he later wrote, "Details of the room emerged slowly from the mist . . . strange animals, statues and gold, everywhere, the glint of gold."[1] When the door was opened Howard found a room full of clothing, food, chariots, thrones, statues, and jewelry. This was put there to assist Tut in the next life. Then the burial chamber was opened and there was a stone sarcophagus, three golden coffins, and the mummy of Tut. The world of archeology was rocked by the discovery of Tut's tomb. While obviously the slab guarding Capone's vault is not the same as King Tut's tomb, it does have the same qualities that fascinate people . . . a calling card left from a different time.

We are fascinated by the discovery lost in time. Imagine. A vault filled with items from Capone's time. If Capone wasn't resting in nearby Mount Carmel cemetery it might have been Capone himself in the vault. But the riches promised go back to Tut's tomb. Archeologists had spent decades searching, but to no avail—not so much for the riches and gold of Tut's tomb, but for the motherlode of information it would provide about life three thousand years before. The vault had the same weird fascination for people reading about it in newspapers for the five years since Harold Rubin made his discovery. The papers painted a vault that could contain cars, bodies, money, booze, torture chambers, no one knew, but put the word *vault* with Al Capone and you have the modern equivalent of King Tut's tomb. For five years people had been hearing about the slab guarding the vault. The slab had become epic in its dimensions. Five thousand pounds of mortar that guarded the secrets of Capone. It must be breached, and it will be breached right after these commercials. But that was all over now.

So now Geraldo has walked over to the entrance to the king's lair. Geraldo is jacked. This is the big payoff. This really is it. The slab will come down. "Let's walk over here," Geraldo says to the viewing audience. "It looks like the slab that seals this mysterious vaulted area is now ready to come down . . .

just one word of caution before we pull it down. . . ." This is where we left off before. Geraldo is standing by the Bobcat that is rumbling, and the well-coiffed operator has his hands on the levers. Here comes the word of caution. "Our tests indicate that this is a very, very deep chamber so don't expect to see gold bars right out front; it's probably not going to work that way. . . ." Geraldo is already telling us we will not see King Tut's gold. No candle in the hole of a plaster doorway glinting off golden cats from three thousand years ago. "This concrete slab is probably the first obstacle we're going to encounter. . . ."[2] Ah, yes, of course. They left many obstacles to stop looters at the entrance of the king. Might even be boobytrapped. Who knows? But Geraldo does know something we don't, but never mind . . . *open the king's lair!*

Geraldo walks over to the yellow hard hats. "John, you guys ready, everybody's ready," he says over the loud purr of the Bobcat. "*Okay, okay, Richard, okay, without further ado, let's take the wall down!*" Geraldo shouts. He begins clapping and chanting. "*Let's take the wall down, let's go, take it down, let's go . . . let's go!*"[3] Coach Geraldo is urging the construction workers on and the camera is on the slab that now has been cleaned up with two cuts down the side to make sure it would fall, and steel guides set up to make sure it fell straight ahead. No one was taking any chances with the king's tomb. It would not do well to have Geraldo flattened by the slab. The bulldozer roars and the chain tightens, and Geraldo shouts out "*Watch yourself, John!*"[4] The chain pulls tight and the slab to the inner sanctum falls like a cement door. No great tearing or wrenching but a sort of flop to the ground. Tim Samuelson will say later he felt the building shake when the slab fell. The engineers had done their work and ensured that slab of concrete would fall perfectly, and it did. So now we are to the moment where John Howard drilled his hole in the door and looked into the darkness of Tut's tomb.

In our world the screen is filled with dust with "Live from Chicago" across the bottom. We can make out some yellow hard hats in the dust and then Geraldo walks in and immediately begins explaining. "It's about like we figured it . . . twenties junk . . . definitely twenties junk."[5] His voice is already apologetic. Geraldo picks up a bottle and urges the workers who have WESTGATE on the back of their blue jump suits to start digging. Essentially, this is a wall of dirt. The slab guarded nothing but dirt and another wall. And this had been explained to us as a vault in a vault; still, it is shocking that the candlelight has not revealed any gold at all so far.

Now Geraldo is walking and explaining what is next:

Now this thing goes forever; the vault that we've indicated as being basically hollow stretches forever so the only way we are going to get inside and empty this place out before our two hours are up is starting another team of workers here, so we brought out the heavy artillery and when we come back the excavation work is going to continue so stay tuned because one way or another the secret is now being uncovered. Okay, let's go![6]

Two men with jackhammers attack the 125-foot-long wall. Coach Geraldo is clapping his hands shouting, "*Let's go! Let's go!*" He is doing a great job filling but there are cracks now. We are twenty-five minutes into the show and the slab that has become world famous has fallen and revealed only . . . *dirt*.

So, the excavation of the king's tomb begins and behind the scenes Geraldo and the producers and everyone else feel a twinge of concern as they go to the first commercial break. But no matter, they have the Bobcat and the dynamite and the second wall to reveal the real secrets of Capone that everyone is waiting for. While the commercials roll people get up for snacks and drinks and yell into the room, "*Did they find anything?*" "*Not yet!*" comes the answer. "*Figures.*" The world is divided into two groups: skeptics and dreamers. Skeptics never believe anything, dreamers believe everything. The dreamers believe there is "gold in them thar hills." They believe that Capone did leave behind fabulous wealth and bodies and cars and gins and suitcases full of money. The skeptics believe none of this. This is just a stunt. A Geraldo-inspired stunt for the fools who waste their time in front of the boob tube. Television is a con and this is just a bigger con. Still, they are mildly curious. *Did they find anything yet? Not yet*, comes the answer.

And we are back from our commercials.

Geraldo is holding the bottle of gin with workers all around him. He seems giddy now. "It's Prohibition gin," he explains. "Now before we totally enter what may have been Capone's private space . . ."[7] he says, walking into darkness out of camera. The production values fall like a balloon whizzing around the room. Chaos and a sense of controlled panic emanate from the construction site. Geraldo is too far from the microphone or there is too much noise. "I think this is an appropriate time," he almost shouts. "I hope you can hear me to find out more about this guy Scarface Al Capone who didn't just control the Lexington Hotel . . . at one point he controlled the entire American underworld and in a perverted bizarre kind of way you could say his was a success story."[8]

And now we are to the first video segment while the crews start to excavate King Capone's tomb.

So now the race is on. Basically, we are back to the men digging up the Valley of Kings to look for any time at all of King Tut, but we are digging up the basement of the Lexington Hotel to look for any sign of Al Capone. So, while the first video segment rolls the bulldozer and the jackhammers tear down the wall and scoop out the dirt for anything that could amount to a payoff for watching a two-hour live program. Tim Samuelson, the Chicago historian, was there when they dropped the wall.

> You can see here's the rubble I thought would be there . . . there's two little bottles. And Geraldo picks up these two little bottles and says we found some old stuff already . . . I get called from upstairs. Tim. You know old bottles, don't you? Well yeah. Come down here. So now I'm in the basement at the scene of the action. And here were two little bottles dated 1948. I said I'm sorry fellas.[9]

Meanwhile, the video rolls that explains Capone was born in 1899 and got his name Scarface from a knife fight in a bar. He goes to work for Johnny Torrio ... the montage of black and white film is broken up by interviews.

But other things are going on behind the scenes of the excavation of Capone's vault. Harold Rubin or Weird Harold, who found the vault in 1981 and is down the street at the Safecracking Party, had his attorney Dominick P. Dolci file a cease-and-desist notice upon the Sunbow Foundation and Patricia Porter, its executive director, for attempting to take credit for discovering the vault. And any profits Sunbow might expect from Monday night's opening are jeopardized by pending litigation. Harold Rubin was interviewed for the broadcast, but his interview was never used in the production. Sunbow also had a suit filed against them by media rights negotiator John Atkins, who claims he was the exclusive agent for the Sunbow Foundation on opening the Capone vault. The suit was for $300,000 charging breach of contract. The 1 percent of profits Sunbow was to receive from the Westgate Group was suddenly in danger. People were smelling money. People were smelling fame. There was a payoff down there in the dirt under the Lexington and all these modern archeologists had to do was find it. . . .

Now, back to the show.

25

The Thompson

April 21, 1986

8:30 P.M. Eastern

The gun that made the twenties roar. Is there a more famous gun in America than the Thompson submachine gun? Tommy Gun. Chicago typewriter. Trench broom. The Thompson was a selective fire submachine gun designed to break the trench war stalemate of World War I. General Thompson was frustrated. Every time his troops overran the trenches the Germans scattered, and they couldn't kill them fast enough. The bolt action carbines were not fast enough to shoot the Germans who scattered like roaches. So, Thompson decided to build his own gun. Thompson thought it would replace the M1903 Springfield in use at the time. He designed it for a hundred-round drum and a twenty-round stick and would call his new gun "the Annihilator."

The Germans could not get away fast enough from the spitting fire of the Annihilator. The British didn't like it because they thought it was too loud, and World War I ended before it went into mass production. After the war the gun found no real function and was regarded as too expensive. But then the gangsters discovered the Annihilator and now referred to it as "the Thompson." A new group of men found the Thompson to their liking and didn't mind the loud report of the gun. Gangsters. Gangsters loved the

Thompson because you always got your man. The gun fired so rapidly that one did not have to aim, just shoot and spray. The reason the Saint Valentine's Day Massacre was so grisly is because two Thompsons were used to murder the seven men. One man shot low and the other high, and they moved the guns back and forth like a garden hose. Al Capone was introduced to the Thompson while eating at a South Loop restaurant in Chicago. A car went by and blasted out all the windows, filling Capone's car with bullet holes. The game had changed, and the Thompson became standard for gangster movies with the mobster hanging off the running board and pouring out a stream of lead. The gun would go on to more fame in World War II when the G.I.s hit the Japanese islands. Lightweight and powerful, it was a beautiful killing machine. Ernest Hemingway would later get hold of one for when he went fishing off Key West and would use it to kill the sharks that came for a piece of his swordfish.

After the video segment ends Geraldo returns, sitting in the main ballroom of the hotel on a sawhorse with another man. "The guys are still digging below," he announces. He is talking with Patrick Healy, the executive director of the Chicago Crime Commission. The interview establishes that Capone made $100 million a year off of booze, but organized crime in 1986 makes $100 billion. Geraldo is holding the two bottles he found in the excavation. "Have you ever seen two bottles of bathtub gin?"[1] No. The bottles were from 1948, but no matter. The interview ends, another commercial break comes along, and then we return to Geraldo, standing in what looks like a bombed-out part of the Lexington Hotel.

We are now thirty minutes into the broadcast and have knocked down the slab but found nothing of value. The excavation is continuing while Geraldo launches off on another segment, except this one is not an interview with old widows whose husbands had been killed by Al Capone—this one is about the Thompson. After commercials we pick up with twenties music and Geraldo standing in the "gym" where he explains that while this was the gymnasium it also "had a more sinister purpose; this was the target practice range for

Capone and the boys and during that time what better weapon to hit what you were aiming at than this one, the Thompson submachine gun? Most civilians called it the Tommy Gun, but the mob called it the typewriter, and with it they wrote a bloody tail of terror." Geraldo then pulls back the bolt and dramatically declares that "if the Colt was the weapon that won the West, then this is the weapon that made the twenties roar."[2]

He then introduces Sherman Tarnoff as a weapons expert. Sherman explains why the gun was attractive to gangsters for its deadly accuracy and ease of use, and then Geraldo announces they are going to demonstrate the gun. Now there is a back story here. Sherman assumed they were going to use blanks to demonstrate the weapons. He was concerned about bullets ricocheting around and hitting someone. But Geraldo insisted they use live ammunition to give the audience at home the feeling of what a Thompson machine gun could do. And so, they loaded up the gun with live ammunition. Sherwin loads the gun and Gerald confirms this is the exact same gun used in the Saint Valentine's Day Massacre. "Weapon loaded?" Geraldo asks. "Weapon loaded and she is on safe."[3]

Geraldo holds the gun up toward the ceiling. "Safeties coming off," Geraldo says. "Weapon's hot." And now the tension in the room comes up. Geraldo has safety glasses on. He aims. No one moves and then he begins firing with bottles exploding on a wall where there are targets of humans posted up. Now comes the next moment that will live in infamy. "They also used this thing with the stock off, didn't they?"[4] Sherman takes the gun and pulls off the stock and explains they did this so they could shoot from a car window. Geraldo turns toward the camera. "Now one point I want to make very clearly right now: this is live ammunition; it's not like the cop shows you see on TV, not like the police dramas where they use squibs or blanks, this is the real stuff, .45 caliber hot ammunition." Now it would seem the demonstration was over. We have seen the power of the Thompson submachine gun with a blast of bullets destroying bottles and sending out fire and smoke from the barrel. But Geraldo is handed the gun a second time with the stock off.

"Gun's hot," Geraldo says and is holding it down like the classic pose of gangsters firing the gun just above the hip. Sherman shakes his head in later interviews about what happened next and he still can't believe it happened. Geraldo Rivera, who was mugged in the hallway of his ghetto apartment when he was a young lawyer and trapped by three men in the hallway of his building later, recalled, "I had backed myself into a corner. I turned to face my attackers. There was an alcove to my right that housed a broom, a mop, and bucket. I reached for the broom and brandished it like a housewife's spear. And then I charged."[5]

Geraldo charged. Just like when he was cornered by the muggers in that New York hallway, he charged with the Thompson machine gun firing live rounds as he went. Sherman had told him, *Do not move off your mark. Stay where I tell you. Do not under any circumstances move off the mark.* It was dangerous enough with live ammo zinging around the room, but now Geraldo Rivera *was charging and firing away*. But really, he had done the same when he charged out of law school and become Geraldo for the defense taking on the cases nobody wanted and defending the poor, the exploited, the downtrodden. Then he was charging with *Eyewitness News* firing away at injustice, the young activist journalist who charged into the Willowbrook Mental Institution and revealed the horrible conditions children were being kept in, and then he was charging and interviewing junkies, dealers, Hells Angels, charging charging charging as he climbed the media ladder, tolerated but never accepted as he stuck a fork in the eye of the broadcasters who looked down on the Puerto Rican Jew who dared to enter the castle. And now he was charging again past the three assailants in his apartment building.

"I knocked over the guy with the knife, but I could not get past the other two. The asshole with the bottle smashed his weapon on the back of my head and then cut me with what remained in his hand. I registered the blows but did not feel them. I continued to fight back."[6] He continued to fight back with his own show where he nearly got fired and then ended up with a network job and began his tenure with ABC. Fighting back when he reached the top rungs of ABC on the show *20/20*. "I jammed the bristled edge of my ridiculous weapon into the face of my assailant and pushed violently. The other two fled."[7] Wounded but not down, Geraldo goes on with his thirty-six stitches and continues firing at the powers that be when he takes on Roone Arledge over the Kennedy story his colleague wants to run, and he sacrifices his career for Sylvia Chase and ends fifteen years with ABC. Unemployed. . . .

Now Geraldo is still firing the Thompson machine gun as he runs off his mark and horrifies everyone in the room. *Is he crazy?* No, he's Geraldo Rivera, and he finishes firing the Thompson in the gymnasium of the Lexington Hotel and Sherman and others feel their arms and legs to make sure they have not been the victim of Geraldo Rivera's massacre where he fires blindly at enemies real and perceived, something the upstart who fought his way up through the trenches had been doing all his life. General Thompson's trench sweeper was put to good use. The decision made by Geraldo to run toward the wall while firing the Thompson machine gun was one he made alone. It was the same type of high-risk, high-reward type of decision he had been making all his life and one with which America has had a long love affair. It was the same one that put him in the basement of the Lexington Hotel with time ticking down.

26

Digging for Capone

April 21, 1986

8:50 P.M. Eastern

After Geraldo terrified everyone in the gymnasium of the Lexington by charging like a banshee with his Thompson blazing away, the production cut away to a long video segment digging up Capone's friends and foes. Geraldo interviews Chicago crime photographer Tony Barati. When Geraldo asks him who he likes better, Eliot Ness or Capone, Tony says Al Capone because he knew what he was about; Ness was just a publicity hound. When Geraldo presses him and says so you liked Capone, Barati pushes back. "Now wait a minute. I liked Capone as a newsman but personally I hated his guts. There's 20 million Italians in this country and 2,000 of them are bums. If it was up to me, I would line up the bums in Soldiers Field and get Jack McGurn to blow them away. That's how much I like Capone."[1]

When we finally return to the basement, Geraldo is pointing to some men working on a wall.

> Welcome back to the basement of the Lexington Hotel. I'll give you a hint as to what is going on. Those fellows are explosives experts; more about that in a second. First, I want to give you a little bit more history. Even though drinking was theoretically outlawed that didn't stop millions of Americans from indulging in their favorite pastime . . . take a look. . . .[2]

We are off to another video montage where Geraldo goes to an old speakeasy called the Green Mill. He interviews a man who tells the story of a jazz singer who crossed Al Capone. Jazz historian Dempsey Travis tells the story of Joe Lewis, a performer who tried to leave the Green Mill for another club.

> Somebody offered him a thousand dollars a week compared to the 650 he was making at the Green Mill, and he accepted it. Three weeks after he left three guys knocked on his door one night and attempted to cut his throat from ear to ear and take off part of his tongue and so it took from 1941 to 1950 before he regained his popularity . . . he couldn't sing, he couldn't talk—all he could do was make motions with his hands.[3]

During a video segment in Cicero while Geraldo is droning on, they suddenly cut away to the back of Geraldo shouting over a jackhammer rattling away in dust-filled light. We aren't sure what is going on. "*Whoa! Whoa! Stop!*" He shouts. "There's a wall . . . we are going to take down." But Geraldo is moving and so is the camera. Geraldo then explains while the jackhammer is blazing away that one man was responsible for getting Capone, Eliot Ness. Then the show cuts to the video montage on Eliot Ness.

Then we are back to the Lexington, where Geraldo is in front of another wall. It is now 8:50 Eastern with only seventy minutes left to find the gold in Al Capone's vault. Men are kneeling down in front of the wall and what looks like little black milk jugs are fastened to the wall. "Okay, guys, as you can see, we have encountered a very substantial obstacle, it's a limestone wall we semi-suspected because there are limestone walls on both sides. Now what we're going to do is something fairly radical." Geraldo begins walking along with Sherman Tarnoff, who supervises the firing of the Thompson machine gun. "He's also an explosives expert. . . ." Men are kneeling in front of the wall. "This is Dennis . . . take it easy." Dennis turns and then turns back to the wall. Geraldo seems nervous. "And Jerry. They're both explosives experts and that is what we are going to do—we are going to take that wall down with careful controlled prepared explosives. . . ." Then he shoves the microphone under Sherman's nose. "Tell me about it."[4]

Sherman looks somber as he explains what is going to happen. "We are going to use 60 percent dynamite sticks, really use two sticks located at the bottom of the wall, the holes are drilled in about 36 inches. We're going to pack them in with sand and we're packing them in there right now. Then we are going to shoot the charge and it's going to lift the wall up and then crush the wall to fall forward." Geraldo nods and, sounding nervous, says, "Okay, I'm all for it. I want to get the wall down to see what's behind it, but I'm curious about one slight detail . . . this is a ninety-year-old building. It's older than ninety years—ninety-five, almost. What's the chances that the explosion will take the whole building down?"[5]

Okay. The city of Chicago had only approved using dynamite in the city at 4 p.m. that day. So, no one was sure if dynamite could be used at all. But Geraldo was justified in being concerned. Dynamite is made of nitroglycerin and sorbents or a stabilizing element such as powered shells or clay. The Swedish chemist Alfred Nobel invented dynamite in northern Germany and it was patented in 1867. Dynamite, which comes from the Greek word *dynamis*, which means "power," was seen as a better alternative to black powder explosives. The nitroglycerin-based explosive was safer than black powder and reduced accidental detonations.

The road to finding a stable explosive like dynamite was fraught with accidents. Nobel's brother Emil was killed in 1864 while experimenting with nitroglycerin. The problem was finding something to mix with; nitroglycerin by itself was too sensitive to motion and could detonate spontaneously. Nobel tried to combine it with other substances like coal, cement, and sawdust, but found fossilized algae was the best for stabilizing the nitroglycerin.

So, this powerful explosive that the city of Chicago almost didn't approve is now going to be used to take down a wall in the basement of the Lexington. But the explosives expert doesn't miss a beat and tells Geraldo, "Well, the problem is here that the wall he was working on happens to be beyond the foundation of the building. It's actually under the sidewalk near the street area, so it has nothing to do with the foundation wall."[6] Famous last words, right? But we now learn that the excavation has taken us to the sidewalk. Capone's vault is outside the building under the sidewalk. Geraldo then turns to the wall. "Okay now, so what is that putty stuff . . . ?" Geraldo motions in the camera man. "Come in with me and take a look at that . . . you just cemented in place." Geraldo then motions to the wall again to what look like small bottles. "What are the black bottle things?"[7]

Sherwin answers. "Those are part of the charges." Dynamite is detonated by a blasting cap that is ignited by an electrical charge, but there is an extra element here. The producers want a spectacle, so flashbang charges have been added, minigrenades the size of a large firework. Geraldo then sweeps his hand across the basement. "Let's go clear the basement, everybody upstairs . . . when we come back from this commercial break . . . we're going to blow that wall up." Geraldo shrugs and laughs. "Let's see what happens . . . okay, clear the basement, everybody out."[8]

The camera pulls back from the front of the hotel lit up by large studio lights. It is 8:50 with seventy minutes to go. This is the last big moment and Geraldo and everyone else knows that with all the digging nothing has been found. *Nothing*. They are approaching the halfway point of the broadcast, and this is the last ace up their sleeve.

Blowing up a wall on live television in itself makes great theater. No one is moving from their television now. It doesn't matter how many commercials are loaded in, and there are many; everyone wants to see that wall blown up because on the other side there might be Capone's millions, Capone's victims, Capone's cars, booze. Who knows? But this wall will be blown up and maybe the whole damn building will come down. You never knew.

"We didn't know. We didn't know if the whole building was going to come down," Allan Grafman, the lead producer, said later in an interview.

> Everything we were doing had not been tried before. Pulling down the five-thousand-pound slab. Dropping a bulldozer into the basement and excavating out the foundation on live TV. It could have fallen down then. This old, creaking, freezing basement had been gutted by vandals and torn apart by the Sunbow Company and now we had been digging for almost an hour, and you just didn't know if it hit the wrong wall or tore down the wrong wall . . . and we certainly didn't know if blowing up a wall under the hotel would bring it all down.[9]

Grafman and others felt a building pall now in the basement. The thought that they could come up empty-handed, had been carefully kept at bay all night, but now it was there. It was on the other side of the limestone wall packed with dynamite and flashbangs for effect. Jobs were on the line. Geraldo's battered career was on the line. This outside the box two-hour syndicated show that had been sold to 181 stations and countries around the world was an experiment in television. Could you offer a two-hour program that elbowed its way into the network lineup and keep viewers from turning away? No one knew. Movies had been moved. Shows canceled. News programs had been moved. Adjustments up and down the television schedule had been made to accommodate this big spectacle called "The Mystery of Al Capone's Vaults" that promised big returns, but really no one knew. It could be a colossal disaster of low ratings and no payoff for the stations that bought the show and the networks that had moved prime-time programming. And if nothing was found . . . nothing . . . really nothing. No. That was unthinkable. For Geraldo. For the Westgate Group. For Tribune Entertainment. A lot more than a wall was about to be blown up.

27

Blowing Up the Wall

April 21, 1986

8:55 P.M. Eastern

So, this is it. The vault, if there is a vault, is on the other side of the limestone wall packed with dynamite. The road to Capone's vault that began when Harold Rubin stumbled onto the concrete slab in the basement of the Lexington in 1981 had finally come with the answer to the question posed by Weird Harold... what was on the other side of the slab? And now, what was on the other side of the wall? *There had to be something.* All of the lights, the helicopters, the satellite trucks, the digging, the preparation, the press, the million dollars paid by Tribune Entertainment, the Sunbow's exploration, the secret stairs, tunnels, speculation, experts, psychics, IRS, medical examiners, historians, producers, Geraldo, all the people watching around the world could not all be for naught. *Something had to be there.* No way the bulldozer, the men with jackhammers and saws working furiously for months and weeks on end, the video montages, the setup, the press that had been intense for the last few months, *no way it could all be for nothing.*

And in that vein the show returns from messages not to the vault but to Doug Llewelyn at the Hyatt Regency and the safecracking party. *"I'm Doug*

Llewelyn and while Geraldo is busy preparing to blast the vault at the Lexington, we are here about twenty-five blocks north of the hotel at the Hyatt Regency in downtown Chicago where a gigantic Al Capone safecracking party is underway."[1] The camera pans back and Doug is standing next to a 1929 Model A Ford police car. He explains this was "the type of car that roamed the streets of Chicago." Now Doug is walking backward and showing us the people who dressed like in the 1920s. We get the feeling these people paid some serious cash to be at this safecracking party. Men are in tuxedos and women are dressed in sequined dresses like flappers. Somewhere there is Harold Rubin and his son, but they don't make the cut for television. The suited-up crowd has been drinking the whole time and watching on a big-screen television as Doug asks if everyone is having a great time and everyone roars back, *YES!*

Doug then rolls a video montage of people guessing what will be in the vault. Money. Bones. Something of significance. Lot of jewelry. Patricia Porter is among those interviewed and says we will find something of some significance. Money. Doug then walks the line of people at the Hyatt. *"I don't know . . . bones . . . cash definitely . . . tickets to Hawaii . . . Prohibition-era stuff . . . a little cash."* Doug then takes the microphone and announces he thinks there will be a lot of money. "So we'll be back at the Lexington right after these messages." It is now 8:58 p.m. After the messages the camera opens on Geraldo in a red hard hat. The messages have pushed us toward 9 p.m.

"We are just about thirty seconds away from being ready to blow the limestone wall that has blocked our progress into the vault space."[2] The camera pulls back and Geraldo in his red hard hat is standing with explosive expert Sherwin with a detonator or plunger between them.

They both turn and look at the far end of the basement. Voices echo around them. "You have something else to wire up," Geraldo calls. "Let's do it here; we are on live TV." Indeed, they are on live television, and they are about to blow up a wall with dynamite in an old hotel basement. The process of blowing up the wall is tricky. Dynamite requires a blasting cap, which starts a small explosion, then triggers the bigger explosion. Nitroglycerin soaked in absorbent material like diatomaceous earth, or some other stabilizer, decomposes rapidly and explodes, blowing out hot gas. This hot gas pushing out creates a shock wave that will crack the wall, then destroy it along with high-pressure gases from the explosion itself. The shock wave has to be enough to destroy the wall but not the building itself. This was Geraldo's fear. Now Geraldo turns to Sherman. "What's going to happen now?"

"Now they are going to wire up the main unit to the Dupont box and they'll be ready, and you'll be ready to blow." Geraldo then has the camera zoom-in on the Capone-era plunger. "We're about ready to go, this is a moment of some drama, got our hardhats on. . . ." Geraldo seems off-balance, moving back and forth. He is nervous. The show is at the halfway point now. One hour has passed and they are about to blow up a wall that will either validate their suspicions or destroy them. "Okay, you guys set . . . everybody set . . ." Geraldo shouts down to the other side of the basement. *"Clear!"*

He turns to Sherman. "What's the classic phrase? Fire in the hole. Fire in the hole!"[3]

He hands the microphone to Sherwin and kneels down by the plunger that in reality is hooked to nothing. It is an antique and doesn't function. Sherman has a button in his hand that will set off the explosion, but to millions of people it looks like Geraldo Rivera is about to blow Al Capone's vault. It is great television. Geraldo carefully lifts the plunger. *"Okay, four three two one. . . ."* Geraldo then pushes the plunger down, fire erupts, and the explosion ricochets across the basement; then a second explosion of fire and smoke. And at that moment Geraldo must have thought, I am good at blowing things up. I blew up four marriages. I blew up my career at CBS after fifteen years and now I am going to blow up what is left of my career in show business. Those explosions began when he took on the news establishment with a hard-charging style that would ultimately change television. But the old order had to be blown up before the new order could come in. And like any great artist you had to blow up what is in front of you and then put it back together in a radical way. Orson Welles understood that.

Right now, there is only smoke and dust rolling out from the basement. We hear Geraldo after the explosions.

"I think . . . I think it worked. What happens now, Sherman?"

Sherman tells him now they are going to check and see if there is any live dynamite that was blown out of the wall. Geraldo turns to the camera. "Okay, so you guys look for duds and we begin sorting through this; now we've blown down one wall, we've pulled down another. We are digging in, we are getting there, we are finding out what's happening. The mystery of Al Capone's vault is being solved one way or another."[4]

Geraldo tips back his hard hat.

"Now remember, there's a lot of mysteries, and we are coming to you live from Chicago."

Now we are off to another video about Chicago while Geraldo and the gang see what the explosion has revealed. The video gives us a quick tour of Chicago, then we are in the basement of City Hall. Geraldo climbs down some stairs and now the camera is down in a tunnel. It is the sixty-mile network of tunnels running under the city. Geraldo explains that Al Capone might have connected the Lexington to the tunnel system used to transport coal and for the telephone lines. "For four months we searched in vain for this tunnel; then we found a clue."

Geraldo's crew had unearthed a secret tunnel that had been built, then filled in. He teases the audience. "We are going to show you this secret tunnel and then we will be right back." They come back and Geraldo is standing in the corner of the basement "where we discovered a secret tunnel system about two weeks ago. . . . This is a real secret tunnel and it's certainly big enough for Capone and his boys to use when they wanted to get out of the hotel in a hurry." Geraldo motions the brickwork, flashes a flashlight into the opening of the tunnel, and explains there was a Walgreens drugstore that was next door. A man who worked for Capone said that whenever there was a raid, Capone went down the secret back stairs and into the tunnel reaching

Walgreens. Geraldo now announces, "We can say that we have discovered one of Capone's secret tunnels."[5]

He isn't saying that's all they have discovered, but the entire world is waiting to see what they discovered not in the tunnels but in the vault. The secret tunnel linked to the larger tunnel system of Chicago is fascinating... *but what about the vault behind the wall that was just blown up?* But not yet. Geraldo comes on to a small, glowing television and explains he came in January and made some fascinating discoveries. Roll tape. It is now 9:10 p.m. and Geraldo and the boys are still using videos to fill. Geraldo swings off to an interview with Pat Porter of the Sunbow Foundation. People are getting fidgety now. *Why after the high drama of blowing that wall have we been inundated with commercials and more videos? What the hell is behind that wall? What is in the vault?* The collective groan in living rooms across the nation is getting louder. We are now brain numb from these background videos. On the far end of the millions of cathode ray tubes people are shouting at their televisions, WHAT IS IN CAPONE'S VAULT???

But not to be. There is a whole segment on Sunbow. Now Geraldo is in Capone's room on the fifth floor and identifying a secret door behind a mirror. Now the video goes to the showbiz people who would come to dinner with Al Capone. An interview with Buddy Rogers reveals that he went to dinner with Capone and was introduced to several senators who were also there in the dining room. When he walked into the lobby there were men reading newspapers with Thompsons in their laps. Capone asks Buddy Rogers to invite Gary Cooper to dinner. Geraldo asks him if he thought of him as a co-celebrity. "That's right. I did."

Now we are back, and the show is breaking down. Geraldo is standing by the Bobcat on a long shot. We can barely hear him as he shouts, *"Nothing new or exciting to report yet, we are still digging!"* But there is something to report. The Bobcat backs up toward the camera and then turns and pivots and the audience can see what they should not see. Behind the blasted-out limestone wall is another wall *of dirt*. A solid wall of dirt. Geraldo cups his hands and yells over the small bulldozers. "When we come back, we are going to Capone's secluded Miami mansion!" Why is Geraldo all the way on the other side and yelling toward the camera? "We are going to talk about an atrocity called the Saint Valentine's Day Massacre after these commercial messages!"[6]

We are well into the second hour now. Less than forty-five minutes to go and the Bobcat and the crew are digging furiously. No matter how many videos they cut to, how many people they interview, the inescapable conclusion is there like an unwanted gas in the basement of the Lexington and now the audience, the producers, and Geraldo are sniffing the foul air of a looming disaster. After almost an hour and a half, they have found nothing so far. And worse, time is running out.

28

Milk Crate Blues

April 21, 1986

9:39 P.M. Eastern

What is amazing is that no one bothered to tell the audience what happened after the wall blew up. No one could bring themselves to tell millions of people that on the side of the wall was a wall of dirt. Tim Samuelson, the Chicago architect, had told the producers that in these old hotels they had service cellars that went out under the sidewalk. And many times, these old vaults were filled in with dirt. That is where they were now. Under the sidewalk and facing the wall of dirt. But they went to videos of the tunnels and more Capone stories while the guys in the hard hats furiously dug. As Sheldon Cooper presciently said, *"Gotta keep shoveling, gotta keep shoveling."*

They only had twenty-one minutes left at this point and it was beginning to look grim. "It got very quiet suddenly in the basement except for the roar of the bulldozer," producer Allan Grafman said later. "Nobody wanted to say what was becoming obvious with every passing second . . . that there might not be anything there."[1] Geraldo himself later wrote:

Initially things went well but about an hour and half into the program I began to realize we were coming up empty. Our excavators had dug up nothing of interest or even collectable value, apart from two 1920s Gilbey's gin bottles and an old road sign. We were blasting, digging, and scraping, and still we had nothing. CC, who had joined me in Chicago after leaving the New Wave with Craig, and the new crew tried to put a smile on the situation during one of our second-half commercial breaks. "This is the most exciting television I have ever seen," she enthused handing me a cup of water. "I love this."

"Don't you realize," I said sternly. "Don't you see what's happening? We haven't found anything. This could be the end of my career."[2]

Something else had been going on as the show progressed. During the commercial breaks and when the videos were rolling, Geraldo went and sat on some milk crates on the dark side of the basement. "He was almost in total darkness," Grafman said later.[3] Geraldo in our interview recalled,

> there were early indications that the fucking thing was going to be empty, and I began to have this creeping sense of dread. My natural cheery optimism was starting to fade as I pulled more into myself. People didn't want to approach me as things went south. I felt closest and safest with the hard-hat guys than the producers at this point. After the nearly cosmic energy of the early part of the show I was now becoming more isolated. . . .[4]

What was Geraldo thinking as he sat on the crates and watched the frantic digging with the minutes ticking away? He was thinking what he told his girlfriend CC. This could be it. He had been fired from CBS under a cloud made worse by CC being caught using a courier to deliver some marijuana. The sharks had come for him. He never played the game, yet he had celebrity other people in the news business would kill for. Now that he was down, they were moving in for the kill. He had taken the Al Capone gig because he needed the money and it was a way back into the spotlight, but now in the damp humus-scented old basement on the milk crates, he saw clearly that this might just be the final torpedo in the good ship *Geraldo Rivera*.

But the show must go on. Geraldo is facing the camera when the network returns from the Capone segment and he is subdued. "Now when we come back besides updating you on the digging that continues even as I speak we're going to show you a little reported side of Scarface Al. It's Al Capone the humanitarian. I know it doesn't sound right but that's after these commercial messages, so stay with us."[5] For the people at home they are asking one question. *Why should I stay with you?* More commercials. More segments. The only explanation to the vault is that they are digging. But people have to stay. Like explorers who are too far up on the mountain, it is too late to turn back. People all across the country and around the world have burned almost two hours, and they have to see the show through to the bitter end. Husbands and wives have split off by now. *"I told you there was nothing there"* rings in family rooms across America. Pizza and hamburgers and hot dogs are souring in stomachs along with beer and Pepsi. Kids are being herded to bed under protest. And it is late on the East Coast. Almost ten o'clock and tomorrow is a workday. A thudding realization not unlike watching a sports team bound to lose has come to viewers. By now the idea of the vault has been lost. They are down to artifacts. The image of opening a vault with Capone's riches is long gone. Now they are men on an archeological dig, and like most digs they are down to looking for clues. No one at home grasps the bad news that everyone in that basement knows now.

There is no vault.

Not in the classic sense of the word. There is no King Tut's chamber where they can drill a hole and push a candle through and see gold. That belongs to the early days when they did drill holes, but those holes only revealed another wall, the limestone wall, then . . . dirt. So, let's take down the slab. Let's take down the limestone wall because that wall is evidence of some sort of chamber. But that evidence has proven false. The second wall was their fail safe. They knew the slab would not reveal much, and this is where they found the famous bottle that turned out to be from 1948. So then the digging out of the second wall began and then the dynamite—and now this was the one that could potentially hide Capone's riches, bodies, cars, whatever. But inexplicably when that wall dramatically was blasted to pieces there was a small space, yes, but then *dirt*. So that was when they went for broke and didn't tell the audience the vault was essentially nonexistent. They just started digging frantically. As Sheldon Cooper of Tribune Entertainment would mutter in his office in ADHD haze, "*Gotta keep shoveling . . . gotta keep shoveling.*"[6]

Take the whole damn building down, if need be, because we have to give the viewers something! They did not tell the audience what was dawning on everyone in that very cold basement: that Harold Rubin's idea born on a freezing day in 1981 under the glare of a flashlight in a dark basement was a hunch that turned out to be nothing at all. Pat Porter and everyone else who had sold the idea to the media to generate revenue for Sunbow and when Westgate came along, Pat Porter, was more than glad to give Doug Llewelyn and John Joslyn the keys to the castle for a cool $50,000 plus a percentage of the profits. It is not unlike bitcoin, where something that has no value is monetized and that gives it value. The slab was the bitcoin and monetized with a promise of Capone's vault extrapolated from gangster lore, but the fact was the five-thousand-pound slab of concrete had no more significance than finding an old bucket.

But the show must go on. The next segment rolls after the commercial break. It is the humanizing side of Capone. He bought baseball tickets for boys. He gave people money. He played Santa at his church. The Great Depression brought about soup kitchens sponsored by Capone. Then two men on a slab in a morgue are shown who Al Capone beat to death with a baseball bat. The segment ends with Geraldo summing up Capone. "Al Capone was probably the most charming and generous mass murder of his time."[7] And then we are back. But everyone is out of ammo now. No more segments. No more interviews. No more shooting Thompson machine guns. No more cutting to Doug Llewelyn on the North Side at the Hyatt safecracking party. No more hidden stairwells or tunnels or secret passageways. No more Capone widows. There was simply no more to talk about. The moment of truth was on the horizon, and no one wanted to face it. Geraldo knew by now he had to take his own medicine, and it was going to be bitter.

But wait. There is one more segment. And they are still digging. The camera is on Geraldo in the semidarkness. "We're still digging and nothing so far. Who knows? We've still got twenty-three minutes," Geraldo says almost apologetically to the camera. "When we come back, we are going to tell you the exciting and somewhat melancholy story of the decline and fall of Scarface Al Capone. And, of course, we will tell you what's happening in the vault,"[8] he says, hooking a finger toward the Bobcat.

They are in uncharted territory now. A two-hour syndicated show was uncharted territory, but a two-hour syndicated show where the promised payoff was suddenly nothing is a disaster. How do you fill for twenty-three minutes? Now there is that groan. It is heard all over the world. Another video. Geraldo is back on his milk crate in the darkness. Now it is an endurance test. People have put their life on hold for over an hour and a half on a Monday night and they will be damned if they are going to bail out now. One more slice of pizza. The crumbs in the bag of chips. The warm beer or Mountain Dew. *Come on, Geraldo, tell me that is not so.* But Geraldo is sitting on his milk crate in the dark. He doesn't want to talk to anyone. He wants to finish this hellish program and disappear. He feels the way he did at the tradeshow when he saw his CBS colleagues. Just hide. *Supreme embarrassment. Shame.* Yes, they could still find something, but it was looking very unlikely. Geraldo was on the milk crate looking down. It was over. He believed this now. He later wrote, "I had been talking in booming broadcast tones for nearly two hours, and my voice was hoarse. For the past half hour our blasts had produced nothing but dirt. We had reached a dead end. There was nothing left to do but fold up our tent." Geraldo had taken a long-shot gig, and he had lost. He just wanted to stay in the darkness, but he had to end the show somehow. The segment covered the murder of a *Chicago Tribune* reporter named Jake Lingle that was blamed on Al Capone. From that moment on the press went against Capone and then

Capone went to jail for tax evasion. Geraldo covers his transfer to Alcatraz, and then his syphilis and dementia, then his last days in his Florida estate. His last days were spent fishing off a dock and he died on January 25, 1947. Capone was buried at Mount Carmel cemetery. He was just forty-eight. His wife Mae, his son Sonny, and a few mourners were the only ones present.

The segment ends and now Geraldo is standing in what looks like a cave. There are men with shovels now, the bulldozer is nowhere to be seen, but it is loud. The men in yellow hard hats are digging into what looks like a sand mountain. "I don't know quite how to tell you this at eight minutes to the hour, but we found another wall in there." Geraldo is holding another bottle. "I wonder if I can get a deposit on a fifty-year-old bottle." He throws the bottle to the side, shrugs, and holds his hands up. "Alright, we'll be right back after these commercial messages. . . . See what we got here."[9]

That is all they have left now. The video segments are now over. Capone is buried. There is nothing left but to run some commercials while two men with shovels dig out another wall. There is no Bobcat, jackhammers, dynamite, explosions, tunnels, slabs being torn down. Just two men with ordinary shovels digging forlornly into the earth. The party is over. This time Geraldo does not return to his milk crate. There is no time. During the break the producers and Geraldo realize it is time to tell the audience the bad news. No one knows it yet, but the third wall they have discovered was to hold back Lake Michigan if it ever flooded. They are basically tunneling across Michigan Avenue now. There is no vault. There is no money. There are no bodies. The IRS is going to leave empty handed. The city of Chicago is going to leave empty handed. The medical examiner is not going to have any old bones to examine. There is simply nothing in the basement of the Lexington Hotel except dirt and bricks and a five-thousand-pound slab that covered a passage to nowhere. There simply was no *there there*. And every person in America and around the world was staring at their clocks and registering that two hours had almost passed.

The Tampa Tribune in an article the following day answered the riddle of the vault plainly.

> Many downtown Chicago sidewalks are hollow, laid over, narrow, subterranean caverns opening to the basements of the stores that line the streets. These are known as "vaulted sidewalks." In the basement of the Lexington the 125 foot long 8-foot-wide vault under the sidewalk was walled up with brick and concrete. Experts say it was done sometime between 1929 and 1932 and appears a rather amateurish job.[10]

So there is the answer and the riddle. The vault is a sidewalk vault that was sealed up in a strange way. This is the humus-rich soil that had grown up the mythology of Capone's vault and now had Geraldo Rivera wondering how to steer his ship from the iceberg dead in his path.

The broadcast comes back from commercial, and Geraldo is holding a portable airhorn. The men in yellow hard hats and blue suits are still scurrying around in the Bobcat. Geraldo holds up the airhorn and blasts it several times. The Bobcat backs up and almost runs Geraldo over as he shouts. *"Kill it, kill it . . . come on, guys. Come on over here,"* he calls out, waving the men over. The men crowd around Geraldo and he faces the camera. "You know when we began opening this wall nearly two hours ago, we had no idea what we'd find inside as it turns out we haven't found very much, at least not yet. In any case I think that we entered. . . ." He turns. "Kill the engine." A man reaches over and for the first time the Bobcat is silenced.

Geraldo begins again, but he is not looking at the camera. He is looking at the airhorn. "We have entered a legend a half-century old that has been resolved. . . . I don't know if we have gone far enough, I mean we found the other wall over there may be more to be discovered, maybe, maybe not. . . ."[11] Geraldo then begins to backpedal, pointing out that they did find some things. "We found the secret tunnel, we found the hidden stairway, we found the other private spaces, we talked to a lot of people. . . ." Like a man pumping water out of a sinking boat, Geraldo is doing the best he can. "We talked to older people whose memories I think otherwise would have been forever lost if it wasn't for this program...." During this whole time the hard-charging Geraldo Rivera is staring down, staring down in shame, remorse. He is looking down at the airhorn and it has the feel of a wake, a wake for Al Capone's vault that never was, and Geraldo is contrite and penitent, and this is not Geraldo Rivera, not by a long shot.

But the biggest emotion in Geraldo's posture, his subdued voice, talking down to the airhorn, is *shame*. And here it comes, the admission. Geraldo looks at the camera now, genuinely crestfallen. "And it seems at least up to now that we've struck out with the vault. I'm disappointed about that as I am sure you are, this is one time in my life that a pot of gold would have been a lot more fun than chasing the rainbows." He is looking down again. "In any case ... get a wide shot here; show my team they worked their hearts out," he says, spreading out his arms. "Come on in, guys, all right...." Geraldo is blocked and then one of the workers bends down. "I hope you've enjoyed the adventure of the chase, you know ... we found some bottles, we found some other artifacts."

The ship is sinking bow first and everyone is in the lifeboats watching the glittering SS *Geraldo* line up for her final plunge. Geraldo is valiantly still pumping, and he will not take a lifeboat.

"... the tunnels around the vaulted space did date back to the time of Scarface Al Capone" ... *Pumping pumping pumping*. "But I don't know our seismic or sonic tests must have been slightly awry because the much-heralded hollow spaces that we were led to believe were in there...." Geraldo has his hands on one of the worker's shoulder. "So, what can I say? I would like to thank my buddies here for doing the job. Thank you for watching...." By now it is obvious Geraldo is filling. The show had ended early, and he was trying to gracefully exit, but not too fast. "I promised all the critics that if we didn't find something I would sing a song...."

Geraldo was about to sing "Chicago Chicago." How this really came about was revealed to me during my interview with Geraldo. This was a controversial moment where many felt Geraldo had simply come up with this as a way to end the show and then walked off into the darkness. "I felt one of three things could happen," he told me. " One, there would be the treasures of Capone in the vault. Two, there would be something in the vault, and we could declare a modest victory. Three . . . there would be nothing, which I didn't really think would happen, but there it was and so I came up with this idea to sing 'Chicago Chicago.' That was my fallback."[12]

Geraldo has now stepped out in front of the workers, and he begins to sing "Chicago Chicago, that toddling town." Then, almost abruptly, strangely, like someone leaving a party suddenly, he is walking, and he waves his hand while the workers watch him. "Alright, I'm gone. I'll see you." He is off camera now and we hear him call back, "I'm sorry. See you next time."[13] It's as if he had left a bar early and called back, *"See you next time."* Here the production values that were held together with Geraldo Rivera momentum crashed to the floor. "The Mystery of Al Capone's Vaults" vanished at that moment, and the viewing audience now saw they really were just in some crappy basement on the South Side of Chicago with an earth mover and a lot of holes dug up.

It is surreal now. The workers awkwardly stare at each other and begin clapping while the Capone music comes up. Geraldo calls back, *"Take it easy."* Take it easy? Another camera catches Geraldo walking into the darkness. *"State Street, that great street. . . ."*[14] He is barely visible and his singing fades away as the workers mill around, unsure of what to do next. The show has ended but no one has really ended the show. The camera stays on where Geraldo disappeared. The credits roll with the sponsors listed; then back to the basement where workers are still milling around.

"I walked right out of the building," he told me later. "Right out of the Lexington and to the bar across the street."[15] And while the credits roll and the camera travels around the basement the producers are in shock. Geraldo had simply walked off. "We were all in shock. He suddenly walked off singing that song and we still had time to fill,"[16] Allan Grafman said later. Geraldo, though, had enough. He had tried valiantly to put a good face on an awful outcome. There was simply nothing to offer to the people who had sat through two hours of television. *There was no payoff.* Geraldo listed what they had found and discovered, but it was not enough, and his body language said it all. It was someone who was supremely embarrassed. The bravado that had carried him all through the show had simply vanished. The assertive Geraldo Rivera was like a coach urging his team on even though they had lost the game and he couldn't face his players. He couldn't face the millions who had watched. This did not happen on television. Not in 1986. You had to give people something for their time and Geraldo could not even offer them an authentic bottle from the era. He could only give the audience tunnels, secret stairs, and lots of people with their memories of a gangster named Al Capone.

Clark Morehouse of Tribune Entertainment had rented a penthouse to watch the show. "We had this penthouse at the Plaza Hotel with an open bar and giant screens, and we served food and when the special ended we said we are fucked . . . it was all doom and gloom among the Tribune people."[17]

Geraldo could not give the audience what they had come to see, the opening of the vault of Al Capone, *because there was no vault*. There was dirt. More dirt. And more dirt. As Geraldo later said to me, "all we found was dirt."[18] The infotainment production that Doug Llewelyn had coined was simply a disaster. It was a televised hoax on an epic scale and all the blame would not fall to the men who put on the show, and pumped up the media, and created the whole concept of the vault. Pat Porter, Doug Llewelyn, and the producers of Chicago Entertainment would not get the public's wrath. That wrath was just beginning to build and was being saved up for one man and one man only, Geraldo Rivera.

PART THREE

THE AFTERMATH

29

War of the Worlds

1938

Mesmerized by carnivals. Drawn to the flashing light. Blown away by World's Fairs. Intrigued by a cowboy turned hunter turned showman named Buffalo Bill. We cannot get enough of the latest thrill. Our Superbowls, our dramatic newscasts, our shocking movies, our outlandish comics, our over-the-top presidents.... We just cannot get enough. Entertainment is at the heart of the American psyche. From the day we are born we are promised riches and fame—if not for ourselves, then for others—and we get the pleasure of watching. But we want to be titillated. We want to be scared to death. We want to be on the edge of our seats as someone jumps out of a closet and frightens us again. It is our birthright now to have never-ending entertainment and we no longer have to wait for the circus to come to town. The circus arrived in our living rooms in the early twentieth century in the form of a disembodied voice—an amazing voice, really, that belonged to a young man just twenty-three years old who scared and thrilled the nation. And everyone heard it. Or so it seemed.

In 1938 Orson Welles was looking for something to wow his audience. He had approached the seventeenth episode of his show *The Mercury Theatre on the Air*, where he was the director, the star, the writer. But he was restless. Where he really wanted to be was Hollywood, but that was not happening—not yet.

Orson had broken into theater at age sixteen in Dublin and never looked back. He couldn't act in the beginning, but he had a one in a million voice. That voice commanded authority, and when he came to New York during the Golden Age of radio he was immediately in demand. From cooing babies to Shakespeare, Orson could do it all. A child prodigy who lost both his parents at an early age, he was a force of nature directing school plays of Shakespeare and then directing *Voodoo MacBeth* in Harlem with all-black actors. It was a smash followed by a fascist *Julius Caesar*. That was a smash. Like Geraldo Rivera, he found fame early and was on the cover of *Time* magazine at just twenty-two. Welles had a prodigious appetite for food, booze, sex, tobacco. He became so in demand he had an ambulance take him from one live radio show to another, walking in just as he went on the air with pitch-perfect timing.

He became the voice of "The Shadow" and became known coast to coast. And now he had been given his own show with carte blanche to do what he wanted. And what did Orson Welles want to do? He wanted to tear things apart. He wanted to stick things back together in a way they had never been before. Welles believe in art for art's sake and pushing the boundaries of every show. Many times, he would be changing lines right up to the moment he went on the air. People who worked with Orson couldn't believe the chaos and the stress of his radio shows and plays. And now he was going to adapt H. G. Wells's novel *War of the Worlds* for the radio. Except he was going to do something no one had done before.

Like the novelty of the two-hour live show the Westgate Group came up with, Orson was going to put on his show as a news program using a breaking news format. The world had just avoided going to war with Hitler's threat in October to invade the Sudetenland. People were being bombarded with breaking news bulletins that stopped shows and paralyzed people with fear. Welles was going to take the plot of Martians coming to Earth and exterminating humans and break the third wall of radio. He was going to make radio part of the show and have a reporter die on the air. When the show began on October 30, 1938, people believed it was a broadcast from a hotel in Manhattan of dinner music until the first breaking news bulletin pulled them away to a town in New Jersey called Grovers Mill where Martians had landed. The tension builds and then the military arrives, and the Martians emerge from cylinders. Then the reporter on the air is incinerated and Orson holds his hands up for six seconds of dead air that shocks people as they believe they just heard a man die from a Martian ray gun.

From here the broadcast builds with momentum and disorientation and goes thirty-eight minutes to the next station break. People tuning from nearby stations hear news in progress reporting on the Martians going toward New York City. The military tries to stop them with planes and troops but are defeated. Now the panic takes hold. Police stations are flooded with calls. Block-long switchboards light up and people cannot get through. A woman sits down with a vial of poison at her kitchen table and contemplates suicide. People drive crazily for the countryside trying to get away from the advancing Martians. People run out of apartment buildings with blankets over their heads against the poison gas the Martians are using. People have heart attacks. People run out of theaters in panic and into churches to drop to their knees. Weddings are abandoned. A woman having a baby finds the hospital suddenly empty. CBS has 126 affiliates, and the terror is broadcast coast to coast. A movie executive in the Redwood Forest driving with his wife hears the broadcast on his car radio and tries to get back home to his kids but runs out of gas. All he and his wife can do is wait for the Martians to come over the trees.

Accidents occur. A man drives through his garage. A woman falls down the stairs of her apartment building trying to get away. People demand gas masks from the police. Others say they can see the fires of New Jersey. A man confesses to his wife his affairs. It is the end of the world, and many people head for the mountains and refuse to come back. A wave of panic fueled by the media sweeps over the country and it continues into the morning with bold black headlines coast to coast. The police finally break into the studio at the end of the broadcast after trying to stop Orson from finishing. The marquis in Times Square flashes the news "Orson Welles terrifies the nation." He and his producer John Houseman are locked into an office and then later released. Orson receives death threats and suits are launched against CBS and Orson. Something must be done as calls for his arrest and cancellation of the show echo through the media universe. People are outraged when they realize the broadcast was a hoax. A man would later try and beat Orson up, claiming his wife committed suicide because of his broadcast.

Orson believes his career is over in show business. He has gone too far. Senators demand an investigation. Censorship of radio is in the air. People swear they will kill Orson on sight. CBS has a press conference the next morning with a contrite, unshaven Orson Welles at the center in a new suit surrounded by reporters. He is Peck's bad boy, and plays it the only way he can. He didn't know. The questions come fast and furious and Orson says he had no idea people would believe it was a real broadcast of Martians landing and exterminating humans. CBS executives carefully monitor the press conference as Orson explains it was just a melodrama and that he couldn't believe anyone would ever think that Martians had *actually landed* in New Jersey. He plays the nice young man who had unwittingly let things get out of hand.

But the demand for punishment and retribution continues after the press conference. Orson and his wife and baby retreat to Woodstock, Illinois, and stay in a cottage on the grounds of his old school. He goes into a depression. He is finished in show business and will never work again. The FCC is deciding what type of action to take against CBS. The lawsuits continue. Orson has created a tsunami. Letters pour in demanding he be fired or jailed. Then, just when all seems lost, Dorothy Thompson, a syndicated columnist, writes an editorial exonerating Orson. Thompson postulates that Orson Welles has done everyone a great favor with his broadcast. He has shown how gullible, how ignorant, how uneducated the American public is. Who would ever believe such a crazy broadcast except a nation of fools? The broadcast of the Martians attacking lasted only thirty-eight minutes, yet the whole world was destroyed. *Who would believe this?* Adolf Hitler and Benito Mussolini would have a field day with the American people. Americans believed anything and Orson had shown this vulnerability beautifully and should be rewarded for it and given a medal. He was only doing his job, and it wasn't his fault a bunch of gullible fools believed that Martians had landed in New Jersey.

And with this one editorial the tide turned for Orson Welles. The twenty-three-year-old looking at disgrace and oblivion was now heralded as a genius of radio. The genius tag had stuck to Orson ever since he was young and now it had been proven again. Brilliant. Campbells Soup came in and sponsored his show with big stars. Then Hollywood came knocking and Orson was offered the chance to make any kind of movie he wanted. It was amazing. He had no experience in the movies, yet the keys to the castle were turned over to him. Just when it seemed he had gone too far Orson got everything he ever dreamed of. In two years, he would direct and produce the movie *Citizen Kane*, which would be heralded as the greatest movie ever made. Orson had walked up to the edge of the cliff and almost fallen over—but in the last minute he turned and found the riches that are reserved for those who risk it all.

30

Revenge of the Suits

April 22, 1986

They had been waiting for him. The first blow was getting fired from ABC. He was down but not out. Now they could administer the coup de grace. He had been a thorn in their side for a long time. The Dan Rather establishment could not stand Geraldo Rivera, and he was going to be hung out to dry. Ever since his gonzo journalism at *Eyewitness News* he had become the counterculture answer to the staid white man. They were the inheritors of the Edward R. Murrow legacy, not this long-haired Puerto Rican guy who busted into mental institutions and smoked pot on television and went into war zones they wouldn't dare to go. He was highly rated and overpaid and had hit the celebrity stratosphere, but he had stumbled and stumbled badly, and now they were going to make him pay for it.

Local and national, they all went after Geraldo Rivera with their knives. "Capone's Vault Special Was Two Hours Wasted," crowed the *Kentucky New Era*.

Whatever else Geraldo Rivera may be it became obvious minutes into a two-hour live television special Monday night that he is no great shakes as a newsman—not this week anyway. "The Mystery of Al Capone's Vaults" will have to go down in history as one of the con jobs of the century, one that prompted millions of television viewers to sit in stupefied attention as Geraldo endlessly led up to the revelation that the so-called vaults contained nothing but a bottle or two, a lot of dirt and debris, and little in the way of proof that the gangster had ever been closer to the basement of Chicago's luxury hotel than his fifth-floor suite of rooms in which he lived and ran his crime land empire in the twenties . . . max that with the unfulfilled promise and you have a good reason why Rivera's stock went down a few more points with a lot of viewers. Perhaps he should become an actor. But there is no real indication that he would be a good one.[1]

The Columbus Ledger's TV critic headline: "**TV Writer Confesses: He Watched Capone.**" Lowering himself to watch the two-hour presentation, he begins with:

Al Capone would have known what to do with Geraldo Rivera and Doug Llewelyn. Me. I had to take my anger out on my poor TV set. Frankly I'm embarrassed to tell this story, but my shrink says I must. Something about cleansing the soul . . . me the guy who warns you about all trash TV. Me the guy who saw right through *Night Court* . . . now I've reached the depths of depravity. Forever more I'll be known as the guy who watched two hours of *The Mystery of Al Capone's Vaults*. . . . Geraldo, who must have been paid well to allow Llewelyn to drag his name and former reputation through the mud, did his best to inform and entertain us as we watched sledgehammers crash into brick. . . . I kept asking myself how the self-proclaimed World's Greatest Newspaper could be affiliated with this.[2]

The Citizens Voice television critic struck a similar tone.

The show was being hosted by the onetime respectable Geraldo Rivera. I figured with Geraldo fronting the two-hour show it couldn't be all bad. Boy, was I wrong . . . in my book Rivera sunk to new depths and for all intents and purposes lost his credibility . . . he also acted as demolition crew foreman—"Cmon guys take it down!"—and a tunnel tour guide . . . but Rivera is not the only person that should come in for public ridicule. You also have to chastise producer Doug Llewelyn of *The People's Vault* or is that *The People's Court*. . . . The show which should have been entitled *The Sordid History of Al Capone* proved to be nothing more than a two-hour buildup to nothing.[3]

The media machine that had pushed Capone's vault for months now turned back the other way and decided to kill the baby they had created. The show they had built up had proven a bust. The Chicago television stations lampooned the show with dour newsmen standing in front of the Lexington letting their viewers know that Geraldo Rivera had struck out. The Westgate Group, Doug Llewelyn, and Tribune Entertainment were essentially let off the hook. The very men who put Capone's vault together and then pitched and hired Geraldo were not the focus of the wrath of reporters nationwide. Geraldo Rivera: he was the villain who had betrayed the trust of millions with his hoax. Media did not understand that Geraldo was essentially a game show host brought in to usher people through the labyrinth Doug Llewelyn and others had constructed. To the media, Geraldo Rivera had done this all by himself.

Geraldo had gone off singing, but once out of range he fell silent and walked back to the producers. Years later he wrote about what happened after the show went off the air. "I shook some hands and beat it out of there as fast as I could. I was obviously subdued, CC was on one arm and she was almost propping me up."[4] The impact of the show's ending was hitting Geraldo all at once. After months of preparation and media and excitement the unthinkable happened. *There was nothing there.* It almost hurt to say it and at the same time it had the quality of a bad dream.

We disappeared to a catfish bar on Chicago's South Side about a block west of the Lexington Hotel. I had promised the construction guys I would meet them for a drink; I was more comfortable with them in my crisis than I was with the suits at the Hilton. These guys had worked their asses off and were ready to celebrate. To them the show was a lark, a nice payday, and a rare chance to appear on television. They had no idea what the broadcast had meant to me or what I had lost with its failure.[5]

Trust. Prestige. A reputation. A career. Geraldo in that South Side bar was reeling from the implications. He had told people for two hours they were going to open Capone's vault to see what was in there. And when they opened the vault, if that in fact was what it was, there was just dirt and another wall. *How could this have happened?* Why didn't he listen to his agent, who told him there was a high risk nothing could be there? "If I was going to anesthetize myself against what happened, these were the guys I wanted to do it with. I ordered a bottle of Cuervo and tried to forget."[6] Geraldo later told the press he got "tequila drunk." And as he did shot after shot he must have spun back through his career. Geraldo would be more comfortable with the construction guys. He had come from blue collar roots in the rough and tumble streets of New York and bootstrapped himself up to a law degree and then a career as a news journalist.

The tequila lulled him away while type was being set for the front pages of newspapers. There was no internet. Newspapers and magazines still ruled. If there had been an internet, then X and Facebook and TikTok and Reddit would have exploded. A mainstream media tsunami welled up, and while Geraldo did shots with the construction workers the great hoax was being served up for a public hungry for revenge for being duped into a two-hour roller-coaster ride that led to nowhere.

This was not the way television was supposed to go. But no matter. In a South Side bar the hurt was beginning to wear off as the alcohol moved in. Geraldo knew his enemies; his old colleagues were all laughing their asses off. The great phenomenon, the media comet that was Geraldo Rivera was now crashing to earth, and this would be it for him. What a pain in the ass he had been to mainstream broadcasters all over the country. They were just doing their job and giving the news, and this young guy comes along and suddenly news is rock and roll and Geraldo is the rock star, and he was making a million dollars a year. Well, that is all over. He is getting his comeuppance after creating the ruckus that had them all dumbing down the news and journalist ethics to get more viewers. He was going to get it in a big way. Bank on it.

Geraldo finished the bottle of Cuervo and was tequila drunk. He was smashed. And it felt good. Better than the crushing voice of defeat in that dark basement. It had all the horror of Dante's Inferno. Yes. He had been in hell with a bulldozer and dust and shouting and noise and dynamite and exhaust and through it all he had been looking for the bright light of a career restart. What had he found was the dark, dirty, dingy basement of his destroyed career. It was hell. *Hell.* And the world would come for him now. But he would simply lock the door on the world. "When CC and I finally found our way back to the Hyatt I collapsed on the bed. In my stupor I barely noticed the stacks of message slips. I did register the constant bleat of the telephone which I tried to ignore until finally telling the hotel operator. I slept like a dead man."[7]

And as Geraldo slept the great presses rolled and the trucks lined up with the early editions. *The Asbury Park Press* led off with the headline, "*Vault Opening Most Pointless TV Show in Memory.*" The critic Bill Carter of the *Baltimore Sun* (this was a wire story) started right in by claiming two hours had been stolen from him on Monday night:

Monday night had a new lieutenant Geraldo fuzz face Rivera. Perfect cover. Used to be a journalist. He lured millions into Capone's former hideout in the Lexington Hotel and fleeced him good. They built a two-hour television show around a pile of dirt and gonzo reporter marching exercise by Rivera. The guy never stood still. He conducted all the interviews on the run literally. He walked along Chicago streets talking to a camera while the rest of the folks in the street looked at him like he was some wacko from New York... as pure documentary, however, this one ranked somewhere between a recreation of "You asked for it" and *The People's Court*.... Let's see, what did we get for our two hours? About 68 commercials, several clips from bad gangster movies, a few highlights from "The Untouchables," a trip to Alcatraz... surely a highlight was a big blast of the vault wall... Geraldo did the right thing. He apologized at the end and obliged with a few bars of Chicago. But he needn't be too ashamed. After all, he was part of history that night. Part of the most pointless television show in living memory. So, keep on walking Geraldo, as fast as you can.[8]

The safecracking party at the Hyatt had ended. Doug Llewelyn and the producers from Tribune Entertainment were not sure what happened either. Producer Donald Hacker would later write, "Geraldo was very depressed. He didn't find anything. People had fun. It was a great two-hour movie with a bad ending."[9] Allan Grafman later commented, "Twenty of us went to a place on the South Side, some honky tonk, and had a drink or two. Some had three or five. I don't know if we even went to bed." Sheldon Cooper, the president of Tribune Entertainment, was more blunt: "It was one of the saddest evenings you ever saw. Everybody was downtrodden." Grafman later wrote, "We thought, oh well that's quite a way to go out. I don't want to say we were fearing for our jobs, but we were fearing for our jobs...."[10]

Now it is early morning and across the country the newspapers land in driveways and hit the newsstands. The *Pittsburgh Press* has a headline on page 1: THE MYSTERY OF CAPONE'S VAULT A BUST.

You have to hand it to Geraldo Rivera, the Tribune Entertainment Company and everyone else involved with "The Mystery of Capone's Vault." When they take a swan dive, they do it on a grand scale. Last night, in what will go down as the media nonevent to top all media nonevents, two hours of television time were taken up to open a vault that did not exist. Two hours to find two gin bottles. It makes the sludge found in the *Andrea Dorea* safe look like the secret of the ages. The plan was to open a sealed vault, billed as Chicago's equivalent to King Tut's tomb, to reveal to a national audience mobster Al Capone's treasure or maybe bodies of his enemies supposedly hidden within. Not only was there no treasure, there was no vault.[11]

Then the article sums up the show on a timeline:

About 8:15 as reporter Rivera shouted encouragement workers pulled down a concrete wall that was supposed to have sealed the vault. They found another wall, this one of dirt and debris. At 9:05 they cleared away the dirt to find another wall which Rivera obligingly blew up by pushing a Capone-era plunger that detonated explosives. At 9:37 viewers were told that "there was nothing to write home about yet." And at 9:52 workers hit yet another wall and Rivera gamely admitted he had struck out with the vault. Sonar equipment had been wrong. There were not empty spaces to be found. . . . You can list Capone's treasure with the search for the seven cities of gold as historical busts. At least Franco Vasquez de Coronado when he explored the southwestern United States in the early 16th century had the good sense not to bring a television crew.[12]

The *Chicago Tribune* proclaimed, "*Capone's hotel vaults full of . . . TV publicity.*" The *Tribune* summed up the show as:

a two-hour television spectacular brought to you by Stroh's beer, Kentucky Fried Chicken and Campbell Soup, among others, ended five years of orchestrated speculation over what, if anything, was embedded in the mammoth blob of concrete lining the foundation of the gang chief's old Lexington Hotel headquarters on South Michigan Avenue. The answer: nothing, save a few empty whiskey bottles. "A legend of half a century has been resolved," said a breathless TV host Geraldo Rivera as he shrugged his shoulders at the end of the show.[13]

The *Los Angeles Times* led with the headline "No Match for Hype." "Seems like we struck out, said Geraldo Rivera, who hosted the telecast playing amateur historian and neophyte urban archeologist."[14] So far the reporting has been tame, but a day out from the broadcast they came with their knives. An editorial in the *Boston Globe* began the bloodbath titled "Inside Geraldo's Head."

> Hello, this is the moment we've all been waiting for. If everything goes as planned we'll soon know the answer to the question people have been asking for decades or since the night before last at the very least. What's in Geraldo Rivera's brain? All of America knows by now that Rivera, the hard-hitting yet sensitive investigative journalist, presided over a never to be forgotten episode in television history Monday night. . . . Millions of Americans clung like limpets to their TV screens for two breathless hours, commercial-packed hours, waiting to see what the mysterious vaults might contain. . . . What secrets did the vaults finally divulge? Nothing but a lot of dirt and trash, which seemed fitting somehow . . . now we have gathered here around Geraldo Rivera's well-shaped head for yet another exciting moment in the annals of investigative journalism. . . .

The columnist then has Geraldo's skull packed with dynamite and asks people what they think is in Geraldo's brain. "I think there's money in it . . . I think you'll find an ego bigger than all the egos at ABC TV combined and that's big. . . . Just what was in Al Capone's vault . . . a lot of rubbish."[15]

The *Los Angeles Times*' review by Howard Rosenberg set the tone and followed suit with the headline "Hole in the Ground Hole in the Head."

> Geraldo Rivera recently was named a semifinalist to be the first journalist in space. Too late. As he showed Monday night he's already in space. We should have suspected the worst when the former *20/20* star and exponent

of "wow" and hero journalism showed up wearing dramatic black, sort of like Zorro ... with Geraldo in town the windy city was never windier. Titled *The Mystery of Al Capone's Vaults,* the live program should have been called *The Mystery of Geraldo Rivera's Shmaltz.* .... Equally mysterious is why so many Americans got sucked by this sprawling spewing scam which Tribune Entertainment syndicated abroad and to a whopping 181 stations in the United States ... Rivera did more than merely host the program. He massaged it. He honked it. He oiled it. He greased it. He oozed it. He huffed it and puffed it ... as viewers were about to discover, there were two empty vaults in Chicago Monday night. One was in the basement of the Lexington Hotel. The other inside Rivera's head. ... He overstated, overrated and inflated it. It was a tight call as to what was more abundant, the bull, the commercials or Geraldo's wardrobe changes. ... In Chicago Rivera showed his stuffy, musty colleagues how's its done. He had gotten down alright, and he had gotten very, very dirty.[16]

The News and Record eviscerated Geraldo and put the whole production in his lap.

Geraldo, who is late of ABC News, apparently came up with the whole idea himself since he is no longer gainfully employed. He recently did a lengthy piece in *Esquire* magazine about how he got fired but never got around to the real reasons. I feel competent in saying having now seen Geraldo open Al Capone's vault, that his dismissal probably had something to do with his disputes with producers, his high salary, his artistic demands, and the fact he is an obnoxious geek. ... I don't know if Geraldo is planning a follow-up. But if he wants to follow the gangster theme, I think I've got a good working title, "Geraldo You Dirty Rat."[17]

The Duluth News Tribune editorial had a more violent reaction to Geraldo: "*Capone's Last Crime was Rivera TV Show.*" The article starts out, "We were all quite disappointed at the outcome of the opening on TV Monday night of the Al Capone vault in Chicago. Some have suggested that the program host Geraldo Rivera's ankles should be tied to bent over birch trees then the trees should be released tearing him limb from limb. I say that is too kind."[18] *The New Jersey Star Ledger* did not mince words:

> Monday night's two hours of watching Geraldo sweat and struggle to make a television spectacular out of nothing at all was pitiful, one of the most embarrassing presentations in the history of the tube. It's about time this guy got caught with his hype down. Rivera, who parted ways with *20/20* because somebody got tired of all his self-promoting bull, had made a career of his kind of sleight of hand with the truth. This time there wasn't even that much suspense involved. Oh, watching Geraldo lock himself into an old cell at Alcatraz was somewhat rewarding . . . but the interviews with the people who had known Capone were dull and unrevealing . . . dull, dull, dull, boring, boring, boring. Poor Jerry has probably lost all his credibility with this one.[19]

The Cincinnati Post joined in the feeding frenzy with "the hoopla over Al Capone's mystery vault has come and gone but it takes a while for the former ABC newsman Geraldo Rivera to recover from Monday night's televised opening of what turned out to be an empty chamber." Even the staid wire services seemed to take delight in lancing Rivera in his role as host, describing him as "breathless and sporting an elegant coif under his hard hat." Bill Carter of the *Baltimore Sun* pronounced the extravaganza "the most pointless television show in living memory."[20] The *Arizona Republic* put the show at Geraldo's feet with "Nation's TV Viewers Let Rivera Bamboozle Them at Capone's Vault." In a searing indictment of Geraldo the article leads with

> We're a nation of suckers . . . how else can anyone explain why viewers tolerated the antics of news personality turned hipster Geraldo Rivera

whose idiotic theatrics and trite commentary fit right in with the show's premise.... We're suckers, it's that simple. And we got fleeced.... Legendary gangster Capone managed thanks to the assistance of triggerman Rivera to pull off one final crime 40 years after his death: the theft of 120 minutes from millions of television viewers. "The Mystery of Al Capone's Vault" was a show without highlights, without entertainment value, and without redemption. Rather, it was an ingenious trap that used a nonexistent vault as bait it made viewers watch more than 70 commercials. . . . Rivera was a complete show-off whether he was demonstrating the operation of a vintage Tommy gun helping blast open the wall . . . the swaggering, hip-talking ABC newsman served as cheerleader and crew chief on the show. . . . We were the suckers while the program's producers and Rivera laughed all the way to the vault, the bank vault.[21]

The Daily Sentinel led with "Prime Time Dud" and then danced on Geraldo's demise:

Throughout his career, Geraldo Rivera has consistently been a practicing proponent of news as entertainment or failing that entertainment as news. That approach climaxed, fizzled really on a live worldwide television broadcast . . . it is certainly a good possibility that we have seen the last of Rivera who dropped the plunger on the biggest prime time dud in the history of broadcast . . . for those who have cringed and bridged at Rivera's outrageous show biz reporting style during his career, watching Rivera shrivel and die in the damp bowels of that hotel on live television was a perverse pleasure.[22]

Columnist William Safire in *The Mercury* led with "BIG AL Capone's TV Laugh."

It is not true that "Al Capone's Vault" opened on national TV Monday night was as empty as Geraldo Rivera's head. Capone's vault had dirt in it. As for

Rivera, who is to investigative journalism what Moammar Khadafy is to diplomacy and as for his nationally syndicated special on the opening of the Capone Vault it should have been clear from the first breathless Rivera words that it was all whoop and no la. Surprises? . . . Least surprising of all was the utter and complete lack of substance to the whole thing . . . a Rivera trademark. . . . People saw Rivera dynamite a wall revealing soil. They heard wild speculation. All classic Rivera. Which is to say, classic garbage. Speaking of a toxic waste problem . . . this was television at its worst, a measure of a medium that has trouble peddling itself. It doesn't need drummers like Geraldo Rivera.[23]

Still other editorial writers gave the two-hour syndicated presentation grudging respect. An editorial in the *Tampa Bay Tribune* titled *Sequels for the Stupefied* explored the idea of a sequel:

A few nights after Geraldo Rivera blew up "The Mystery of Al Capone's Vault" on live TV and discovered a couple of mysterious old liquor bottles, one local station actually aired a rerun of the pseudo-event. That made about as much sense as deciding to run the replay of a baseball game that was rained out in the top of the first inning after the umpires had sat around for two hours discussing the weather with Joe Garagiola. Still, a lot of people must have watched "The Return to the Mystery of Al Capone's Vault" just to make certain they hadn't missed anything the first time around . . . at least one viewer wrote in to say she'd like to see a sequel.[24]

The Canadian papers were not much better. The *Windsor Star* led with "Geraldo's Hype Better Than His Story." The first line sets the tone: *"What canard! What a sham! What a flim flam!"* And it gets worse:

Little did I realize taking my garbage for a ride Monday night was the perfect preparation for a viewing of "The Mystery of Capone's Vaults." The audience was also taken for a ride Monday night in a two-hour, overhyped television show which promised to share the contents of Al Capone's secret vaults... Geraldo Rivera, a master of hype, acted as host and head engineer for the production which didn't even do a good job recreating Capone's story... the production ended with Rivera apologizing for the lack of the contents to me and walking off singing a song about Chicago. Viewers shouldn't be surprised Geraldo was involved in something that failed to live up to its billing. You see, he doesn't always live up to his billing either. The 42-year-old former storefront lawyer's name wasn't always Geraldo Rivera. His father's name is Cruz Allen Rivera. And his mother's name is Lillian Friedman. However, Rivera was calling himself Gerry Rivers until New York's WABC-TV was looking for a Hispanic to add to its staff. Suddenly he was Geraldo Rivera again and got the job.[25]

The *Irish Independent* was a simple *Capone's Vault—Zero*. *USA Today* led with *Stonewalled by Capone*. The massacre of Geraldo Rivera went on and on. But no one had seen the victim since he got tequila drunk. As he was being turned over the spit of national media, some wanted to talk to the charred corpse of news journalism... *but where was he?*

31

Redemption

April 22, 1986

6 A.M.

On the eighteenth floor of the offices of the Tribune building Allan Grafman opened the door to the president of Tribune Entertainment, Jim Dowdle's office. He was nervous and faintly hungover from the dinner the night before at the bar across from the Lexington Hotel. Geraldo had sat at one end with the construction guys. "We were all just relieved to be away from the scene of the crime if you will," he said later. "There had been nothing in the vault and if the ratings were bad then the advertisers and the stations would be angry and then there was the public reaction. . . . Jobs could be on the line."[1]

There was a skeleton crew of reporters and secretaries, and Allan walked directly to the fax machine in Dowdle's office. He had one hell of a headache and like Geraldo had tried to distance himself from the thudding reality of what had happened in the basement of the Lexington Hotel. They all put a good face on it and Doug Llewelyn and John Joslyn proclaimed the show a great success. Sure, it was a great success for them. They didn't pay a million dollars for a basement of dirt. Because that, in the final analysis, is what they found. *Dirt*. Lots of dirt. Even the two bottles they found were from 1948. There was not one shred of Prohibition paraphernalia in the basement of the

Lexington. Not a bottle cap, not a bottle, no guns, no shoes, no money, no old radios, magazines, newspapers. Nothing but dark brown dirt that they removed by the ton to reveal more dirt and yes, there were the hidden stairs and the adjoining tunnel to the tunnel, but the main show, the reason the whole country, if not the whole world, was watching was CAPONE'S VAULT. And they could not even find the vault to open it to be disappointed. All they could do was dig and dig and dig and dig and basically that is what they did for two hours on live television. *They dug!* And blew up a wall in a very exciting moment on live television that revealed . . . wait for it. MORE DIRT.

And so now Allan and Peter Marino and Donald Hacker were wondering if they still had a job because they had built this edifice called Al Capone's vault and the damn thing just toppled over. It was hollow. There was no there there. It was like that Wendy's commercial that had been hitting the airwaves. WHERE'S THE BEEF? There was no beef. There was no bun. The Lexington Hotel, that hulking relic from the nineteenth century, was just another old building that eventually would be torn down. And Harold Rubin, Chicago's Porn King, who had started the ball rolling, Weird Harold, was just some guy who had broken into the hotel looking for anything to sell. Well, he had found the vault, and they had sold the vault, and the damn thing blew up in their hands.

Allan stared at the fax machine. It would tell him if he had a job or not. If the ratings were low, then he had better start looking and he was already hearing about the media backlash. People were pissed. And why shouldn't they be? They should have just put something there. They should have opened the damn thing or blown up the wall first or done something. It was the reason the networks wouldn't touch it. *What if nothing is there?* They wouldn't take the risk. It was the reason ABC wouldn't let Mike Wallace be the host. They didn't want Mike Wallace splashed with the sewage that was all over Geraldo Rivera now. This was a career-killing moment. Whole networks and whole news divisions were fired when things like this happened, although he couldn't think of a disaster on television that matched this. No, they had definitely broken ground. *This was simply the biggest disaster on television he had ever heard of.*

And now. Now the fax machine was turning on. Allan stared down. The machine was buzzing. The paper was queueing up. The light showing transmission was glowing and now blinking. Yes, the overnight ratings were coming. Yes, they were. This would tell the tale about the syndicated disaster so far called Al Capone's vault. Allan looked down and waited for his future. He frowned. "We weren't sure if were reading it right," he said later. "We generally didn't look at overnights... so I wasn't sure the numbers were correct... then I realized the numbers were right. I can still feel it now...." Allan paused and shook his head. "I had never seen numbers like this before... the numbers were fricking unbelievable."[2] Clark Morehouse, the vice president of sales, recalled, "I think it was Grafman or somebody said, *Clark, you got to see this... it was simply unbelievable.*"[3]

*

Geraldo Rivera was waking up to a changed world. He had been severely inebriated and had refused all calls. He later wrote:

> The first contact with the outside world was with my parents calling from Sarasota, Florida, where they were living in the RV I had bought for them. The operator had the kind sense to put them through. "Everybody's talking about the show," my mother announced with misplaced glee. It was the worst possible news. I knew the show would pull through the roof numbers in Chicago where it was a local phenomenon but the only way I had gotten from last night to this morning was in convincing myself that the interest would be diluted through the rest of the country. Without the local spin, I hoped, I prayed there would be no compelling reason for people to tune in. Maybe the damage to my reputation would be confined to one city.[4]

That was how bad it was. Geraldo was hoping nobody had been watching. He was so sure the disaster of Capone's vault was a career killer that he hoped it stayed local, and the national press would ignore this strange moment in television history. He was now betting against himself and the show. For the last four months the push to publicize the two-hour live broadcast had known no bounds. This was going to be his comeback, and he wanted the world to be watching. But like someone who forgets their lines in a play, Geraldo had woken up hoping the world had largely ignored their Chicago-based infotainment documentary. The best he could hope for now was that the show was such a failure people didn't tune in or they turned it off and it would be relegated to the junkyard of failed television programs that most people never saw.

Geraldo's mother then threw another bomb on Geraldo's lap. A childhood friend, Frankie De Cecco, was dying from cancer. Geraldo was reeling from the disaster of Capone's vault and now there was this. He felt like crawling back into the bed and never coming out of his room in the Hyatt.

After calling Frankie's wife, he then spoke to his friend. Geraldo sat on the bed with CC and felt like he could not face the world. Not now. Not like this. There was a knock on the door. He had ordered breakfast from room service. "I put on my bathrobe to answer it," he wrote later, "and found an elderly, rail-thin black man, his wiry arms sticking out from his too short white coat. He reminded me of a Pullman porter. The man recognized me, and his face lit up like a pinball machine. The news about Frankie was still sinking in for me; I was also hung over, both from the drink and the embarrassing broadcast, my despair was obvious. The old man put one of his long arms around me and said, 'Man you feeling bad?'

'Yeah,' I said. 'I'm feeling pretty bad.'

'About that program.'

'That,' I allowed. 'And other things.'

'Well shoot,' he said. 'Don't be feeling bad about that program. Not your fault there was nothing there.' And then he patted me on the back, wheeled his cart into place and left."[5]

It was the only time anyone had ever said to Geraldo Rivera it was not his fault.

None of the producers had told him this. None of the sponsors. No one. A simple concept, a simple truth delivered by an old black man delivering his breakfast. "The exchange brightened my mood considerably and distracted me from Frankie. Maybe the response to the show would not be what I feared. Maybe I was not the laughingstock I thought I was. Maybe the silent majority of television viewers would not blame the messenger for the bad news."[6]

Geraldo was now hoping that if a lot of people saw the broadcast, they would not see it as his fault. He would not be tarred and feathered for dragging people along for two hours and then giving them nothing. He was pinging from one hope to another. Maybe no one saw it. And if they saw it, they would not blame him. After all, he didn't say there was anything there. He said *there might be* something there. He was really the hired gun who had a job to do. He began to eat his breakfast but then he realized this was just a pipe dream. No. They would come for him. They always did. His detractors who made sure he was not let into the club. The respectable club of journalists who turned up their noses at his unorthodox approach to reporting on the news. His very appeal was that he was not one of the benchmark broadcasters molded in the Edward R. Murrow pantheon. But hadn't Murrow broken ground by reporting live on the Blitz in London when no one was doing it? He had broadcast sometimes for twelve hours straight while the Nazis bombed London. He too had risked his life multiple times and set new standards, but he was accepted. He was a WASP, while he, Geraldo, was a Puerto Rican Jew who had fought his way up and would never click with the Ivy League set.

When the old man left, I saw the dozens of message envelopes piled by the door. I was too scared to open them but collected them and put them aside.

CC and I looked at the pile all during breakfast. I began to think that the messages contained the keys to my future. That they would tell me whether I would ever work again. [7]

Geraldo was feeling the heavy weight of despair again. He had to face the truth. His career might have ended last night at 10 p.m. Eastern when he faced the camera and admitted they had found nothing at all in the basement of the Lexington Hotel. What was he thinking? Who would hire him now? He was a punchline. A joke that would live on forever whenever anybody brought up "The Mystery of Al Capone's Vaults." Yes. It was all over. Geraldo drank his coffee and heard another knock at the door. "CC went to answer it," he remembered. "It was Doug Llewelyn. The hotel operator would not put him through, so he came calling. 'I know he's not taking any calls,' Doug said, as CC fumbled for some excuse why I could not see him. 'It's okay. Just give him this.' He handed her a slip of paper. 'Make sure he sees it. Tell him that him that in a week nobody will remember the damn thing was empty.'"[8]

CC walked back, handed Geraldo the paper, and he opened it and stared. Geraldo sat back in his chair and read it again and again. "The overnight ratings. The numbers eclipsed any I had ever seen attached to a single television program. New York Fifty share. Los Angeles Sixty-five share. Chicago Eighty-two share. Eighty two percent of all Chicagoans watching television last night were watching our program!" Geraldo simply couldn't believe it. The ratings showed that people all over the country had been watching "The Mystery of Al Capone's Vaults." "It was a staggering number. CC was reading over my shoulder and then we looked at each other and started laughing. We nearly choked we laughed so hard. Half that rating would have been a smash hit. We were delirious."

"It was the most amazing turnaround. A life-affirming experience . . . it affected my whole life,"[9] he recalled in our interview. Geraldo went back through the numbers again. The ratings were scarcely believable. Then he saw the national ratings for the show. The final tally was 34.2 national, which showed that over thirty million households watched the two-hour show based on opening a vault that might have had something to do with Al Capone. The implications of the ratings hit him like a load of bricks.

> The moment, displacing what only seconds before had been seen as an unqualified disaster ... was like reading the returns from an election route. I was transformed from a has-been to a hot property. My career was not over, I knew, but had just begun. And all because of a silly high concept stunt that had failed to deliver on its titillating promise. I had done better work but never to such a vast audience. Whatever our winged monster of a program turned out be, it crapped on the networks.[10]

This was some payback. He had hidden at the convention advertising the show from his colleagues out of embarrassment, but now Geraldo had succeeded in the one area the establishment networks held higher than anything else ... *ratings*.

"We absolutely crushed the competition in the ratings, benefitting from a wind of hype and a high-voltage combination of substance and live theater." Geraldo was beginning to glean that they had inadvertently broken new ground in television. They had violated all the rules, a two-hour live show based on a single concept that might or might not pay off. Geraldo would write later, "The thrill of commercial victory was made even richer against the overwhelming negative reviews and the embarrassment of digging for a vault that turned out to be virtually nonexistent."[11]

The show had broken new ground and set a new bar as the highest rated syndicated show in the history of television. "What made the show even more remarkable was that the show was aired on a makeshift network of independent stations, in many markets we were carried on weak signaled UHF stations."[12] Geraldo was now seeing the tremendous odds the show had overcome. It was not a network. It was the product of a concept sold to stations and countries all over the world for one night one off of strung-together stations . . . it had disaster written all over it, yet the ball was hit so far out of the park there was no point of comparison. A 34.2 national rating. That is what came over the fax at the *Chicago Tribune* office where Allan Grafman and the other producers shouted so loudly the reporters came running from their desks. Not only would they keep their jobs, but the overwhelming success of the program set them up. They had done the impossible and now Tribune Entertainment could do whatever it wanted. The company with *The Farm Report, A Night at the Movies,* and just a handful of stations broadcasting had just knocked the big networks on their ass. Of course they yelled. They yelled and yelled and yelled.

And Geraldo finally opened the envelopes piled inside his door brought by the room service waiter.

> The envelopes contained congratulations from every Tribune executive and from friends and family and former colleagues. And buried in the pile were twelve job offers, from every television syndicator in the business: Paramount, Viacom, Columbia, King World, Taft Group W . . . twelve job offers! I could not believe the sudden turn but then I understood it for what it was. Everything follows success in Hollywood. And I was the glamour boy of the moment.[13]

Years later when I interviewed Geraldo, he thought about the old room service waiter who brought him the messages.

> The black guy coming into the hotel room still is the most vivid in my mind. The old man came in when I was in a deep funk. The booze had worn off and I was hungover and here comes this angel of mercy with the messages and the congratulations and the offers . . . whenever I see old black men I always associate them with that moment.[14]

The job offers would eventually stretch to twenty-two. It was a lesson Orson Welles learned when Hollywood came knocking. Nothing succeeds like success and the show had blown away all expectations. For the local stations the program was a great success. These stations had bought the show along with advertising segments. On April 23, 1986, *The Detroit Free Press* ran an article that summed up the success of the syndicated program: *Vaults were empty, but TV ratings were Gold.*

> They didn't find anything in Al Capone's vaults, but WKBD Channel 50 is laughing all the way to the bank. Nearly 700,000 Detroiters tuned in Monday night to view "The Mystery of Al Capone's Vaults," a live, nationally syndicated special that scored the highest rating of any syndicated special in the history of television. The two-hour program from Chicago with host Geraldo Rivera registered a 39.8 rating and attracted 53 percent of the viewing audience in Detroit . . . this compares with this year's Super Bowl telecast which in Detroit drew a 46-point rating. . . . In Chicago, where the program originated, WGN-TV scored a 57 rating and captured 73 percent of the viewing audience. KTLA-TV in Los Angeles had a 46 rating and a 61 percent audience share while KWGN-TV in Denver collected a 41 rating and 61 shares. . . . Even though the ballyhooed dig into Capone's vaults in the bottom of the Lexington Hotel produced zilch, no money, no bones, no nothing, the big ratings easily soothed television's bottom line. "Advertisers were dying to get in on the show, says Channel 50's Henry . . . Channel 50 logged only a smattering of viewer calls protesting the limp ending to the show. "Probably this morning all over Hollywood, they're making clones of Al Capone's Vaults," NBC Entertainment President Brandon Tartikoff joked during a press conference with TV critics Tuesday. . . . And the show isn't over for Channel 50. As part of the syndication deal, the station agreed to air the special twice. "The Mystery of Al Capone's Vaults" minus the mystery will be shown at 11:30 p.m. Saturday.[15]

On April 23, *The Birmingham Post Herald* ran an article from the United Press International wire. *Some Folks Just Won't Let It Rest. Digging to Continue in Capone's Vault*. "Don't touch that dial. An official of the production company that brought you The Mystery of Al Capone's Vaults said yesterday digging will resume in the basement of the Lexington Hotel."[16] In a departure from the juggernaut of Geraldo roasting editorials there was only one in the *Princeton Daily Clarion* that put the show back on the audience. *Audience Should Have Known Hotel Vault Might Be Empty*. The article points out that:

> Many people said that it was disappointing, and it cannot be denied that finding money, bodies or gangster paraphernalia would have made the show more interesting. But it seems to me that this was an "honest" show and there wasn't much to be disappointed about. . . . Geraldo Rivera and company presented a two-hour show worth watching and by asking questions the public was induced to build expectations out of perspective. The audience always knew there was no guarantee of finding anything. . . . People expecting too much became their own victims, it seems to me. It was a good show and to me it seemed like good entertainment.[17]

A lone voice in a sea of catcalls. Like Dorothy Parker's editorial that exonerated Orson Welles by saying he was just doing his job, the thought that the audience had some role to play in "The Mystery of Al Capone's Vaults" is novel and obvious. The only way the show worked was if the audience put their own expectations and fascination with Al Capone into the mix. How could anyone really believe Al Capone's millions were in a dirty basement sealed in a bricked-up vault? But millions of people did, and like someone cheated at cards they blame the dealer rather than admit they should never have sat down in the first place. It was always much easier to blame the messenger, which it seemed almost everyone was doing.

Viewers' reactions to the eviscerating reviews began to surface as well. *The Los Angeles Times* published letters to the editor regarding the reviews:

> You should be ashamed of yourself and your cruel and really stupid review of Geraldo Rivera and "The Mystery of Al Capone's Vaults." Mr. Rivera did

very well indeed with a cream puff of a story. He kept it going one way or another. You missed the point. You were looking for a pot of gold as does a child. You missed all of the story of Al Capone's Prohibition murders, prison, his life, his death . . . you missed a good piece of history while you were sucking your thumb waiting for the gold to be revealed. Do grow up. There is never a pot of gold.[18]

The only thing that came through loud and clear in your review was unfortunately not what the show was about but your obvious utter contempt for Geraldo Rivera. I thought a reviewer's job was to be as objective as possible or at least be able to hide his obvious prejudices. Shame on you!

The program certainly confirmed the good sense and justification for keeping Geraldo Rivera out of Celebrity Hall. I'm sure you have reduced rage and restored calm and peace of mind for thousands of viewers who were seriously imposed upon by the entire program.

Bravo for your perfect review of Geraldo Rivera's Capone Carnival. The puffed-up extravaganza was oddly symbolic of Rivera's self-aggrandized career all these years. Since he first exploded on the tube with his purple exploration of the Willowbrook School Story in New York, all the hyperbole, the tears, the ranting, the raving, the oohing and ahhing and all the posturing have led to the opening of Geraldo's door. And what do we find? What we expected all along. Nothing.[19]

And there were a few who saw into the future and understood what "The Mystery of Al Capone's Vaults" really was about and where it would end up in the pantheon of television history. An editorial, "Once and Future TV Spectacle," in the *St. Louis Post-Dispatch* took a shot at the way the syndicated show would come to be regarded.

For the first 15 minutes of "The Mystery of Capone's Vault" I actually felt sorry for ex ABC News correspondent Geraldo Rivera. . . . By the time the show ended two hours later I realized that Rivera had managed to associate himself with what is sure to become classic television. . . . Years from now we will still talk about the Al Capone vault special. We'll complain about what a rip-off it was. We'll recall that we sat for two hours waiting to see what amounted to a few old bottles and a lot of dirt. . . . The point is *we'll remember it.* Given the torrent of material that pours through television screens in the 1980s, being remembered is no small achievement. . . . I've heard complaints that some viewers felt 'taken.' . . . Give me a break. That's like playing three card monte on the streets of New York and getting upset when you lose. They didn't have Walter Cronkite as host of this thing, you know. It was Geraldo Rivera, a guy who changed his name from Jerry Rivers so he would sound more ethnic . . . the Capone TV special was an unrepentant, thoroughly amoral, gloriously awful spectacle that would have made P. T. Barnum envious. It was the pure distilled essence of pop culture as tack and spellbinding as a pulp novel or an old Marvel comic book, and just as purely American.[20]

32

Capone's Vault

People waited for the circus to come to town once upon a time. In the early part of the twentieth century the circus was the only entertainment people had outside of their town. We were a nation of towns then. Small, agrarian-based centers scattered across the checkerboard of the United States. Most people didn't have a car, and few could afford to take a train anywhere. But the circus brought the world to the town, and everyone marveled at the freaks, the lions, the man shot out of a cannon, the very exotica presented under the hot, popcorn-scented air. We lived for it. And when the World's Fairs were put on in the big cities people would ride the tops of boxcars to get there. We just wanted something outside of our everyday life to take us somewhere else. From Buffalo Bill's Wild West show to Orson Welles's broadcast we yearn to be thrilled, scared, titillated, and taken away from the thudding existence of our short time on the planet.

We live in a time now when we have a thousand shows at our fingertips. It is amazing and overwhelming and a challenge each night to determine what we shall donate our hour or two hours or three hours to. Movies, sitcoms, documentaries, television has evolved into vast platters of epicurean tastes that almost drown us with their plentitude. But that was not the case in 1986. Television was still dominated by the networks. Let's back up. People in 1986 still watched television as their primary source of entertainment. No internet. No streaming. Yes, there were VCRs, but these were one-offs. The core of our watching was still dominated by three networks, with cable just beginning to edge its way in. HBO was still the funny service that gave you movies on demand, but most people did not have HBO. They had four channels or a cable box of strange channels where most were unwatchable.

Into this landscape comes a special. A two-hour live special based on a bet that a vault discovered in the bowels of an old hotel in Chicago had Al Capone's riches, victims, cars. And on live television they were going to open this vault. And this was on a Monday night: a very down night for television. "The Mystery of Al Capone's Vaults" stood out like a diamond among the coal. A live, two-hour program breaking into Al Capone's vaults? Now the allure of the gangster who was bigger than life during his time is brought to life. Yes. Al Capone. He had been immortalized in movies and folklore. Part Robin Hood, part gangster, part celebrity . . . he was a magnet. Before the internet, Al Capone had the kind of fame reserved for movie stars, and so he was essentially dug up for one last dance. This new kind of television Doug Llewelyn dubbed "infotainment" stood out because it was unorthodox.

An overlooked reason for the high ratings of the show was timing. An article in the *Wausau Daily Herald* came out on May 1, 1986, and explained how "The Mystery of Al Capone's Vaults" could not have been timed any better. "*Golden Ratings Capone's Vaults drew most viewers.*"

> When Geraldo Rivera opened Al Capone's vaults, he found nothing but high ratings . . . one example of how opportunistic programming can exploit the networks in between week of predominantly reruns and rejects. The so-called "black week" comes after the end of the traditional prime time season and before the May sweeps. For that week the A. C. Nielsen Co. doesn't supply age sex and income demographic breakdowns, so the networks schedule mostly fresh productions for the key month of May. Tribune Entertainment's syndicated "The Mystery of Al Capone's Vaults" was a treasure bust but a ratings bonanza. National ratings for the April 21

special won't be available until Friday, but if they parallel Nielsen's 12 city overnight, the program would beat even the top-rated Cosby show. . . . Al Capone's vaults with Rivera as host was shown on 181 stations many of them network affiliates immediately reducing the networks' exposure for their shows by about 5 percent. The network share of the tuned in audience that night was 49 percent when it is usually in the 70s. If original programming keeps performing at extraordinary levels during black week more advertisers will start focusing on that week and it will become a major TV week.[1]

Al Capone had done it again. He had stolen the viewers from the big networks when they had their pants down with reruns and lackluster shows. It was a brilliant move by Tribune Entertainment. A Monday night of blah programming when the networks were looking toward May, and here comes this show that takes almost half the network viewers and hijacks them for two hours. And now people are suddenly waking up and considering that the Gods of television might be missing something when an upstart production company cobbles together a syndicated show that blows everyone out of the water. In the weeks following "Capone's Vaults," producers were dusting off syndicated proposals at programming meetings all over Hollywood.

The television ethos up to this point was that you never did something unscripted. You had to deliver to the audience, and to offer the unknown was something television was not familiar with. Something might be there and something might not. But those people who waited for the circus knew all about the unknown. Would the man shot out of the cannon survive? Would the lion tamer be mauled? Would the trapeze artist fall? Accidents did happen. It is the allure of sports; no one can predict the outcome. So it was with "Al Capone's Vaults." What the hell was in there? And for two hours we would wonder and sit in that circus tent and wait for the explosion. And so, we went on the ride. Pull down the slab and see what's there. Dig up to a wall and see what's there. Blow up the wall and see what's there. And then finally dig and dig and dig until we see nothing is there.

And so, we leave the circus and walk home in the warm twilight, and we are satiated. Maybe we didn't see the clowns, maybe we didn't see the man shoot out of the cannon, the elephant, the lions, the freak lady, the freak dwarf. But we went for the ride, and at the end of it we were all satisfied *because it was the ride we were after, not the payoff. The ride.* That is what was found in Capone's vault: the knowledge that even though nothing was there, at the end of two hours *we had loved the ride anyway.* The thrill every time Geraldo Rivera said something was about to happen, and like a great circus master, he kept us enthralled the whole time. And so we left Capone's vault not knowing that we had just seen the future of television. *Reality TV* had arrived because "Capone's Vaults" demonstrated a basic truth: *it was the journey, not the destination.*

And today, with every reality show in the world on television, from truckers to cooking shows to fishermen to coal miners to celebrities who we lived with for a few hours each day to everything we can think of, they owe it all to the two-hour presentation on April 21, 1986, where a small production company put on a program no one thought had a chance in hell of succeeding. It was based on the premise that something unknown is better than something known. And so, the circus leaves town, and we are disappointed, because for a while we lived in that bigger world, but it will come back one day.

So, what was in Capone's vault? A couple of gin bottles, yes, but the treasure was the future of television. In one of those bottles was a message, and it said be bold, take risks, and break the present for the future. And if they had found something, it would have been some old early television embedded in all that dirt under the sidewalk. And when those workers lifted that cathode ray television up and stared at the curved screen they would have seen a reflection. It would have been the reflection of ourselves. That's television. Television is *us;* our own projected selves with all our foibles, hopes, dreams, and desires. Suckers? Yes. Yes we are, in all our human glory.

EPILOGUE

Why do we go into the haunted house? Why do we thrill to the movie that puts us on the edge of our chair or go on the roller coaster that makes us think we are going to die? Because humans love the ride, the adrenalin rush that we look for over and over again. The people who tuned in to their televisions on that Monday night on April 21, 1986, were looking for a thrill. Why not? Our lives are somewhat homogeneous now. We avoid risk. We live a controlled existence somewhere in the buttery middle class. And we prefer it that way and are amazed to hear the stories of daredevils, explorers, or gangsters. Evel Knievel knew very well what people were after when he tried to jump the Grand Canyon with millions watching on television. Television allows us a voyeurism that was not available to the generations before us. Radio began to allow people to participate in an experience vicariously, and when television and movies came we sat in amazement as the world performed its daring feats in our living rooms. And sometimes we get more than we bargained for. Orson Welles told everyone Martians had landed and were exterminating the human race and we believed it. Geraldo Rivera told us Al Capone might have left millions of bodies behind in a basement of a hotel on the South Side of Chicago and we believed it.

Geraldo Rivera is a man who has written four books and received 150 awards over the span of his career including three national and seven local Emmy awards, two Columbia Du Pont journalism awards, two Scripps Howard journalism awards, and the George Foster Peabody Award, but still has not received credit for breaking the third wall of television. What he did on that cold night in April was open the gate for all the cooking, trucker, rockstar, bounty hunter, cop, survival, dancing, singing, Kardashian shows that offered nothing more than reality. The very thing Geraldo was crucified for was his biggest contribution to the evolution of television. Geraldo came out from behind the curtain and said look; we are going to try something on the air that may or may not work out, we simply don't know.

What followed was COPS, *American Idol*, *Dog the Bounty Hunter*, *Dancing with the Stars*, *The Osbournes*, *Jerry Springer*, *Duck Dynasty*, *Ice Road Truckers*, *Survivor Island*, *The Bachelor*, *The Real World*, *Shark Tank*, *The Apprentice*. The list goes on and on, but it all started with a group of producers who came up with the idea to have an "unpredictable" format with an unpredictable host who had no teleprompter, no path to follow. And when the dust literally settled after the wall was blasted and there was literally nothing, then that is when the Wizard of Oz's curtain was pulled back by Dorothy's dog. Even as the Wizard commanded us *to ignore the man behind the curtain* we could not. It was too damn fascinating and when Geraldo faced the camera and sang "Chicago Chicago" in defeat, that was the final wall of television coming down. We now knew what was behind that screen, people just like us. That was an amazing moment and the fact we wanted to see it again, opened up the flood gates.

The skewering of Geraldo continues to this day.

> Critics, cartoonists, comics and commentators began roasting me mercilessly. The lampooning continued for weeks. I became everyone's punch line and some of it was pretty funny stuff. Andy Rooney joked on *60 Minutes* he was planning a live television spectacular around the excavation of the space behind his office wall. *Saturday Night Live* reported that my next project would be the examination of the unknown soldier. And Johnny Carson suggested I unearth the cement encased Chernobyl reactor.[1]

To this day people have strong reactions to Geraldo Rivera. Whenever I mention I am writing a book on Capone's vault there is usually a visceral response. He is still that lightning rod.

Geraldo Rivera was confronted with lots of job offers from the big studios and networks but chose to return to Tribune Entertainment. Tribune Entertainment had an idea that appealed to Geraldo. "Ever since Phil Donohue left us," Sheldon Cooper said later, "we had been looking for someone to replace him on a daytime talk show. Someone who could play morning, afternoon, whatever. Geraldo seemed like a good fit, and I talked to everybody about it, and everybody got excited about it except Geraldo. He wasn't too sure I think at first. And I said to Geraldo you know there's nothing to invent here except to do it in your own style. The format has already been invented by Phil, and he's done it very well with it and now Oprah's doing very well with it. But you do it in your own style."

Another article appeared in the *Chicago Tribune* on October 7, 1986:

These days everyone may get a network or syndicated talk show for fifteen minutes. The exciting news from the Los Angeles basin is that Geraldo "It's in here somewhere" Rivera will commence working on a talk stunt show tentatively dubbed *Geraldo Live!* ... The show syndicated by Tribune Broadcasting Company ... admirers of vintage TV chicanery will recall Mr. Rivera's foray through the bowels of the Lexington Hotel and *The Mystery of Al Capone's Vaults* last April. ... Rivera mucked around in the hotel basement and came up with a beer bottle, a 57 rating and a 73 share. That means 1.7 million TV households in the Chicago area were having their pockets picked and loving every minute of the fleecing. ... Rivera's career has wound down into a kind of pseudo-investigative slap and tickle ... as long as Winfrey and Phil Donahue prosper television programmers will remain convinced that no talk show format is too extreme, that no manifestation of foaming conversational lunacy is too excessive. So why not go with Geraldo ... smart money and dumb television would indicate his time has come around again.[2]

The Westgate Group in 1987 produced another two-hour live show, "Return to the Titanic . . . Live," with Telly Savalas as host. The high point of the show was when an assistant pursuer safe found on the ocean floor was opened and found to contain a black purse with 161 coins. The ratings again were at record levels with 22 million families watching the show. The Lexington Hotel would never be renovated. The Sunbow Company would eventually give up and the hotel was torn down in 2000 and replaced by a high-rise of apartments. Al Capone's millions have never been found. On April 23, 1986, Doug Llewelyn told the press that digging will resume in the basement of the Lexington Hotel. "We believe there is something there whether it is a vault or a tunnel or whatever. We feel until we are satisfied there is nothing there we will continue."[3] And he said the entire process would be videotaped. Digging did continue for several days as reruns of the syndicated show were shown across the country. No one was bothered that Capone's vault was empty and didn't really exist at all. People just wanted the ride.

Geraldo Rivera went on to host and produce the daytime talk show *Geraldo* for eleven years. The show had controversial guests including skinheads, white supremacists. A famous brawl resulted in Geraldo's nose being broken and the term *trash TV* was coined by *Newsweek* to describe his show. From 1994 to 2001 Rivera hosted *Rivera Live*. He became a Fox News correspondent and covered the war in Afghanistan. He hosted the Fox News program *Geraldo at Large* and in 2020 a one-hour segment, "I Am Geraldo," celebrated his fifty-year broadcasting career. In 2023 he left Fox News after twenty-three years. He joined NewsNation in 2024 as a correspondent-at-large.

In a final interview with Geraldo, he thought back on the show. He was in his backyard in Cincinnati while we talked. "My life is a lot smaller now. I go to New York for a week, and I have a home studio where I can broadcast from. . . ." I can hear him walking as I ask another question. "You know they will probably put on my tombstone, 'He opened Capone's vault and nothing was there.'"[4] Geraldo laughs.

But seriously, I think the success of "Capone's Vaults" came from several things. It wasn't copying anything. It was a live show. I had been on ABC for fifteen years and I was a popular senior correspondent on *Good Morning America* and *20/20* was a very popular show . . . but really the live aspect of it was brilliant because you did not know what was going to happen and if it went badly then careers were on the line and people could lose jobs.

Geraldo paused. "I think it could happen again. After 'Capone's Vault' you had the reality shows move in like *COPS* and others. . . . I think inadvertently we had paved the way for those later shows." Geraldo is walking again in his backyard; then he stops and pauses.

"You know . . . you just can't fabricate the sincerity of surprise."

He is silent.

"Wow . . . I just saw a hawk. He just took off. God . . . he's big."[5]

Yes, he is. At eighty-one, Geraldo Rivera continues to sail the high seas.

On June 18, 2025, *The New York Times* reported that for the first time more people were streaming content than watching broadcast television and cable combined. That one-eyed cyclops that stares back at us had changed again. "The Mystery of Al Capone's Vaults" remains the highest-rated syndicated show in history.

NOTES

Preface

1. *Salt Lake Tribune*, "Capone's Vault to Share Secrets on Live Television," https://www.newspapers.com/image/613817356/?match=1&terms=capones%20vault%20to%20share%20secrets%20on%20live%20television%20
2. *Detroit Free Press*, "Assault on Big Al's Vault," April 21, 1986, https://www.newspapers.com/image/99313261/?match=1&terms=Assault%20on%20Big%20Als%20Vault%20
3. *Philadelphia Inquirer*, "Experts Speculate," May 18, 1985, https://www.newspapers.com/image/173553337/?match=1&terms=What%20Will%20Be%20found%20hidden%20in%20capones%20vault%20
4. *Knight Ridder Wire*, "Al Capone's Vault to Be Pried Open on TV," Show. https://www.newspapers.com/image/426487160/?match=1&terms=Al%20Capones%20Vault%20to%20be%20pried%20open%20on%20tv%20show

Prologue

1. "'The Mystery of Al Capone's Vaults'—(1986)," Rearview Mirror Media, May 25, 2020, YouTube, https://www.youtube.com/watch?v=jUEYhIp5SG0

Chapter 1

1. Louise Hutchinson, *Chicago Tribune*, "Capone Slept Here," January 29, 1962.
2. Ibid.
3. Ibid.
4. Laurence Bergreen, *Capone: The Man and the Era* (New York: Simon & Schuster, 1994), 34.

5 Ibid., 310.

6 Ibid., 311.

7 Adam Selzer, *Speaking Ill of the Dead: Jerks in Chicago History* (Boston: Globe Pequot, 2012), 190.

Chapter 2

1 Josh Levin, host, *One Year: 1986*, podcast, season 3, episode 3, "The Mystery of Al Capone's Vault," *Slate*, September 1, 2022, https://slate.com/podcasts/one-year/s3/1986/e3/al-capone-vaults-geraldo-rivera-television-mystery

2 Ibid.

3 Ibid.

4 *Chicago Tribune*, "Capone's Old Hotel Now Just a Tomb," June 18, 1981, https://www.newspapers.com/image/386900270/?match=1&terms=capones%20old%20hotel%20now%20just%20a%20tomb%20

5 Scripps Howard wire service, "Al Capone Slept Here and Now Women Give Hotel a Facelift," May 28, 1985, https://www.newspapers.com/image/302268576/?match=1&terms=Al%20Capone%20slept%20here%20%20and%20now%20women%20give%20old%20hotel%20a%20facelift%20

6 Ibid.

7 Ibid.

8 Ibid.

9 *Chicago Tribune*, "Capone's Vault Still in Dark," May 3, 1985, https://www.newspapers.com/search/results/?keyword=capones+vault+still+dark

Chapter 3

1 *Los Angeles Times*, "Capone Hotel to Be a Women's Museum," January 24, 1985, https://www.newspapers.com/image/390413963/?match=1&terms=capone%20hotel%20

2   Associated Press, "IRS Places a Tax Lien on Hotel to Get Share of Capone's Loot," May 26, 1985, https://www.newspapers.com/image/607097731/?match=1&terms=IRS%20PLACES%20A%20TAX

3   Jake Rossen, "An Oral History of When Geraldo Rivera Opened Al Capone's Vault," Mental Floss, May 14, 2025, https://www.mentalfloss.com/article/78842/oral-history-30-years-ago-geraldo-rivera-opened-al-capones-vault

4   Ibid.

5   Allan Grafman interview with the author.

6   Ibid.

7   Ibid.

8   Ibid.

9   Rossen, "When Geraldo Rivera Opened Al Capone's Vault."

10 Associated Press, "Capone's Vault May Be Opened by California Film Company," August 27, 1985, https://www.newspapers.com/image/997555289/?match=1&terms=capones%20vault%20may%20be%20opened%20%20by%20california%20film%20company%20

11 Allan Grafman interview with the author.

12 Rossen, "When Geraldo Rivera Opened Al Capone's Vault."

13 Ibid.

14 Ibid.

15 Ibid.

16 Ibid.

17 Clark Morehouse interview with the author.

18 Ibid.

Chapter 4

1   Geraldo Rivera, with Daniel Paisner, *Exposing Myself* (New York: Bantam, 1991), 145.

2   Ibid.

3   Ibid.

4   Ibid.
5   Ibid.
6   Ibid.
7   Ibid.
8   Ibid.
9   Ibid.
10 Ibid., 135.
11 Ibid., 174.
12 Ibid.
13 Ibid., 181.
14 Ibid., 182.
15 Ibid.
16 Ibid.
17 Ibid.
18 Ibid.
19 Ibid., 243.
20 Ibid., 260.
21 Ibid., 266.
22 Ibid., 419.
23 Ibid., 426.
24 Ibid., 427.

Chapter 5

1   Laurence Bergreen, *Capone: The Man and the Era* (New York: Simon & Schuster, 1994), 312.

2   Jonathan Eig, *Get Capone: The Secret Plot That Captured America's Most Wanted Gangster* (New York: Simon & Schuster, 2010), 191.

3   Eig, *Get Capone*, 84.

4   Ibid.

Chapter 6

1. Geraldo Rivera, with Daniel Paisner, *Exposing Myself* (New York: Bantam, 1991), 3.
2. Ibid.
3. Ibid.

Chapter 7

1. UPI, "*Andrea Doria* Yields a Safe," August 27, 1981, https://www.newspapers.com/image/532979495/?match=1&terms=Doria%20Yields%20a%20safe%20
2. Associated Press, https://www.newspapers.com/image/146796284/?match=1&terms=andrea%20doria%20
3. Ibid.
4. Ibid.

Chapter 8

1. Bruce Moffat, *Forty Feet Below: The Story of Chicago's Freight Tunnels* (Glendale, CA: Interurban Press, 1982).
2. Ibid.
3. *Albuquerque Journal*, "Al Capone's Vaults," April 21, 1982.
4. Ibid.
5. Ibid.
6. *San Francisco Examiner*, https://www.newspapers.com/image/461400824/?match=1&terms=tunnels%20capone%20
7. Allan Grafman interview with the author.
8. Ibid.

Chapter 9

1. Jonathan Eig, *Get Capone: The Secret Plot That Captured America's Most Wanted Gangster* (New York: Simon & Schuster, 2010), 209.
2. Ibid.
3. Ibid.
4. Ibid.
5. Ibid.

Chapter 10

1. Geraldo Rivera, with Daniel Paisner, *Exposing Myself* (New York: Bantam, 1991), 5.
2. Geraldo Rivera interview with the author.
3. Rivera and Paisner, *Exposing Myself*, 5.
4. Ibid.
5. Clark Morehouse interview with the author.
6. Rivera and Paisner, *Exposing Myself*, 5.
7. Ibid., 6.
8. Ibid.
9. Ibid.
10. Ibid., 7.
11. Ibid., 6.

Chapter 11

1. Allan Grafman interview with the author.

Chapter 12

1. *San Francisco Examiner*, "Capone's Legacy," January 19, 1986, https://www.newspapers.com/image/461400824/?match=1&terms=capones%20legacy%20

2. Geraldo Rivera interview with the author.

3. Geraldo Rivera, with Daniel Paisner, *Exposing Myself* (New York: Bantam, 1991), 438.

4. Ibid.

5. "The Mystery of Al Capone's Vaults," YouTube, https://www.youtube.com/watch?v=jUEYhIp5SG0

Chapter 13

1. Jonathan Eig, *Get Capone: The Secret Plot That Captured America's Most Wanted Gangster* (New York: Simon & Schuster, 2010), 236.

2. Ibid.

3. Dennis E. Hoffman, *Scarface Al and the Crime Crusaders* (Carbondale: Southern Illinois Press, 2010), 91.

4. Ibid.

5. Eig, *Get Capone*, 273.

Chapter 14

1. Geraldo Rivera, with Daniel Paisner, *Exposing Myself* (New York: Bantam, 1991), 209.

2. Ibid.

3. Ibid., 212.

4. Ibid.

Chapter 15

1. Jonathan Eig, *Get Capone: The Secret Plot That Captured America's Most Wanted Gangster* (2010), 273.
2. Ibid.
3. Ibid.
4. Ibid.
5. Ibid.
6. *Chicago Examiner*, January 16, 1974.
7. *New York Times*, February 10, 1978.
8. Eig, *Get Capone*, 347.
9. Ibid.
10. Ibid.

Chapter 16

1. Geraldo Rivera, with Daniel Paisner, *Exposing Myself* (New York: Bantam, 1991), 290.
2. Ibid.
3. Ibid.
4. Ibid.
5. Ibid.
6. Ibid.
7. Ibid.
8. Ibid.

Chapter 17

1. Jonathan Eig, *Get Capone: The Secret Plot That Captured America's Most Wanted Gangster* (New York: Simon & Schuster, 2010), 374.
2. Ibid.
3. Deirdre Capone, *Uncle Al Capone* (ReCap Publishing, 2010).

Chapter 18

1. United Press International, "Capone's Vault Still a Mystery," https://www.newspapers.com/image/183518705/?match=1&terms=capones%20vault%20still%20a%20mystery%20

2. *Spokane Review*, "Geraldo Rivera Returns to TV with Capone's Vaults," April 20, 1986, https://www.newspapers.com/image/572598203/?match=1&terms=Geraldo%20Rivera%20Returns%20to%20TV%20with%20capones%20vaults%20

3. Ibid.

4. *Wichita Eagle*, "Opening of Capone's Vault May Close Rivera's Career," May 21, 1986, https://www.newspapers.com/image/701836653/?match=1&terms=opening%20of%20capones%20vault

5. Ibid.

6. Ibid.

7. *Knight Ridder*, "Al Capone's Secret May Only Be Stale Air," https://www.newspapers.com/image/831637552/?match=1&terms=capones%20vault

8. Ibid.

9. Ibid.

10. Ibid.

11. Ibid.

12. Ibid.

13. Allan Grafman interview with the author.

14. Knight Ridder story, https://www.newspapers.com/image/831637552/?match=1&terms=capones%20vault

15. Fred D. Pasley, *Al Capone: The Biography of a Self-Made Man* (Edizioni Savine, 2020).

16. Ibid.

17. *Washington Post*, "TV Stations Eager to Air Vault," April 21, 1986, https://www.newspapers.com/image/1110544441/?match=1&terms=TV%20Stations%20Eager%20to%20Air%20Vault%20

18. *Oakland Tribune*, "Recess Is Over, Viewers Will See a New Geraldo Rivera," April 3, 1986, https://www.newspapers.com/image/758699998/?match=1&terms=Recess%20is%20over%20viewers%20will%20see%20a%20new%20geraldo%20rivera%20

19. Ibid.

20 Ibid.

21 Jake Rossen, "An Oral History of When Geraldo Rivera Opened Al Capone's Vault," Mental Floss, May 14, 2025, https://www.mentalfloss.com/article/78842/oral-history-30-years-ago-geraldo-rivera-opened-al-capones-vault

22 *Slate* interview, https://slate.com/podcasts/one-year/s3/1986/e3/al-capone-vaults-geraldo-rivera-television-mystery

Chapter 19

1 Geraldo Rivera, with Daniel Paisner, *Exposing Myself* (New York: Bantam, 1991), 440.

2 Geraldo Rivera interview with the author.

3 "The Mystery of Al Capone's Vaults," YouTube, https://www.youtube.com/watch?v=jUEYhIp5SG0

4 Ibid.

Chapter 20

1 "The Mystery of Al Capone's Vaults," YouTube, https://www.youtube.com/watch?v=jUEYhIp5SG0

2 Ibid.

3 Ibid.

4 Ibid.

5 Ibid.

6 Ibid.

Chapter 21

1 Commercial, "Al Capone's Vaults."

2 Mitch Nednick interview with the author.

Chapter 22

1. "The Mystery of Al Capone's Vaults," YouTube, https://www.youtube.com/watch?v=jUEYhIp5SG0
2. Ibid.
3. Ibid.
4. Reddit.
5. "The Mystery of Al Capone's Vaults," YouTube.
6. Ibid.
7. Ibid.
8. Allan Grafman interview with the author.
9. "The Mystery of Al Capone's Vaults," YouTube.
10. Ibid.
11. Ibid.
12. Ibid.
13. Ibid.
14. Ibid.
15. Ibid.

Chapter 23

1. "The Mystery of Al Capone's Vaults," YouTube, https://www.youtube.com/watch?v=jUEYhIp5SG0
2. Ibid.
3. Ibid.

Chapter 24

1. Zahi Hawass, *The Golden King: The World of Tutankhamun* (New York: Penguin Random House, 2006), 108.
2. "The Mystery of Al Capone's Vaults," YouTube, https://www.youtube.com/watch?v=jUEYhIp5SG0

3   Ibid.
4   Ibid.
5   Ibid.
6   Ibid.
7   Ibid.
8   Ibid.
9   Ibid.

Chapter 25

1   "The Mystery of Al Capone's Vaults," YouTube, https://www.youtube.com/watch?v=jUEYhIp5SG0
2   Ibid.
3   Ibid.
4   Ibid.
5   Ibid.
6   Geraldo Rivera, with Daniel Paisner, *Exposing Myself* (New York: Bantam, 1991), 60.
7   Ibid.

Chapter 26

1   "The Mystery of Al Capone's Vaults," YouTube, https://www.youtube.com/watch?v=jUEYhIp5SG0
2   Ibid.
3   Ibid.
4   Ibid.
5   Ibid.
6   Ibid.
7   Ibid.

8. Ibid.
9. Allan Grafman interview with the author.

Chapter 27

1. "The Mystery of Al Capone's Vaults," YouTube, https://www.youtube.com/watch?v=jUEYhIp5SG0
2. Ibid.
3. Ibid.
4. Ibid.
5. Ibid.
6. Ibid.

Chapter 28

1. Geraldo Rivera, with Daniel Paisner, *Exposing Myself* (New York: Bantam, 1991).
2. Ibid.
3. Allan Grafman interview with the author.
4. Geraldo Rivera interview with the author.
5. "The Mystery of Al Capone's Vaults," YouTube, https://www.youtube.com/watch?v=jUEYhIp5SG0
6. Allan Grafman interview with the author.
7. "The Mystery of Al Capone's Vaults," YouTube.
8. Ibid.
9. Ibid.
10. *Tampa Tribune*, April 22, 1986, https://www.newspapers.com/image/336231396/?match=1&terms=capone%20vault%20sidewalks%20
11. "The Mystery of Al Capone's Vaults," YouTube.
12. Geraldo Rivera interview with the author.

13 "The Mystery of Al Capone's Vaults," YouTube.

14 Ibid.

15 Geraldo Rivera interview with the author.

16 Allan Grafman interview with the author.

17 Clark Morehouse interview with the author.

18 Geraldo Rivera interview with the author.

Chapter 30

1 *Kentucky New Era*, "Capone's Vault Special Was Two Hours Wasted," April 23, 1986, https://www.newspapers.com/image/1053701509/?match=1&terms=capones%20vault%20special%20was%20two%20hours%20wasted%20

2 *Columbus Ledger*, "TV Writer Confesses He Watched Capone," April 23, 1986, https://www.newspapers.com/image/857087203/?match=1&terms=capone%20

3 *The Citizens Voice*.

4 Geraldo Rivera, with Daniel Paisner, *Exposing Myself* (New York: Bantam, 1991), 441.

5 Ibid., 442.

6 Ibid.

7 Ibid.

8 *Baltimore Sun*, "Vault Opening Most Pointless TV Show in Memory," https://www.newspapers.com/image/377806417/?match=1&terms=geraldo%20capone%20

9 *Slate* interview, https://slate.com/podcasts/one-year/s3/1986/e3/al-capone-vaults-geraldo-rivera-television-mystery

10 Jake Rossen, "An Oral History of When Geraldo Rivera Opened Al Capone's Vault," *Mental Floss*, May 14, 2025, https://www.mentalfloss.com/article/78842/oral-history-30-years-ago-geraldo-rivera-opened-al-capones-vault

11 *Pittsburgh Press*, "The Mystery of Capone's Vault a Bust," April 22, 1986, https://www.newspapers.com/image/146171943/?match=1&terms=the%20mystery%20of%20capones%20vault%20a%20bust%20

12 Ibid.

13 *Chicago Tribune*, "Capone's Hotel Vaults Full of TV Publicity," April 22, 1986, https://www.newspapers.com/image/388627957/?match=1&terms=capones%20hotel%20vault%20full%20of%20publicity%20

14 *Los Angeles Times*, "No Match for Hype," April 22, 1986, https://www.newspapers.com/image/342834850/?match=1&terms=capone%20no%20match%20for%20hype%20

15 *Boston Globe*, "Inside Geraldo's Head," April 23, 1986, https://www.newspapers.com/image/437564524/?match=1&terms=capone%20inside%20geraldos%20head%20

16 *Los Angeles Times*, "Hole in the Ground Hole in the Head," April 23, 1986, https://www.newspapers.com/image/437564524/?match=1&terms=capone%20inside%20geraldos%20head%20

17 *News and Record*, "Geraldo You Dirty Rat," April 24, 1986, https://www.newspapers.com/image/943197359/?match=1&terms=geraldo%20you%20dirty%20rat%20

18 *Duluth News Tribune*, "Capone's Last Crime Was Rivera TV Show," April 23, 1986, https://www.newspapers.com/image/1163662977/?match=1&terms=capones%20last%20crime%20was%20rivera%20tv%20show

19 *New Jersey Ledger*, April 23, 1986, https://www.newspapers.com/image/1112993620/?match=1&terms=capone%20geraldo%20vault%20

20 *Baltimore Sun*, April 22, 1986, https://www.newspapers.com/image/377806417/?match=1&terms=geraldo%20capone%20

21 *Arizona Republic*, "Nation's TV Viewers Let Geraldo Bamboozle Them at Capone's Vault," April 23, 1986, https://www.newspapers.com/image/120246266/?match=1&terms=capone%20vault%20

22 *Daily Sentinel*, "Prime Time Dud," April 23, 1986, https://www.newspapers.com/image/537941943/?match=1&terms=prime%20time%20dud%20

23 *The Mercury*, "Big Al Capone's TV Laugh," April 23, 1986, https://www.newspapers.com/image/424798716/?match=1&terms=big%20al%20capones%20tv%20laugh

24 *Tampa Bay Tribune*, "Sequels for the Stupefied," April 27, 1986, https://www.newspapers.com/image/336231696/?match=1&terms=capone%20vault%20geraldo

25 *Windsor Star*, "Geraldo's Hype Better Than His Story," April 23, 1986, https://www.newspapers.com/image/504264895/?match=1&terms=geraldos%20hype%20better%20than%20his%20story%20

Chapter 31

1 Geraldo Rivera interview with the author.

2 Allan Grafman interview with the author.

3 Clark Morehouse interview with the author.

4   Geraldo Rivera, with Daniel Paisner, *Exposing Myself* (New York: Bantam, 1991), 442.

5   Ibid.

6   Ibid.

7   Ibid.

8   Ibid.

9   Geraldo Rivera interview with the author.

10 Rivera and Paisner, *Exposing Myself*, 445.

11 Ibid.

12 Ibid.

13 Ibid.

14 Geraldo Rivera interview with the author.

15 *Detroit Free Press*, "Vaults Were Empty but TV Ratings Were Gold," April 23, 1986, https://www.newspapers.com/image/99314358/?match=1&terms=vaults%20were%20empty%20

16 *Birmingham Post Central*, "Some Folks Just Won't Let It Rest: Digging to Continue in Capone's Vault," April 23, 1986, https://www.newspapers.com/image/794877865/?match=1&terms=%20digging%20in%20capones%20vault%20to%20continue%20

17 *Princeton Daily Clarion*, "Audience Should Have Known Hotel Vault Might Be Empty," April 23, 1986, https://www.newspapers.com/image/794877865/?match=1&terms=%20digging%20in%20capones%20vault%20to%20continue%20

18 *Los Angeles Times*, Letters to the Editor.

19 Ibid.

20 *St. Louis Post Dispatch*, "Once and Future TV Spectacle," April 23, 1986, https://www.newspapers.com/image/140993331/?match=1&terms=once%20and%20future%20tv%20spectacle%20

Chapter 32

1   *Wausau Daily*, "Golden Ratings Capone's Vaults Drew Most Viewers," May 1, 1986, https://www.newspapers.com/image/272764126/?match=1&terms=golden%20ratings%20capones%20vault%20drew%20most%20viewers%20

Epilogue

1. Geraldo Rivera, with Daniel Paisner, *Exposing Myself* (New York: Bantam, 1991), 446.
2. *Chicago Tribune*, "Geraldo Vaults from Capone to Talk Show," October 7, 1986, https://www.newspapers.com/image/388781034/?match=1&terms=geraldo%20vaults%20from%20capone%20to%20talk%20show
3. Ibid.
4. Geraldo Rivera interview with the author.
5. Ibid.

SELECTED BIBLIOGRAPHY

Interviews

Allan Grafman
Clark Morehouse
Mitch Nedick
Geraldo Rivera

Books

Bergreen, Laurence. *Capone: The Man and the Era*. New York: Simon & Schuster, 1994.
Capone, Deirdre. *Uncle Al Capone*. ReCap Publishing, 2010.
Edgerton, Gary. *The Columbia History of Television*. New York: Columbia University, 2009.
Eig, Jonathan. *Get Capone: The Secret Plot That Captured America's Most Wanted Gangster*. New York: Simon & Schuster, 2010.
Hawass, Zahi. *The Golden King: The World of Tutankhamun*. New York: Penguin Random House, 2006.
Hazelgrove, William. *Al Capone and the 1933 World's Fair*. Lanham, MD: Rowman & Littlefield, 2017.
Hoffman, Dennis E. *Scarface Al and the Crime Crusaders*. Carbondale: Southern Illinois Press, 2010.
Moffat, Bruce. *Forty Feet Below*. New York: Interurban, 1982.
Pasley, Fred. *Al Capone: The Biography of a Self-Made Man*. Edizioni Savine, 2020.
Rivera, Geraldo. *Exposing Myself*. New York: Bantam, 1991.
Rivera, Geraldo. *The Geraldo Show*. New York: Benbella Books, 2018.
Selzer, Adam. *Speaking Ill of the Dead: Jerks in Chicago History*. Boston: Globe Pequot, 2012.

Newspapers

Arizona Republic
The Baltimore Sun
Birmingham Post Central
The Boston Globe
Chicago Tribune

Cincinnati Post
The Citizens Voice
The Columbus Ledger
Daily News
Daily Sentinel
Detroit Free Press
Duluth News Tribune
Kentucky New Era
The Leader Post
Los Angeles Times
The Mercury
The Miami News
New Jersey Ledger
Oakland Tribune
Orlando Sentinel
The Philadelphia Inquirer
The Pittsburgh Press
Princeton Daily Clarion
Saginaw News
Santa Maria Times
Spokane Review
The Star Ledger
St. Louis Dispatch
Sun Journal
Tampa Bay Tribune
United Press International
Washington Post
Windsor Star

Podcasts and Websites

Apple Podcasts: 1986: The Mystery of Al Capone's Vaults
Archive of American Television: Geraldo Rivera Discusses the Mystery of Al Capone's Vaults
AV Club: When Geraldo Opened Capone's Vault
Entertainment: Geraldo Rivera's Failure Launches His Career
Grunge: The Untold Truth of Al Capone
Media Village: The Mystery of Al Capone's Vaults
Mental Floss Interview
Slate Interview: The Mystery of Al Capone's Vaults
Vanity Fair: The Mystery of Capone's Vault
YouTube: "'The Mystery of Al Capone's Vaults'—(1986)"

INDEX

Ahern, Michael 102
Alcatraz 114–15
Ali, Muhammad 38, 42, 73
Alis, Bob 32
Anderson, Elga 57
Andrea Doria, opening of safe 27, 55–9
Anselmi, Albert 70
Arafat, Yassar 42
Arizona Republic review of show 210–11
Arledge, Roone 3, 40–1, 108, 109, 110–11, 169
Atkins, John 164

Baird, John Logie 78
Baltimore Sun review of show 205–6, 210
Barker, Willis 20
Beatles 37, 38
Barati, Tony 171
Belin, Édouard 78
Berman, Marty 97
Billet, Stu 23
Birmingham Post Herald review of show 223–4
Bogart, Humphrey 91, 92
Bonnie and Clyde 91
Boston Globe review of show 208
Braun, Jeanette 156
Braverman, Chuck 40
Braverman, Sheri 40
Bulova watches 79
Burke, Rio 156–7

Cagney, James 91, 92
Capone, Al. *See also* "The Mystery of Al Capone's Vaults"
   celebrity of 68–71
   discovery of white slab of cement at Lexington 19–22
   impact of, on Chicago 45, 46–7
   Lexington Hotel tunnels 64–5

   lifestyle of 9–10
   personality 11–12, 155–6
   in prison 113–16
   Prohibition 11, 12
   as public enemy number one 89–93
   Saint Valentine's Day massacre 47–9
   speculation of what was behind second wall 2–5
   tax evasion 101–5
   vault discovery reported 83–7
Capone, Mafalda 71
Carnarvon, Lord 159
Carson, Johnny 232
Carter, Bill 205, 210
Carter, Howard 159–60
Carter, Jimmy 40
Cermak, Anton 15
Chancellor, John 97
Chase, Sylvia 3, 40, 109–10, 169
Chicago Tribune review of show 207–8
Chicago tunnels 61–5
Cincinnati Post review of show 210
Citizens Voice review of show 202–3
Cleveland, Grover 18
Collins, Judy 38
Colosimo, Jim 137
Columbus Ledger review of show 202
Cooper, Gary 181
Cooper, Sheldon
   "Gotta keep shoveling" 183, 186
   influence of *Andrea Doria* show on 59
   proposal for show 25, 26, 28–9
   Rivera as possible replacement for Donahue 233
   sad mood following the show 206
Costa, A. 48, 49
Costner, Kevin 89
Creeden, John 70
Cronkite, Walter 95, 97, 226

Cruickshank, Cynthia (CC) 40, 110, 125, 184, 203, 205, 218, 220
Cummings, Homer S. 114

Daily Sentinel review of show 211
Dawes, Rufus C. 45, 46, 49–50
De Cecco, Frankie 218
Denver, John 38, 39
Detroit Free Press review of show 223
Dixon, Jeane 127
Dolci, Dominick P. 164
Donahue, Phil 233
Donaldson, Sam 97
Dowdle, Jim 25, 98, 215
Downs, Hugh 40, 41, 110
Duluth News Tribune review of show 209–10

Enright, Dan 79
Esposito, Carmelita 156, 157
Esposito, Diamond Joe 156

Farnsworth, Philo 78
Fitzgerald, F. Scott 12
Fonda, Jane 39, 42
Fournier, A. 78
Fox, Michael J. 117
Fraley, Oscar 89–90
Frank, Bobby 46
Friedman, Lillian 213
Friendly, Fred 32

Gardella, Kay 96
Geritol 79
Giancana, Antoinette 22
Giancana, Sam 22
Gimbel, Peter 56–8
Goldstein, Louis 47
Grafman, Allan
    Chicago tunnels 65
    dynamiting wall 175
    high ratings of show 222
    Nielsen ratings 81
    proposal for show 25–7
    somber mood due to lack of Capone discoveries 183, 192, 206, 215, 216–17
    uncertainty of vault contents 123, 150
Grateful Dead 38
Great Depression 47
Green, Dwight 103
Green Mill 172
Griffin, Jim 51–3
Guinta, Joseph 70
Guzik, Jake 48

Hacker, Donald 28, 29, 206, 216
Hall, Monty 23
Harlow, Jean 91
Harrison, George 34, 37
Hatos, Stefan 23
Healy, Patrick 166
Hemingway, Ernest 166
Henderson, Parker 48
Hoover, Herbert 67–8, 92, 104
Horowitz, Michael 39
Houseman, John 198
Howard, John 161
Hughes, Irene 127

Internal Revenue Service 27, 151–2
Irey, Elmer 89
Irish Independent review of show 213

Jackson, George W. 61
Jackson, Michael 42
Jagger, Mick 40
Javits, Jacob 36
Javits, Marian 36
Jennings, Peter 120
Johnson, George 68, 69
Johnson, John 33–4
Jordan, Michael 117
Joslyn, John
    Capone show pitched 23–5, 26–7, 28
    deal with Porter for show 186
    proclaims show a success 215
    show preparation 65
    uncertainty of vault's contents 123, 124, 128

INDEX

Keach, Stacy 38
Kennedy, Ethel 3, 110
Kennedy, John F. 3, 39, 110, 125
Kennedy, Robert 95, 110, 125
King, Carole 39
King, Martin Luther, Jr. 95
King Tut 159–60
Kissinger, Henry 36
Kristofferson, Kris 39

Lanham, M. P. 47
LaRue, Victor 103
LeFrak, Francine 39, 40
Lennon, John 31, 34–5, 37, 38, 73
Lewis, Joe 172
Lexington Hotel
    Capone's presence in 9–10
    discovery of white slab of cement 19–22
    history of 17–19
    pre-show preparation 85–7
    Sunbow Foundation development of 23–4
    tunnels 64–5, 84, 180–1
Lindbergh kidnapping 46
Lingle, Jake 90–1, 187
Llewelyn, Doug
    criticism following Capone show 202
    deal with Porter for show 186
    early stages of Capone show 51
    idea and development of show 23, 24–5, 26
    informs Rivera of show's high ratings 220
    pre-show hype 84, 128
    proclaims show a success 215
    at safecracking party 156, 177–8
    show preparation 65
    start of Capone show 138
Lodge, Henry Cabot 12
Loesch, Frank J. 67
Los Angeles Times review of show 208–9, 224–5

Mack, Willard 70
Madonna 117
Mailer, Norman 34, 40
Malone, James 70
Marin, Cheech 38
Marino, Peter 26, 27, 28, 216
Masterson, John 23
Mattingly, Lawrence 102
McCartney, Linda 39
McCartney, Paul 39
McCormick, Robert 90
McGovern, George 95–7
McGurn, "Machine Gun" Jack 12, 171
McLean, Don 39
Mercury review of show 211–12
Midler, Bette 38, 39
Mitchell, John 37
Moneypenny, David C. 113
Monroe, Marilyn 3, 40–1, 109–10, 125
Moran, George (Bugsy) 11, 12–13, 15, 46, 49
Morehouse, Clark 27, 28–9, 74, 192, 217
Morgan, Linda 56
Morici, Vito 113
Mr. T. 137
Murray, Bill 98
Murrow, Ed 32
Murrow, Edward R. 201, 219
"The Mystery of Al Capone's Vaults." *See also* Capone, Al; Rivera, Geraldo
    allure of live show 143–6
    criticism of 201–13
    discovery of vault within a vault 147–53
    dynamiting a wall 172–75, 177–82
    idea and development of 23–9
    no dramatic Capone-related discoveries revealed 183–92
    perspective on 227–30
    setup of show 137–41
    slab removed 160–4
    start of show 133–6
    Thompson machine gun 166–9

Nash, Jay Robert 122
National Association of Television Producers and Executives (NAPTE) show 73–6

Nednick, Mitch 145
Ness, Eliot 28, 89, 113, 171, 172
New Jersey Star Ledger review of show 210
News and Record review of show 209
Nielsen ratings 80–2
Nixon, Richard 95–6
Nobel, Alfred 173
Nobel, Emil 173
Novak, Edward J. 62

O'Banion, Dion 46
O'Connor, John 34
O'Connor, Sinéad 144
One-to-One Foundation 36
Ono, Yoko 31, 34–5, 37, 73
O'Reilly, Bill 144

Pasley, Fred D. 123
Paul, Ronnie 32
Persky, Constantin 77
Peters, Jon 109
Pittsburgh Press review of show 206–7
Plimpton, George 55, 56, 58
Porter, Patricia 192
  deal with Westgate for show 186
  dispute with Rubin over discovery of vault 164
  IRS lien for vault contents 24, 152
  pitch for show 24–5, 27, 127–8
  purchases Lexington Hotel 21–2
  at safecracking party 178
  uncertainty of contents of vault 83, 139
Presley, Elvis 42, 109
Princeton Daily Clarion review of show 224
Prohibition 11, 12

Rand, Sally 118
Randolph, Robert Isham 49–50, 90
Rather, Dan 201
Reagan, Ronald 42, 117
Rignoux, Georges 78
Rio, Frankie 70, 71
Rivera, Cruz Allen 213
Rivera, Geraldo. *See also* "The Mystery of Al Capone's Vaults"
  agrees to host Capone show 51–3
  around-the-world sailing trip 41–3
  background 31
  Capone show pitched to 28–9
  career after Capone show 231–5
  criticism following Capone show 201–13
  day after show 217–26
  early career 34–6
  forced resignation at ABC 107–11
  job loss at ABC 3
  Lennon, John 37
  McGovern endorsement 95–7
  at National Association of Television Producers and Executives show 73–6
  on network shows 39–41
  no dramatic Capone-related discoveries revealed 183–92
  overview of hours leading up to dynamiting second wall 1–5
  pre-show preparation 84–7
  pre-show publicity 118–26
  rumored cocaine problem 98–9
  sets up premise of Capone show 137–41
  slab removed 160–4
  smokes joint on air 38–9
  start of Capone show 133–6
  stretches out time as vault within a vault is discovered 147–53
  Thompson machine gun 166–9
  Willowbrook 31–4
Roberto, Dominick 157
Robinson, Edward G. 91, 92, 103, 151
Roche, Patrick 45–6
Rogers, Buddy 181
Rolling Stones 38
Rooney, Andy 232
Roosevelt, Teddy 42
Rose, Judd 75–6
Rosenberg, Howard 208
Rosenwald, Julius 90
Rubin, Harold
  background and speculation of Capone contents in hotel 17–21, 119, 122

discovery of wall and vault in hotel
    126–9, 216
files cease-and-detest notice with
    Sunbow and Porter 164
at safecracking party 156, 178
speculation of vault contents 139, 177
Rubin, Jules 18, 19, 156
Ruth, Babe 102

Safire, William 211
Saint Valentine's Day massacre 13–15,
    45–50, 166
Samuelson, Al 27
Samuelson, Tim 86, 139, 147–8, 161, 163,
    183
Sansoni, Dennis 151–2
Saturday Night Live 144–5, 232
Savalas, Telly 234
Scalise, John 70
Schillizzi, Sal 57
Schofield, Lemuel B. 70–1
Secret Six 90, 91, 92
Sha Na Na 39
Shanks, Bob 107–8
Sheehan, Bill 38–9
Shepardson, Tim 127
Shumway, Leslie 101–2
Silverman, Fred 108
Simmons, Pete 136
Slick, Grace 39
Smith, Liz 40, 110
St. Louis Post-Dispatch review of show
    225–6
Stack, Robert 28, 89
Starr, Ringo 34
Stemple, Herbert 79
Stills, Stephen 38
Stockholm 56, 58
Sunbow Foundation 21, 23–4, 26, 27, 119,
    152, 164

Tampa Bay Tribune review of show
    212
Tarnoff, Sherman 167–8, 169, 172–4,
    179–80

Taylor, Robert 47–8
television, history of 77–82
Thomas, B. J. 39
Thompson, Big Bill 10, 15, 68
Thompson, Dorothy 80, 198
Thompson, General John T. 13, 165, 169
Thompson, Hunter S. 34
Thompson machine guns 13–14, 165–9
Torres, Jo Ann 110
Torrio, Johnny 12, 164
To Tell the Truth 78–9
Travis, Dempsey 172
Tribune Entertainment 25, 26
Trohan, Walter 14–15, 45
Trump, Donald 42

Van Doren, Charles 79
Vidal, Gore 40
Vonnegut, Edie 33, 34, 36, 39
Vonnegut, Kurt 33, 34, 35–6, 40

Wallace, George 95
Wallace, Mike 28, 96–7, 216
Walters, Barbara 40, 110
Warhol, Andy 40
War of the Worlds 196–9
Warren, Clinton 10
Wausau Daily Herald review of show
    228–9
Weingold, Dave 32
Weintraub, Jerry 37–8, 108, 109
Welles, Orson 80, 195–9, 224, 231
Wells, H. G. 196
Westgate Group 26, 27, 123, 164, 234
Whaley, Ven 122
Wilkerson, James 103, 104–5
Willowbrook (mental institution) 31–4
Wilson, Frank 89, 92–3, 101–2, 104, 113
Windsor Star review of show 212–13
Winfrey, Oprah 26, 117, 233
Withers, Bill 39
Wolfe, Tom 34, 40
World's Fair (Chicago) 45–6, 49–50, 118

Zapruder, Abraham 39

ABOUT THE AUTHOR

William Elliott Hazelgrove is the national bestselling author of ten novels and fourteen nonfiction titles. His books have received starred reviews in *Publishers Weekly*, *Kirkus*, *Booklist*, Book of the Month Selections, ALA Editors' Choice Awards, Junior Library Guild Selections, Literary Guild Selections, History Book Club Selections, History Book Club Bestsellers, Distinguished Book Award, and optioned for the movies. He was the Ernest Hemingway Writer in Residence where he wrote in the attic of Ernest Hemingway's birthplace. He has written articles and reviews for *USA Today*, *Smithsonian Magazine*, and other publications, and has been featured on NPR's *All Things Considered*. *The New York Times*, *Los Angeles Times*, *Chicago Tribune*, CSPAN, *USA Today*, and *World News Tonight* have all covered his books with features. More information can be found at www.williamhazelgrove.com.